THE LOG OF
BOB
BARTLETT

THE LOG OF
BOB
BARTLETT

The True Story of Forty Years of
Seafaring and Exploration

Captain Robert A. Bartlett

FLANKER PRESS LTD.
ST. JOHN'S, NL

Library and Archives Canada Cataloguing in Publication

Bartlett, Robert A. (Robert Abram), 1875-1946.
    The log of Bob Bartlett : the true story of forty years of seafaring and exploration / Robert A. Bartlett.

Includes index.

ISBN 1-897317-00-X

    1. Bartlett, Robert A. (Robert Abram), 1875-1946. 2. Arctic regions--Discovery and exploration. 3. Scientific expeditions--Arctic regions--History. 4. North Pole--Discovery and exploration. 5. Ship captains--Canada--Biography. I. Title.

G635.B3A3 2006   910.9163'2   C2006-903919-4

© 2006 by Flanker Press

PRINTED IN CANADA

FLANKER PRESS
P.O. BOX 2522, STATION C
ST. JOHN'S, NL, CANADA A1C 6K1
TOLL FREE: 1-866-739-4420
WWW.FLANKERPRESS.COM

Cover Design: Adam Freake

Originally published by G. P. Putnam's Sons, Blue Ribbon Books, New York, 1928

11 10 09 08 07   2 3 4 5 6

We acknowledge the financial support of: the Government of Canada through the Book Publishing Industry Development Program (BPIDP); the Canada Council for the Arts which last year invested $20.1 million in writing and publishing throughout Canada; the Government of Newfoundland and Labrador, Department of Tourism, Culture and Recreation.

To my mother

CONTENTS

FOREWORD

TO THE 2006 EDITION OF
THE LOG OF BOB BARTLETT
BY PAUL O'NEILL

When a book already has a foreword written by the author, providing another may seem illogical. However, the original foreword to the first edition of *The Log of Bob Bartlett,* an autobiography by the captain himself, introducing the reader to a gripping narrative of his legendary experiences, is a personal one that seems a part of the *Log* itself. A foreword to this present edition serves to bring the work to the attention of new readers. Much has happened to Captain Bob's reputation over the nearly eighty years since the work was first published in New York by G. P. Putnam's Sons to the present time, when Flanker Press has brought it back to a new readership.

During the in-between years, Bartlett has become acclaimed internationally, as well as locally, as the province's most valorous hero. There have been others from Newfoundland and Labrador who have done truly remarkable deeds on water and in the trenches of Europe, but none grip the imagination as do the heroic actions of Captain Bob while exploring the Arctic. It is fitting that a monument to him has been erected on the beach at Brigus, and his home in the community, Hawthorne Cottage, which dates from 1830, has been preserved as an extremely fine museum by the Historic Sites Association.

The American poet Carl Sandburg said, at the dedication of the Overseas Press Club in New York, "Valour is a gift. Those having it never know for sure whether they have it till the test comes." In the intervening years since the first edition of Bartlett's autobiography, we have all come to know for sure that when the test came he had the rashness and bravery that makes a man valorous. To read the story of his life is like having an armchair chat with this great Newfoundlander, so down-to-earth is his style. His book is where the corned beef, cabbage, and pease pudding are cooking and you can catch the scent.

Born to the sea in Brigus, he said that the very salt smell of the schooners moored there was a beckoning lure for any small boy living "right at the edge of the sea" and he found it irresistible. I know the feeling myself, having spent much of my boyhood right at the edge of the sea in Conception Bay's biggest cod-fishing settlement, Bay de Verde, where my father, grandfather, and great-grandfather, like the Bartletts of Brigus, operated schooners and fishing punts for generations.

Captain Bob's experiences on land, as he told an admirer at the Explorers club of New York, always made him glad to go to sea again in spite of "rotten meat, frozen fingers, lice and dirt." Those were the least of the challenges he had to meet beginning at the age of seventeen. Being with the American Robert E. Peary when he discovered the North Pole, as the youthful master of Peary's ship the *Roosevelt*, is just one of the many incredible stories he tells in this remarkable book.

The Log of Bob Bartlett should be on the must-read list for all students in Newfoundland and Labrador, as well as for every other person. Bob's life, and the lives of all the Bartletts, made him what he was, a young lion who without pretense treaded his way to becoming our provinces's greatest hero. We should all be uncommonly proud of him and how he mastered events in life. This new edition by Flanker Press provides us with an understanding of Captain Robert A. Bartlett, the man, the myth, in his own words.

FOREWORD

TO THE 1926 EDITION OF
THE LOG OF BOB BARTLETT
By Captain Robert A. Bartlett

It seems there is a fashion of writing forewords to books. I had not intended doing it—after all, a sailor isn't apt to be fashionable. But two things made me change my mind since I have logged off the chapters of this story of mine.

Just after we got back from the Baffin Land Expedition of the summer of 1927, I received a letter. I have had a good share of letters in my time, some of them flattering (plenty contrary!), and many from really important people. But never came a pleasanter, more surprising letter than this one. I wanted to use it in my book. But the book was written.

"We will make a berth for it," I said to myself. "A foreword is the place. If the book cannot carry that additional sail, she's not fit for sea anyway."

Here's the letter*, and that's all I know about this cheerful friend:

November 4, 1927

Captain Bob Bartlett
c/o Explorers Club,
47 W. 78th Street,
New York, N.Y.

Dear Bob:

I don't know who is paying you wages at the moment but I do know the whole world is in your debt. If your salary were based on the value of your services to mankind and your employer, you would be in the millionaire class, but damn it Bob, that isn't the way with mankind. An inventor hits on a lucky device for polishing teeth and pulls off a fortune-you, not only take care of yourself, but a dozen tenderfeet through 1,000 miles of Arctic waste, and what?-Draw maybe just enough to carry you, while you are trying to find another job. But, we love you just the same. We admire your fearless courage, your clear head, your mastery over the forces of nature, your rugged grandeur, for you really are a master of men and natural forces-a giant among pigmies.

In 1,000 years you will be more famous than today. But, meanwhile hasn't mankind a duty? I think so, and I have one too, namely, to do my little bit, which is to divvy my assets to the extent of a Fifty, which I am enclosing herewith.

I have known you a good many years, but I don't want you to know my real name, lest you might hesitate to accept the cheque. Just consider it a little payment on account of the great debt the world owes to you, and which under no circumstances is it ever apt to pay.

Sincerely yours,

(Signed) Jedediah Tingle

Address—
Care of American Trust Co.
209 Montague Street,
Brooklyn, N.Y.

* Reprint from the Bowling Green Column of the New York *Evening Post*.

Mr. Jedediah Tingle

Occasionally, in recent years, various people have been startled to receive a letter, most charmingly phrased, expressing gratitude for something they have done or painted or written or said, and signed Jedediah Tingle as a pseudonym, but they have found that the cheque was perfectly valid and cashable or the book worth reading.

Now one of the most pleasing adventures we have had lately was a call from Mr. Tingle himself. He did not come, we must explain, to exert his benevolence upon ourself, but to consult us about a certain phase of his recreation of secretly rewarding, in a modest way, those whose works appealed to him. He did not tell us his real name, and we have no desire to know who he is, other than that he is a thoughtful businessman who has found great delight in these mysterious gestures of helpfulness. To identify him would not only necessarily put an end to his cheerful avocation, but would also deprive the situation of its unique charm.

The secret circle of those who have received these letters from Jedediah Tingle is a curiously assorted one. We have had some of the letters shown us, in the past, by those who have received them. These letters have gone to cabinet ministers and to obscure, struggling poets, to great writers and to unknown heroes. But the point is this—while Mr. Tingle tells us he has greatly enjoyed the occasional acknowledgements that have come to him by being addressed to the banks on which his cheques are drawn, certain individuals and newspapers have made determined attempts to unmask his innocent secret. We should like to ask all managing editors and others to be good sports and not spoil this admirable innocent generosity by trying to discover its source.

Christopher Morley

* * * * * *

The undersigned feels mildly resentful at being called a "pseudonym." He harbours a strong suspicion that he is the living incarnation of his own great-grandfather whose name he has taken and who in turn came from generations of Abou Ben Adhems.

In 1820, they placed his bones in a country graveyard in the Middle West, now an abandoned tangle of grasses, briars, and broken trees, but that event was probably merely an episode in an eternal mission, which is to bring smiles and tender thoughts to the great in heart—in high and low places. To comfort and cheer those who do exceptional things, or suffer.

Jedediah Tingle

——

The second reason for this extra literary top-hamper is this. I have been reading a book by a great explorer, a man who has accomplished really big things. It is an amazingly unhappy book. He seems to want to quarrel with all the world. As he writes it, nearly everyone is a rascal, a fake, and incompetent. It is all bitterness and recrimination, without a trace of good humour anywhere.

Well, after I read as much of that as I could stand, I was sort of sick at heart, and really sorry for this poor man who so easily could have remained as big as his fine record. And at once I said to myself, "If there is any of that kind of sour spirit in this yarn of mine, my log is never going to be launched at all."

Well, I read my book all over again, changed a bit here and there, and threw a few paragraphs overboard. It is my book now about the way I would like to have it—although of course I wish it were more interesting and better written.

At least there is no meanness in it; and, I think, no bitterness and no criticism. I am not taking a swipe at anyone. I am not trying to open up old sores and air old grievances. At the worst, at least it is all set down with a smile.

My log is just a simple yarn of a plain man—a man not particularly well-equipped, who has seen a lot of life in queer ways; who has had his share of success and discouragement and excitement; and who is grateful for what life has given him in adventures, fun, and friends. And I hope the book finds a fine fair wind to take it to the harbour of its readers' friendship.

R. A Bartlett.

CHAPTER I

THE TROUBLE WITH WOMEN

I have been shipwrecked twelve times. Four times I have seen my own ships sink, or be crushed to kindling wood against the rocks. Yet, I love the sea as a dog loves its master who clouts it for the discipline of the house.

"How does it feel to face death?" This is a question that has often been put to me.

"That depends," are always my first words in reply. And it does. Because, if the peril is short and swift, as when a man points a gun at your head, that is one thing. But if you have to cling, half frozen, for many hours to the rigging of a sinking ship, not knowing which moment may be your last, that is another sort of shiver altogether.

One misery I have been spared, the feeling in the face of death that I was leaving wife and children behind me. I never got married. I don't think a seafaring man ought to because women so often break your heart. A fisherman I knew got wrecked on the Labrador one winter. He left his wife in a snow dugout while he went to the nearest village for food. When he got back to his wife, he found the dogs had eaten her. He never got over the shock; which shows what a care and sorrow a woman can be under some circumstances.

Naturally, my life has been mostly with men, hard men, good and bad men, brave men and cowards; but men all the time. With one good look I can tell what a man is like. A couple of questions and I know his character. I can tell whether a man can be counted on or not in a pinch. I can almost say how he will behave when he dies.

Yet, strange to say, I have learned a great deal about women too. I don't claim to understand them. They probably don't understand themselves. But I know how a woman acts under circumstances, and why. Maybe it is this knowledge that has kept me a single man. Women don't often go where I have gone. However, curious to relate, there have nearly always been women on my most exciting voyages.

When I went close to the North Pole with Peary, we had Eskimo women aboard the ship. When the *Karluk* sank in the middle of the Polar Sea one black January night, with the temperature fifty-four degrees below zero, one of the bravest persons in our party was an Eskimo woman—a wife and mother.

Once I was shipwrecked in the North Atlantic and it was a woman that smiled when the great moment of disaster came. The biggest influence in my forty years of going to sea has been a woman—my mother. She is still alive and now and then still tells me where to get off.

You might say it is not fair to look on Eskimos in the same light as one would look on white women. That is not true. An Eskimo woman cooks and sews, gossips and laughs, loves her babies, and worries about her husband every bit as much as any white wife does.

There was Inuaho on Peary's ship the *Roosevelt*. She

was a fine bronze study as she sat stripped to the waist sewing away on her skin boots. Her name wasn't easy to say so we called her "The Black Mare," from the long ebony locks that hung over her shoulders.

One day Inuaho came to me on the ice outside the *Roosevelt* and said:

"Captain, you watch my man?"

I could see her hands were gripped tight and her eyes were wide open.

"Sure I watch him. Why?"

"Because Pearyaksoh (the big Peary) do not care if he die. My man go where Peary go. I am afraid."

I patted the girl on her back and told her the best I could that I wouldn't let anything happen to her man. That summer her baby came; its father was one of the first human beings to reach the North Pole. In 1917, I returned to Greenland and told the story to the sturdy little hunter growing up.

In 1914, the *Karluk* sank north of Alaska. She was crushed to kindling wood in the ice. We were many miles from the land. The weather was dreadfully cold. In the biting wind, the powdery snow drifted ceaselessly across the wild and broken icefields. It was a gamble whether we should ever get back. Four men started off towards Alaska and were never heard of again. The rest of us struggled down to Wrangell Island. The trip took weeks and was filled with terrible hardships.

We had an Eskimo woman along. She was our seamstress. She was not trained to sledge work for she had lived a sheltered life in the little village where we had picked her up. She was not like the North Greenland Eskimo. I should say that she was as unprepared for hardship as most white woman. Did she whine? Listen:

"Where in hell are my boots?" I yelled at the top of my lungs in the confusion that followed the sinking ship. Nobody paid attention.

Five minutes later I felt a woman's fingers on my wrists. I whirled around in the dusk and flying snow. There was Inaloo.

"I fix Captain's boots," she said.

I grabbed them out of her hand. I suddenly noticed her lips were bleeding.

"Somebody hit you?" I asked.

"No."

"Well, what in the devil is the matter with your face?"

"I chew Captain's boots."

Then I realized that she had dashed into the cabin, at risk of her life, when the ice was crushing the ship, and saved my spare boots. I knew they were wet and in bad shape. She had taken them out and in the Eskimo way had chewed the thick leather into a pliable state and filled the soles with grass. In the cold and snow, and with the hard hide, she had split her lips in twenty places. But she had saved my feet.

In the long hard weeks that followed, she was like that all the way. Time after time she helped bind up frozen fingers; she went easy with her share of the grub when we were short; she mended our clothes and cleaned our boots; and she was always there with a smile when things looked darkest.

White woman are just as brave and just as fine when they have to be. Of course when it comes to wearing fandangles in competition with other women for the eyes of a man, she has got to be on the job if she is going to make progress. But jam her up against a stone wall of necessity and I'll stake my hat on the average woman being full-and-by with the best of us.

I remember one girl down the Newfoundland coast. She was from a good family in Halifax. She fell in love with a young sailor and went with him to live outside of a little village near my home. I suppose the excitement of being married and living in a new country carried her along the first year or two. She was pretty free and could visit about while her man went to sea. But children came along one after another, and pretty soon she was tied down as much by poverty as by her brood.

The sealing season begins in March. Men are poor in Newfoundland. Late in February, after they have cut enough wood for their families and when their winter supply of salt fish is getting low, they begin to go down to St. John's to join the sealing fleet. Usually they walk. Young men think nothing of covering hundreds of miles or so overland, through deep snow and blizzards.

The bad part of it is after they have gone through two months, maybe three, of hard sealing life, they come back with total earnings as low as $15! Sometimes they make $50 for a sealing cruise; sometime $300—but that is very rare. Usually it is around $25 to $60.

Think of it. This $50, let us say, represents the total season's earning for the head of the family. Some of it goes for the man's outfit and clothing. Some of it he wastes on knickknacks for the children. After three or four months of ice, and snow, and cold, and incredible toil, he goes back to his woman with maybe only $25 in cash!

That spring, the girl I am telling about kisses her man goodbye. All the little children kissed him goodbye—five of them, as I remember it. He had to go. The $25 or $50 he would bring back must pay for the flour and medicine and tools vital to the life of the little family.

Three days after he left it came on to blow. Snow mixed with the wind. The little shack where lived the mother and her children became isolated. It was isolated for a month. In the third month, the mother broke out and got help to bury one of her babies. Meanwhile she cut wood and boiled salt fish and waited for her man to bring back $25.

He never came back. After a while the girl gave up. She let people come and help her support the children; she was a good sport about it. She went right on working and made enough money so that she could have her little house. She fished and chopped wood like a man. She did not forget that her man had gone down in the sealer *Southern Cross* in a brave effort to provide for her. The children were half his and to this day she tries to carry his load as well as hers.

I have an idea that all women are good to start with. The trouble with so many of them is that they have too easy a time. Maybe I am wrong. Maybe if they didn't have an easy time they would lose that ornamental edge which catches the eye of a man skilled in a woman's fine points. Anyway, I know plenty of cases where my theory holds true.

There was a good girl I knew who turned her nose at lots of fine young fellows because they didn't have enough money or hold down big jobs. She was out to marry a captain. She finally did.

Now some captains like to take their wives to sea with them. But all sailors know that a woman on board ship is bad luck. I once sailed as second mate with a captain who took his wife along. She brought misfortune from the day we cast off until we reached port again.

On the second day out I fell down the hatch and nearly put out one of my eyes. My shin had to have four stitches taken in it. Next the first mate broke his knuckle when he swung at one of the deckhands. The sailor dodged and the mate struck the oaken pin rail with his unprotected knuckles.

The worst tragedy came in the second week out. Our steward had a bad knee. I suppose it was rheumatism. He suffered terrible pain. You know the average merchant ship doesn't carry a doctor. She has a medicine chest aboard with a book of directions. When anybody is ill the captain opens the chest and treats them according to the book. If he gets the symptoms wrong, or reads off the wrong page, then there is old Nick to pay.

When the steward complained about his knee the captain's wife insisted on taking charge. She got the book out of the medicine chest and read it all the way through from beginning to end. I think that's what set her adrift. Anyhow it turned out afterwards that she treated the steward for something on page 109 when what he had was on page 209. He became terribly ill on the second day of treatment and just before we reached port he passed away. There was an investigation and the captain got in a lot of legal trouble that

I don't think he ever cleared up. Next time he put to sea his wife stayed home where she belonged.

Yes, I have sailed all over the globe and often been shipwrecked. And I have handled some thick-skinned humanity in my time. But my greatest danger and my toughest task always has been the womenfolk.

I remember once I had just rounded to from a cruise to the West Indies. I had a cargo of bananas on board that had to be discharged. As the job would take some days I stowed away in a boarding house. The housekeeper was a fine upstanding woman of about forty. I could see right off that she was built for hard work and heavy weather. Though she had a nice face she would never take a beauty prize.

The second night I came home for supper she had a rose in the vase up on my bureau. About two minutes after I had come in and was about to cast adrift for a bath, I heard a knock on the door. It was my hostess.

"Everything all right, Captain?" she asked.

"Fine as a fiddle," says I.

"Can I do anything for you?"

I wanted to tell her she could get out, but instead I said, "Yes, you can. If you will wait a minute you can take this shirt and send it to the laundry."

Would you believe it, she was insulted! Before I knew from which quarter the wind blew I was apologizing. And the minute a fellow starts to apologize he's in irons. I mean at a disadvantage. Within ten minutes that woman had tears coursing down her cheeks. I don't know whether it was my apologizing or whether she was laughing at me. Anyway it ended up with my taking her out to the movies. She had the cargo hooks in me fore and aft.

I tell you it was a narrow shave. Even now I don't know how I escaped. But I got a room at a different place the very next day. I could see there were breakers ahead with that boarding-house keeper. Luckily she wasn't there when the expressmen came for my ditty bag.

I have heard that a sailor has a girl in every port. Lots of sailors have. But by a girl is meant a sweetheart. And a sweetheart to a sailor doesn't always mean what it means to other people. That sounds a little complicated. It is complicated. Women are the most complicated things in life.

I think my worst encounter with a woman happened at a house party I once attended. I suppose the host thought it would be fine to have a sea captain along; sort of give his party a touch of atmosphere. Several of the guests were yachtsmen and there was a big swimming pool in the back yard; so it might have been called a seafaring party, I suppose.

But I was all out of kilter there. The people were very rich and every time I turned around I bumped into a servant in livery. But I got through the dinner all right and was doing well with the evening—it was a nice moonlit, summer evening—when someone proposed that we all go swimming. I didn't mind swimming but the suggestion was that we go swimming with all our clothes on. No doubt the wine had made my friends reckless. Being a teetotaller, I was not so enthusiastic at the idea.

Like most sailors I travel light. I had only one suit of clothes with me, one suit of underwear and one pair of shoes. So when that happy crew began to move towards the swimming pool with the idea of jumping in "all standing" I was faced with a problem.

I was puzzled as to whether I should turn around and run, or whether I should throw off some of my clothes and make the best of a bad bargain.

Just then two ladies took hold of my arm and began to propel me towards the pool. I back-watered hard. But there was no escape. I figured if I could only get my coat and pants off I would at least have some dry clothes to put on when I got out.

With a quick move I suddenly shook myself clear and peeled off my coat. Before they could grab me again I slipped out of my pants and started off on a run for the pool. It was about twenty yards away. There was a loud shout as I did so. At once several of the ladies came running for me and began to pull at my shirt. You would hardly think ladies would act like that even after a little wine. Before I knew it I was pretty nearly down to rock bottom so far as clothes went. Terribly embarrassed I dove in.

Of course there were loud cheers when I came up. I refused to get out of the pool until my host brought me my overcoat.

Experiences like that make a seafaring man glad to get to sea again.

I could go on for a long time telling about my experiences with women; some of them good, some bad; some funny and some tragic. Naturally these experiences have brought me to pretty definite conclusions about the fair sex.

One of these conclusions is that while they may be fair in the sense of looks, they aren't in the sense of justice. An old lady once exclaimed to me:

"Why, Captain, you have the cleanest hands!"

"Well, why shouldn't they be clean, madam?" said I.

She giggled foolishly. "Oh, because you are a sea captain."

You see she just had a deep conviction that all sea captains had dirty hands; and probably nothing in the world would shake that unfair prejudice out of her.

On the other hand I think most women are braver than men; certainly they are more plucky. I have heard many a man whine; I've never heard a normal healthy woman in her right mind whine.

I like a woman's judgment, too. Old as I am, and I'm old enough to be a grandfather, had I shipped a wife in youth, I still write and consult my mother's judgment if I possibly can before making any important decision.

I like a woman's temperance and moderation. This may seem a funny thing to say when there's so much outcry against the modern flapper and dissipated young married woman. But I don't believe all this truck. Let the young things be gay and the brides be free—so long as they are decent. And when you come to heave your sounding lead among the two sexes you'll find it's the women far more than the men that have kept to the deep safe channels of health and good citizenship.

Good women are the best company in the world: this from a confirmed bachelor, too.

Pound for pound, thought for thought, a competent woman will work even with the best of men.

A woman is more constant in every way; more consistent, too, if you don't go and upset her with emotions we men don't understand.

Woman's home-keeping instinct is the sailor's salvation; maybe it's the world's too.

If women are bad luck at sea, they're equally good luck on the beach.

I am sorry I have never married. This has been the greatest loss in life; but then it's also probably been some poor woman's gain.

CHAPTER II

A MANGY LION

A life of adventure takes on a queer shape towards its finish—that is, unless a man be rich and can fashion its shape to his heart's desire.

I was in the Explorers Club of New York not long ago when a friend of mine came in accompanied by another gentleman. My friend introduced his companion and then, excusing himself, left. I was struck by the eagerness with which the companion plied me with questions:

"My, you fellows are lucky who can go exploring!" he exclaimed.

"Yes," said I. "It's all right while you're exploring. You get used to rotten meat, frozen fingers, lice, and dirt. The hard times come when you get back."

He looked surprised. He was a businessman and probably spent his entire life since college moored to a desk.

"But I thought that was the finest part of it all. Don't you go to banquets, lecture, write stories, and get interviewed a lot?"

"Yes, we do."

"And aren't you always more or less preparing for the

next voyage looking up a ship and gathering supplies together and that sort of thing?"

"Yes, that's true, too."

"And don't people make a lot of you? I mean to say, isn't an explorer something of a social lion?"

I had to laugh at that. And right away I had to agree, because there was some truth in what the fellow said. But I couldn't give him the whole truth without revealing a good many private matters that I have never spoken of until I penned these lines.

I was just a young fellow when I got back from Peary's polar trip. I had lived a seafaring hard life and had never known what a real luxury was. So I was pretty much set up when under Peary's guidance I got myself a suit of evening clothes and sat down to ten-course dinners with a lot of great men. At first it was like going to a circus. And the figure of speech that calls the guest of honour a lion proved to be an accurate one. For the guests of honour are animals that everybody comes to look at.

Curiously enough I didn't discover I was a lion until after about ten years of it. Then it began to dawn on me that the smiles and cordiality passed out were not always genuine. It was come-along stuff. People who wanted me to do tricks, so to speak.

I didn't have any real tricks, any more than old Silver King did. He was the big polar bear I brought back in 1910, after I'd taken Paul Rainey and Harry Whitney hunting in Greenland. I admit that sometimes when I got enthusiastic about the Eskimos or a little bit sore about the Cook-Peary business, I used to come out with language that wasn't exactly refined. And when I got to describing the muck and gurry of a seal hunt I had to push the English tongue pretty hard to get the colours somewhere near the real picture; and once in a while I used to talk loud, sometimes when everybody was piping down. You see, a man's lungs get a bit powerful after bawling orders to windward against a gale. I shall always be more at home on quarter-deck. I suppose I even waved my hands around sometimes. In other words I was "putting on a show." I was a lion—an animal out of the zoo, too damn tame to bite anybody, but strange enough for people to enjoy looking at once in a while.

But all this didn't come home to me until I got to be a mangy lion.

The trouble was I fell into a spell of drifting in the years after the war. I really ought to have been at sea. Thirty years on the ocean does not fit a man for a shore job. But there I was teetering on the fence, neither going to sea nor becoming established ashore. I had had too much exploring to get any kick out of a straight job of skippering; and the plans I had for flying to the North Pole or the South Pole somehow wouldn't come to a head. I wasn't getting anywhere. I wasn't making any money. I am not sure that I was even making any friends.

Thus I can say perfectly frankly that I was just a mangy lion, a has-been who was being carted around to a free dinner here and there in hopes that he would break out into some rich sea tale and stage a freak monologue free of charge.

This is a delicate subject I am on, for I have so many

good true friends that I wouldn't for the world step on their toes or be ungrateful. But I have to admit that in those drifting years I gathered a wide circle of acquaintances who had only a passing and selfish interest in me.

I remember one big dinner I went to. It was in a private house. There were all men present, most of them millionaires. The host certainly put on a lot of dog. There were servants in livery standing all around. I felt as if I were at the President's reception or something of the sort.

After about eight rounds of cocktails we sat down. As I was a teetotaller I was good and sober. Outwardly everybody was sober too. But there was an exuberance about the crowd that was unmistakably artificial.

It was a good gang. They were lively and full of jokes and many of them good sportsmen. But I could see how the whole party was working around me. The moment was bound to come when my host would, in effect, push me forward and nudge me in the back with, "Bartlett, do your stuff."

As he had no doubt primed his guests they would all be waiting for the invisible signal and turn my way expecting me to put on a good show.

I tell you it was a pretty nasty feeling. I admit I was getting a good dinner in high-class company. With my small bank account I couldn't afford anything like it. But a wave of feeling came over me that I would much rather be starving in the street than play the part of a hired clown for a group of money masters.

Sure enough, when a lull in the conversation came, the host sang out:

"Well, Bob, how are you making out?"

"All right," said I, "all right. Don't I look all right?"

I didn't recognize my own voice. It was flat and unfriendly. I heard somebody near me say, "Give him a drink; his has died on him."

Before I could control my anger, I turned around and retorted sharply: "I don't drink."

"Gentlemen," loudly announced the host, "you have sitting before you the only he-man in the world who is a tee-totaller!"

Cheers and applause mixed in with ribald remarks met this observation. I felt my neck get hot. My fingers itched to beat some of the sneering wine-flushed faces around me.

"Who got to the Pole?" shouted a thick voice across the table.

I didn't even look up. I went right on eating although I couldn't swallow. My food stuck in my throat.

The host made two or three other attempts to draw me out. But he failed. I had seen the light at last. I was just a mangy old lion and too old to be put through the hoop any-more. I was ashamed to be rude and maybe snarl a little. But that was only human.

I was in too deep to stop all of a sudden. There were engagements that I couldn't cancel. Also the true friends were mixed up with the false friends. To escape with dig-nity the trap into which I had blindly walked, was not easy.

One party I got into on false pretenses. I was told there weren't going to be any strangers there. It was held in a fine big house that I loved and I knew I should have some conversation with a man I admired for years, besides living for a few hours in the soothing atmosphere of the perfect luxury inherited money can buy.

Imagine my horror when I discovered my friend wasn't going to be there at all! Instead, some of the younger people were having a dance. The guests weren't all young; many were my age. But they weren't my kind.

As usual there was a lot to drink and the party got rougher and rougher. I don't set myself up to be any saint, but I certainly didn't belong there. I tried to sneak away soon after midnight.

Just to show that I am not a prude I will tell about one night when a special friend of mine got started drinking and being foolish and I wouldn't leave him. He was a man a little bit older than I was, too. He was worth a great many million dollars.

I followed him to a gambling club up in the fifties in New York. I went in with him just as sober as I am right now. We checked our coats and were about to go in to where the tables were when he turned to me and said:

"Bob, I want you to keep some money for me."

He shoved a roll of bills into my hand. He had only a second or two because I saw some of his friends coming from the other side. I didn't look at the money but jammed it down in my jeans only too glad to be of help.

I got home about three o'clock in the morning after a not altogether unamusing evening. While I was undressing I suddenly remembered the money. I reached in and pulled out the bills. Imagine my horror when I discovered that my friend had given me sixteen 1,000-dollar bills! I'd never seen so much money in my life. I was scared stiff. I locked the door and put the washstand against it. Ordinarily I sleep with all the windows open because I hate close air. That night I kept them all closed and latched. The next morning, I felt just about as groggy from the frowst as my friend must have felt from his dissipation.

I steamed through breakfast over the trick he had played on me. Then I had an inspiration. I would get even with him.

That afternoon I met him at his club.

"By the way, Bob," he said, "didn't I give you some money last night?"

"Look here," I told him with affected irritation, "you've got to stop drinking. You didn't give me any money. When a man gets all tanked up with liquor the way you did last night he doesn't know what he does."

"Gracious goodness!" he muttered. Those were his actual words. (Think of a man giving away $16,000, forgetting what he has done with it and using language as thin as that when he remembers it!)

I strung him along for quite a while. Finally I gave him his sixteen 1,000-dollar bills. He wasn't very excited after all. But then he was a millionaire. He tried to give me one of them, but I refused. Even a mangy lion sometimes knows whose hand to lick.

A rich friend took me down in the country 100 miles or so from New York to spend the night with him. I stayed there a week. I found the people he invited were a friendly crowd and they were interested in outdoor things. I must say it was a pretty temperate party. Of course there was a good deal of drinking; there always was in pre-prohibition times. I suppose there is yet.

The thing that stuck in my mind about this party was the endurance people showed in exercising as well as in eating and drinking. I don't mean children either; I mean people in their forties and fifties.

Yet one of them who was interested in the north said to me: "You must be made of iron to stand that life up there in the Arctic."

"I have a good digestion," I admitted.

"But doesn't it wear you out to live on a raw meat and pemmican diet and drive a dog team for miles and miles every day?"

I agreed it was hard work.

"How long does it take you to get over it?"

"Depends on the trip," said I. "Usually there isn't any 'getting over it' as you call it."

I didn't tell my questioner that for three days I had been going through just as hard a life as I ever did in the Arctic. And I figured it was going to take me longer to get over the results of those three days of high-speed house party than any seven days I ever spent on the Polar Sea.

I mean that hardships are pretty much a matter of the point of view. After I have put in twenty hours of eating rich food and talking to fat ladies and rushing here and there without any particular plan I am just about exhausted. Before I know it I begin to have indigestion in my head as well as in my stomach. As for the fatigue of being polite every minute of the day to people you don't like, or never heard of before, I think that's about the worst chore in the world. At the end of that party I admitted to my host I had had a fine time; and I did. But I had to recuperate. It was ten days more before I felt normal again.

The same sort of thing applies to my experiences downtown in New York. I mean down among the businessmen in what is known as the financial district. I have some fine friends there. They still ask me down to lunch once in a while and sometimes get me to sit in their offices while they do business. I always enjoy the adventure of it, same as any of them enjoy bear hunting, I suppose.

But I swear it tires me just to sit and look at a modern business executive at work. I remember one man especially. He has three telephones on his desk and two secretaries. He'll grab a telephone and say: "Hello! Sure, what will you pay me?" And while the other fellow is answering him he'll turn to his secretary and begin dictating a letter.

"That isn't enough," he'll shout back into the telephone and reach for the other telephone that has just begun to ring.

"Make it dinner," he'll yell into the other telephone. And then come back to the first telephone and snap: "Add five per cent."

I got so dizzy one afternoon watching him go through this acrobatic performance with those telephones and secretaries, and two or three people standing around and talking to him at the same time, that I had to go put my head out of the window. A seafaring life may be hard work but it never drives anybody crazy who isn't crazy already. I'll take my punishment in the Arctic any day.

Sometimes I have gone down to Wall Street actually on

business. I remember the time I went to Hudson Bay in the steamship *Algerine* as mate and what came of it. On board we had a well-known rich man, Mr. Arthur Moore. He invited me to visit his office next time I came to New York.

So a year later I took my life in my hands, put my gold watch in an inside pocket and went down to Wall Street to see if I couldn't get some financial backing for Admiral Peary who had been so kind to me.

I found Mr. Moore, Sr., and he gave me a letter to Mr. William Rockefeller, urging me at the same time to give up Arctic work and get a job in the Standard Oil. That sounded pretty heavy. I began to wish I were back on my ship. When I went to present the letter I stopped on the steps of 26 Broadway. I tossed up a coin, heads I go in, tails I don't. It came tails. That afternoon I saw Mr. Jesup by appointment. He said to me: "As long as I live I'll see Peary has enough money to work with."

Altogether that was a bad day. I met a number of rich gentlemen and they were very courteous. But they seemed absorbed in their business. Finally it was all put up to Mr. Morris K. Jesup whether I got the money for Peary or not. I had to wait until five o'clock to know the answer.

Thinking of my mother and home and wishing I could see both I bought a newspaper and slipped into Trinity Church to rest my troubled mind. I sat down in one of the back pews and opened the paper, being careful to not make any noise, and began to read. It was a much more typical thing for a seafaring man to do than most people realize.

Just about the time I was comfortable a loud voice said: "Get out of here! Why are you profaning God's temple by reading a newspaper?" It was a shock and a surprise. My eyes may have been on the paper but my thoughts were never far from the Christian atmosphere in which I sat.

I looked up at the vestryman but his face was hard. The Devil must have laughed as I turned red and went out.

That night Mr. Jesup gave me the good news that he was going to help. But as I started to say, I do not feel that he or any of the other big men had worries any greater than a fishing captain can have.

Right in the past year I spent $2,000 to fit out our cod-fishing trip in the steamer *Viking*. Down east I took on about 200,000 pounds of green codfish and had them dried for Mediterranean trade. When I got back I had to sell them at a low price because the market was off. I had to pay my crew $1,600. This left me without any money and I still owed $2,600. If some of those fine gentlemen I met in New York were up against a thing like this, with every penny of their capital sewn up tighter than a drum, they would know what real worry is.

CHAPTER III

THE SEA IS A HARD MASTER

The early years of my life were spent with my father and uncles in the Newfoundland sealing fleet. Then I got into the banana trade, mostly in the West Indies, from which I was graduated to command of a full-fledged ocean tramp steamer, sailing to all oceans of the globe. For the past thirty years I have been going to the polar regions, with some sealing between expeditions. I was master of Peary's North Pole ship, the *Roosevelt*, and I commanded a troop transport during the war, when I held rank in the United States Naval Reserve. At no time since my boyhood have I been for over a month on the beach save whilst recovering from one voyage or preparing for another.

I was born on August 15, 1875, in the little village of Brigus, in Conception Bay, Newfoundland, where for 150 years my forebears have lived. The Bartletts of Brigus have always been seafaring people. When Thomas Jefferson was President of the United States, the Bartletts were cod fishers on the Banks and down to Labrador.

My people came originally from the west coast of England, Devon, and Dorset. On my father's side they were big-boned folk, very dark in complexion and with coarse black hair. These are still sometimes called the "Black Bartletts of Brigus," and the reason of it goes clear back to Drake's day.

In 1588, the Spanish Armada, with the flower of Spain on board, cruised north to make all England Spanish. But by one of the overrulings of fate a great storm arose and the proud fleet was dashed to pieces on the rock-ribbed coast of western England and Scotland, from Land's End to John o' Groats.

From these ships hundreds of Spanish soldiers and sailors were washed ashore, dead and alive. Many were so well treated by the coast folk that there they stayed. Thus came to the Nordic Bartletts a strain of somber Spanish blood, accounting not only for their complexion and hair but, some say, for the independence and the airs still found among them.

These castaways from the Spanish ships found happiness and contentment for a time. The beautiful English girls, coupled with luscious Devonshire cream and a countryside of rare loveliness, held them for a while. But a roving spirit seldom stills. The newcomers began to look, not north, but west; and many, including my forebears, set forth.

My people reached Newfoundland at Brigus and settled there. The hard stern coast no doubt reminded them of their native heath: the surrounding country of woods, streams, downs, and hills was not unlike bleak western England. Mostly in the old country they had been fishermen and sailors. Now in the new land they soon found cod, salmon, and seals in plenty. Yet it was a hard place in which to settle down. The weather was unfriendly; the seasons short. But in Newfoundland, at least, the pioneers were monarchs of all they surveyed. Timber was there to build boats; and enough soil for small gardens, though not so productive as that of the old country. They came to stay, and stay they did.

In the earlier days, the first settlers lived right on the shore. They depended chiefly on the sea, catching cod and seal in tiny boats. But as they prospered and began to understand conditions in the new country, they built larger boats so that they could go off shore.

In the year 1800, old Billy Bartlett built a boat large enough so that he could go off shore and meet the great spring migrations of seals as they came down from the far north in March and April to whelp off the Newfoundland and Labrador coasts. Billy Bartlett's watchword was "Follow On," and to this day he is known as "Follow On Bartlett." Follow on he did, going away up the Labrador coast in his little shallop (for that's all she was) and returning back to Brigus loaded down to the gunwales with skins and blubber of seals.

Now began the Golden Age in Brigus. The town reached its crest fifteen or twenty years before I was born. Four hundred or so sailing craft swarmed in Conception Bay ports in those days, and on them likely 10,000 men made prosperous voyages. Sealers and fishermen they were mostly. As a youngster, I can remember the long lines of vessels berthed along the wharves of Brigus, their masts towering, their yards and rigging a fine marine forest, the very salt smell of them a beckoning lure for any small boy living there right at the edge of the sea. In those fine days the shipping brought the far places of the world close to our little port. . . . And now, there's not a sailing vessel hails from all Conception Bay. And Brigus, a sacrifice to the age of steam, is scarce an echo of its proud yesterdays.

Despite these sadly changed conditions my family still all follow the sea and love it. Of course in recent years our vessels have been mostly those of steam. However, down in our hearts we are old-fashioned "windjammers" and think of the sea in terms of wind and rigging; and we tend to choose our men for their mechanical perfection. It is out-of-date to feel this way, I know. And the comforts of modern life on the ocean are great. But somehow the toil and misery of early years has got into my blood to stay; which seems to me to be only natural when I think of the seafaring that preceded me.

No person living ashore can believe the hardships that men on the old sailing ships went through. Shortening sail in a gale, for instance, often meant hours on the upper yards in biting cold without one bit of shelter. At that time we did not wear fine slickers the way we do now. Our costume consisted of heavy blanketing drawers, a couple of flannel shirts, wool sweater, pilot cloth reefer and trousers homespun. On our feet we wore homespun knitted stockings and leather boots. This was before the days of fancy modern oilskins.

Our food consisted of boiled flour pudding and pork, served out in the middle of the day three times a week. This mass was about the colour of cement and almost the same consistency. Tea sweetened with molasses and hard biscuit and butter, completed our rations. No soft bread ever. But any time the ships were in the ice and whenever the galley was free we could roast or stew our strong seal meat, which was thrown away after skinning. The trouble was that very often for days we didn't get any seals; and it was seldom we could get the galley. Wood was scarce and the cook was rarely in good enough humour to let us mess round his quarters.

Most of the early captains had little or no education at all. Some of them unable either to read or to write. Yet they all fished from March to June anywhere from Cape Farewell to the Gulf Stream, often without charts, almanacs or sextants. And when the time came for them to bear up for home they pretty nearly always made good landfall. This was really remarkable, considering that the ice was always adrift and ships wandering in all directions out of sight of land.

Notwithstanding such dangers and hardships relatively few lives were lost. Of course in some bad seasons more ships were lost than in others. And when competition grew keen many of the masters took terrible chances for the seals; which meant more chances of losing their vessels. For instance, they would work into leads of open water along shore with no ice between them and the land to act as a fender. As a result if the wind changed and set the ice on shore there was no chance the doomed vessel would escape.

Generally the ice on the outside kept the water smooth so if the ship got nipped and was crushed the crew could get out of her and walk to another vessel or to shore. But sometimes they were caught in narrow strings of ice. If a gale of wind were blowing and a heavy sea running, the ship would then be pounded to pieces amid the broken ice and heavy swell. At such times the crews would have a hard time to get through, and always many drowned on the way.

My great-uncle, Captain Isaac Bartlett, had a pretty bad time one year when he was out late in the spring in his brig, *The Brothers*. He was hunting old seals well north of Cready, Labrador. A knockdown northeast gale came on, forcing him to run for the tight ice which lay along the coast in a strip some seventy miles wide. He found an opening and for twenty-four hours enjoyed a safe shelter among the old floes. But the wind kept up for several days; and to make matters worse the ice moved at a great rate south. Gradually it opened out and the swell increased. The continuous gale gradually split up the heavy floes. At length the pack in which Uncle Isaac's ship lay brought up on the land. With all the grinding it had had this ice was now just trash filled with the growlers. The latter were heavy, blue ice, just as hard as the very granite on shore, and each piece weighing many tons, pounding at the little ship. It was simply hell let loose. No ship ever built would stand such punishment. Finally the hull of *The Brothers* collapsed, but her crew managed by sheer good luck and good judgment to get to the shore by clambering over the ice. They were wet and shivering but some longshore fishermen took them in and so saved their lives.

Several other ships were lost the same day with all hands on board, all within a mile or two of where *The Brothers* went to pieces. The brig *Huntsman* drove over a small reef just awash at high water. With the impact of the ice, caused by gale, she drove through a saddle in the reef. One man out of a crew of forty-five jumped on the reef as she passed through.

The story of this man is a strange one. The next day, at about 11 a.m., some of the shipwrecked crews from the other ships were on the hill at Battle Harbour, which later became Dr. Grenfell's main Labrador Station. Looking toward the reef which is about three miles away the unhappy men thought they saw something moving. No ship was in sight not even the wreck of the *Huntsman* which had gone over the shoal or reef the previous afternoon leaving no trace. The men kept looking and after a while they came to the conclusion that it was a survivor of the ship's crew. But they could do nothing because of the awful weather. The next day the gale spent itself and ice moved off the shore. At once those ashore launched a boat and went out to the reef they had been watching. It is almost incredible that they took from the rock the lone survivor of the *Huntsman*. The poor fellow had been there sixty hours soaking wet and in the bitter cold with both of his legs broken. He was in bad shape, but he lived to make many a cruise after that.

Other Bartletts have found the sea a hard master, too.

In 1869, Captain John Bartlett went as far north as the Devil's Thumb in Melville Bay, Greenland. With him was Dr. Hayes, the famous American explorer. In 1874, another uncle of mine rescued Captain Tyson and other members of the Hall expedition who had been forced to abandon their ship in a blinding snowstorm off Lyttleton Island, Greenland. After seeking refuge on the ice they drifted south from October until April on a big floe. Another great-uncle, Captain John Bartlett, lost twenty-four of his men on his brig, the *Deerhound*. Old Nathan Percy, one of the survivors, told me the story:

"In company with us," so he tells it, "were eleven ships. But ourselves and Norrand Sam (the captain of the other ship) were the only ships which put down their punts that morning. The weather didn't look good. We dropped all our punts, then wore round and reached back to pick up the first one, the distance being about five or six miles back. Presently it began to snow. We were at the sixth punt dropped and five punts were still out. Captain John kept reaching back and forth under close reefed topsails, frantically hoping to find the missing punts. But the ice had broken up with the gale so we had to seek the heavy ice for safety.

"The next morning at eight o'clock, we ran upon a punt on a pan of ice. The crew of four men belonged to Norrand Sam. They had given up all hopes of being saved and were so weak and frozen that they had to be hoisted on board. We, in the *Deerhound*, were pretty well in line of his track when he reached back because we kept working to windward. This was what saved them. We lost on the *Deerhound* twenty-four men out of the crew of forty."

To give some idea of the sort of public spirit existing in my early days in a community, I would like to cite a case I knew about personally.

A vessel had been listed out and her crew began sheathing her. The weather looked sociable. Before night it was the usual thing to upright a vessel under such circumstances. But this time the owners took a chance of letting her stay over, in order that the crew could work on her promptly in the morning the next day. Unfortunately a gale of wind rose during the night. In the morning, there was no sign of the vessel. She had sunk. I remember this was in the middle of winter and with hard frost of at least twenty degrees below zero.

But the people didn't hesitate. Within a short time a crowd was mustered and every man in the neighbourhood responded. With the help of two other vessels they raised the sunken craft to the surface before night, pumped out her water, and made her ready for her crew to work on her at daylight the next morning. A tough job, I tell you, in the cold and wind and wet. Yet no one ever thought of asking any pay, either for the use of the vessels which had raised her or for the work which the men had done in getting her righted.

Recently when home old Nathan Percy (who helped raise her) and I were talking about it. Percy is near the 100-mile mark. He voiced an opinion, with which I was forced to concur, that if such a thing happened recently the old vessel would have to stay where she had sunk.

My father has been fifty-four springs to the seal fishery and only once had he had a man die on board. This death was caused by lack of nutrition. The man had been working hard at logging before coming on the ship and had not been eating nourishing food. He had walked a long distance to reach the ship from his home, and had worn himself down. On getting on board he contracted a cold which further reduced his vitality and he succumbed to it.

Men dying on board of a sealer have always been

brought home to be buried. A rough coffin is made of narrow boards, the seams of the box callused with oakum and then pitched. Usually one of the crew has had experience in preparing a body for burial. He does the job. The body is washed and clean clothes put on it. Coarse salt is then packed around it. The shroud keeps the salt in place. Lint or gauze is laid on the face and a pint of rum poured over it. Then the shroud is sewn up from head to heels. The body is then put in the box or coffin and this placed on deck to remain there until the ship reaches port when it is immediately passed on to the undertakers. The present practice is still about the same.

Of course medical help was scarce or quite absent in the early days. I have been to the seal fishery many times with as high as 300 men on board and no doctor. I have seen one of the sealers set another sealer's leg and the job was so good that when the ship arrived in port there was no occasion for the hospital doctor to reset the limb. The man had no anesthetics either. I have seen cuts in the head several inches long and deep, sewn with an ordinary needle and thread, and no ill effects.

I could go on and write a book just about the tough times a sailor man has; about his narrow escapes and his sufferings. But I must say, too, that for every foul day there's a fair one. Many is the compensation in adventure and contentment of life aboard a blue-water craft. But few who have not followed the sea can understand the feelings of one who has.

I remember once when I told a writer friend of mine I'd never marry because I loved the sea, he said:

"You don't really love it. It's a kind of insanity you fellows get, wanting to be wet and cold and ill-fed. When you say you love it and tell about the romance, it's all bosh!"

My friend was wrong. The mariner's life is just as full of adventure and romance as story writers and poets make it out to be. More so. In fact, sometimes I think a man who's been to sea all his life is far luckier than the landlubber.

But the sea is a hard master, and that's no mistake. Just ask any seafaring man that knows.

CHAPTER IV

MEANT FOR A MINISTER

As I was the eldest son my mother resolved that I should enter the ministry. So at fifteen I was sent to the Methodist College at St. John's, Newfoundland. But the spirit of my fathers was in my blood. The sea was calling me.

At seventeen I gave up the struggle and went with my father to the seal fisheries. Sealing is still a hard life. As I have already described, often a blizzard sweeps down while the men are away from their ship. Then, with no shelter and frequently without food, they wander about for hours, sometimes days. As many a staunch Newfoundlander has become numb and dazed at such a time and has lain down and died, we have many "sea widows" at home. Hard as it was, this was the life that ran in my blood.

Let me tell you a little incident in my own early experience to show how tough a young man has to be for that work. One time I was with a gang shooting old seals and we came to a lead of water separating us from a fine bunch of animals. As the lead was too wide to jump across, I took off my clothes without hesitation and plunged in. Remember this was early spring, with the temperature close to zero. I wouldn't do the same thing now for a cask of gold.

The water was terribly cold, but I swam across. I was so numbed that I found it hard to climb up on the sharp ice on the other side. Finally I crawled out with shivering limbs and chattering teeth. The other fellows threw my clothes and rifle across. With shaking fingers I got dressed and ran hard in the direction of the seals to warm up. It was a tough twenty minutes, I tell you. That evening the captain offered me a tot of rum for the unusual number of seals I had killed. As I don't drink, I didn't take it. But I remember how fine I felt when he looked me up and down and suddenly exclaimed: "You'll do, boy! You'll do!"

My first command of any craft came the next summer, when we were down at our family fishing station that had been established years before at Turnavik on the Labrador. This particular season the fishing was poor and my father was much worried.

June that year was full of raw fog and loose ice, both of which slowed things up all along the coast. Also the fish seemed bewitched. We simply couldn't find them. For three weeks I had been away with the traps seeking favourable opportunities to set them. It was pretty mean work, for we had no permanent shelter and only the sails of our small boat kept the weather from us at night. Living this way in our oilskins and long boots was anything but comfortable. About this time my father decided that he would send the schooner farther north. He had everything in readiness for the start when I put in an appearance with my trap boat. The first intimation I had of his plan to make a master of me was when I heard him say sharply:

"The schooner is all ready, Bob. I want you to take command and seek for fish."

I could hardly believe my ears. But mechanically I assented.

"All right, sir," said I, scarcely realizing that I had at last got my first command. Just a small fishing schooner, to be sure. But a real seagoing craft at that.

Like every youngster I lacked confidence in myself. Always before, Father had been with me to help and give counsel whenever I had been at the helm. Now I hardly knew how things were going to turn out. However, I went to the master's room aboard the vessel, changed my clothes, had a good wash-up and turned in to sleep. On awaking I felt greatly refreshed and cheered in spirits. I said to myself, "Now buck up! Father has every confidence in you, and he knows what he is about."

In an hour I had the gear shipshape, hove up and away I went. It was blowing down the "tickle," as Labrador inlets are called, and there was thick fog; but I kept on and at length reached the place around the cape where I decided to look for fish. Now I had never been so far north, and the naked unlighted coast was all new to me; but I was no worse off than many of my predecessors who had gone for the first time on the same quest.

I soon saw that the point we had reached was no place for us. So I kept north, going in and out of the bays, seeking all the information I could. I had some narrow escapes from rocks and shoals; but they only made me more determined. At length I reached a spot where I found fish. Never have I been so thrilled. It was late in the season and at times snow fell. But by holding on there as long as possible we were fortunate in securing quite a good fare of fish.

Thus came my real start in sea life at the age of seventeen. I have never regretted that experience. I had commanded a ship and brought her safe home loaded with fish. It made me confident, self-reliant and observant; and the responsibility was of incalculable value in my future work.

The first voyage I made outside the family schooner came the following year in an old square-rigger outward bound from St. John's with a load of dry fish for South America. When the impulse hit me I told no one, but went right down to the dock and enrolled as a common sailor before the mast. Then I walked to the hotel in St. John's where he had put up after that summer's fishing cruise which had just ended and told my father what I had done. To my surprise he did not object, though our schooner was already loaded with supplies for our return to Brigus.

After a little he said: "How will it be about your mother?"

"Won't you tell her?" I asked him.

But he would not. "No, you are her son. You have got to tell her yourself."

Although I weighed nearly 200 pounds at the time, about twice the size of the woman who bore me, I hated to face the music. But, the next day, I plucked up my courage when we got to Brigus and told my mother it looked as if the time had come for me to go off on my own hook.

Her eyes filled with tears. But, like Father, she did not try to stop me although I could see it hurt her terribly to think of my being away from home months at a time.

In the end she said: "I never intended you to go to sea, boy. But if you will persist in going, I cannot stop you."

I am happy to tell about her bravery, for she is still alive and has followed me in her mind's eye all over the Seven Seas, and clear to within a few miles of the North Pole.

Now before I go ahead and tell about the ill-fated first cruise, I want to make it plain that I was not one of those drifters who end up at sea because they have no real home, little of luxury and perhaps but a tithe of the vast blessing of parental love God means a man to have. For if ever a man had much in material things to keep him home, 'twas I. That my mother planned for me to be a minister had no bearing on the case. What counted, and what made hard the struggle in me against inborn yearning for the sea was one of the finest homes in Newfoundland; a home full of love and happiness; wonderful parents that knew no task that did not somehow fit into the welfare of their children; and a whole fishing village full of friendships that dated back more than 100 years between our family and the hardy folk about us.

My father and mother grew up when Brigus was at its best. Conditions there were then the same as in New Bedford, New London, Mystic, Stonington, and other New England places in their eras of prosperity. There was plenty of money in Brigus at the time; no unemployment; ten children to a family; and everywhere a great pervading happiness. It was the golden age of Newfoundland.

Grandmother Bartlett was boss in our tribe. Grandfather Bartlett, for all his ravings on the after deck, did not have much to say about the raising of his "kids."

"Abram, while I live, I reign," was Grandmother Bartlett's ultimatum on the beach. And reign she did. A good, kind woman, but as full of authority as ever a skipper at sea. In family affairs she set the course and steered it, come fair or foul, to the bitter winter day she died.

It was in my grandparent Bartlett's home that I was born. The house had high ceilings, and was plastered with homemade lime from basement to roof. The large rooms were furnished with old English furniture, mostly brought from the old country. In the lower floor were French windows with long crimson curtains and heavy mahogany rods in well-polished brass rings. I remember the rich Brussels carpet, the big mahogany table in the centre of the room, the open fireplace with its brass fenders and andirons; the quaint marble clock on the mantelpiece; the rich crimson and gold paper on the wall.

I can picture a snowy winter's evening with a lot of Brigus youngsters in to supper. The different games such as Bagatelle. The stories told. I can recall my grandmother asking us all about happenings at school, and listening attentively to every word of it. Much chatter about skating, coasting, hunting, and trouting. The girls whispering their affairs. Never-to-be-forgotten days!

Evenings one of my sisters would play the piano. Up and down the long wide hall we would dance waltzes, mazurkas, reels, polkas, lancers and quadrilles. It was an open house and always had been. Indeed, some of the boys' and girls' parents had been entertained as youngsters there a generation before we were born!

Grandmother lived well but simply. We ate enormously of her milk and cream, hot biscuits and jams, poultry, vegetables and roasts; a provender that produced a hardy group.

While I was still a child we moved to another house; we occupied one end of it, and a family by the name of Crosby lived in the other part of the house. With mother, the youngsters came along very fast. The Crosbys had a large family, as did we; but theirs were all grown-up, except a boy name Jack, my own age. His father was a well-to-do merchant with schooners and wharves and all that. Jack Crosby later became a man of a large family, and he held in turn about all the executive offices of the Newfoundland government. A few years ago he was knighted. Some day he may be Premier.

From March until May, Father would be away sealing; from June until October he fished on the Labrador. When the Crosbys moved to St. John's to go into the hotel business we went and lived with Grandmother Leamon (Mother's mother) who was all alone in her cottage called Hawthorne. All the houses in Brigus had names. Hawthorne Cottage is still one of the showplaces of Brigus.

I was fond of both my grandmothers, especially so of Grandmother Leamon. She was very fair, small, vivacious, full of fun, almost always on the go. Wherever she visited, people wanted her to stay longer. She was a born "mixer." Like a born seaman she had the eyes of a hawk. A spot on her carriage or harness, or the horse not well curried, she instantly noted. She had a will of iron. Anywhere she wanted to go, go she would. She could dance, sing, and play the piano. She waltzed in great style.

Her husband died young. She never remarried; a shame, I think, as so many men were crazy over her. But it gave the neighbours something to talk about, wondering which bachelor she was setting her cap for.

Wintertime in Brigus, from Christmas to the end of February, was one riot of parties, dances, bazaars, concerts, and the like. They were delightful days of Arcadian simplicity, when there were no debts and port wine was a shilling a bottle.

My mother in her girlhood was gay, sang and played well. She was church organist for years. Now that her own girls have grown up they have taken this position over from her. Some of the Bartletts were High Church Episcopalians; some were Congregationalists. But as Mother and Father were Wesleyan Methodists, never in all my life have I seen a playing card in our home. Only once have I seen strong drink there—that was when father had grippe. He almost died; indeed, the doctor had given him up and prescribed brandy. It was a long time before Mother agreed. Even then Father never got his drink. He lived. And the brandy was thrown away.

I cannot say that all Newfoundlanders held the same scruples. Rum flowed like water in those early days. The cost was generally only about five shillings a gallon for pure ninety per cent stuff. At that rate every man could afford his grog, morning, noon and night. Heaven help the knave who might be foolish enough to attempt to doctor it.

Nearly all of the old captains had their favourite pub or saloon. Once "aboard the hearth" in a warm armchair many of them would forget that they had any particular business or that their families required food. Hours they spent swapping yarns telling of their experiences. Despite the general hospitality men from outside villages coming to visit would usually be the signal for trouble. Old grievances would be renewed and new ones started. A free-for-all fight was no uncommon occurrence. As a boy I remember the terrific excitement such fracases would cause. At these times it behooved the constables to make themselves scarce for the sealers had no love for policeman. I recall one of them in particular, however, who never ran away and as a result received many hard knocks. But I can vouch for it that he gave just as many and often a little harder ones in return.

There are many interesting characters about these old pubs. One elderly sea captain had a gray pony called Billy. Along about 9:00 a.m. every morning Billy was brought around to the captain's door and away they would start. Everything was plain sailing until the first pub was reached. Then old Billy would anchor right there; the captain would climb out of the wagon and go in; and, no matter who might get into that wagon before the old man came teetering out and got in, not an inch would Billy be budged.

Since then I have sometimes seen his grandchildren driving the old nag. The horse would go along pretty well until he came to one of the usual haunts of the captain's and then he'd stop dead. And he wouldn't move unless someone got out and got in again. This done, Billy would go along as unconcernedly as though such a thing as a pub never existed but come to another and the same performance had to be gone over again!

Money was plentiful in those early days. With the

many avenues for revenue open to a man, especially sealing, it was seldom that all of them failed during one season. And since, as I have just said, those were the days of prohibition, nearly every master had a well-stocked cellar. As a result it was often a difficult thing for the poor womenfolk to round up their lords at mealtime since masters were always around sampling each other's stock. But this was also in the good old days when servants were plenty and never thought of kicking either at late dinners or extra company and meals were seldom served on the dot.

Visiting these old scenes today, it seems impossible that they could have been the centre of such open-hearted genial hospitality and gaiety. Alas, most of the fine old mansions have crumbled to dust with their owners.

Father's code was a terribly strict one even in other things besides drink. I never heard Father curse, or saw either Mother or Father drink or smoke. Though both had been raised in homes where there was plenty of liquor, card-playing and dancing, when Mother got a home of her own she had none of it. Father read prayers morning and evening. When Father was away sealing, Mother read prayers. It was a stiff change from the freedom of Grandmother's place.

Sunday with us kids was a day of church service and Sunday school. Father read aloud to us the *Christian Age*, an English paper; the Sunday School column in the Montreal *Weekly Witness*; and three other church papers. He had also read *Josephus*, *The Pilgrim's Progress*, Thomas à Kempis's *Dante*, and Rehan's *Life of Christ*. I think the one I liked best was *Josephus*.

I never did like Sunday School. Grandmother Leamon's house was my Sunday School. There, from her, I learned a lot about old Bible days, which she told to me as no teacher in a Sunday School could.

Ah, but those were golden Sunday afternoons with Grandmother Leamon! The western sun shining in through the windows of that fine old place, a little lad in velvet clothes and Eton collar sitting up in a chair before the open fireplace, with its crackling logs and the kettle on the hob. Then came the singing of the kettle, the fast fading daylight, the drawing over of the curtains, and Grandmother Leamon busy over the tea things. There were the big silver urn and teapot, the wonderful thin real Chinese teacups with pale pink flowers all over them; and finally all the good things to eat that a hungry boy would like. Then out again into the starry night, crisp snow underfoot, and home to my soft eiderdown bed, where Mother would hear my prayers.

Often did I lay awake in those days thinking over many things my nurse had told me. She was the spinster daughter of an old Brigus fisherman, and a great reader. She had read every book in our house and all of the Sunday School library. Some of the latter were chock full of hellfire. She gloried in telling me about these. I spent many an uncomfortable hour in bed trying to figure out how folks could ever stand to burn in hell forever and ever; what sort of book God kept all the names in of those who did bad and good things; and what sort of a man God was to be able to do this sort of bookkeeping.

Growing up we were always in awe of our parents.

"Children should be seen and not heard" was the rule in those days. I never was chummy with my father until I grew up. He was a stern man. I have heard but few men or women ever call him by his first name, even those who, as boys and girls, played and grew up with him. It was always "Captain" or "Skipper." I always had to "sir" him; and, when speaking to Mother, to say, "Yes, Mother" or "Yes, ma'am."

I wouldn't dare to come in Father's presence with my cap on, nor would I in any way be familiar or salacious. One time I had just come into the smoking room of the Crosby Hotel in St. John's to see Father. I remember he was standing by the big open fireplace at the end of the public room. Someone began telling a rough story. Father gave me one look and I cleared out quicker than you could clear a gantline.

Mother can knit, sew, do fancy work, nurse, run a store, a ship, a church, a school, a farm, a garden, or a political meeting. She is loved by everyone in Brigus, old and young. Her name is a household word in the village. She has had lots of trouble. She lost a daughter in childbirth. Three children died young. My brother Rupert, the apple of her eye, was killed during the World War in France. Another brother, Lewis, contracted anthrax in Mesopotamia in 1916.

Mother went through days of adversity when thousands of dollars were lost in one season of sealing and cod fishing. She endured anxious days when Father and his men went sealing and cod fishing amidst storms and hard fortune, with the wives, mothers and children at home. If tragedy came, Mother was always the one to whom the stricken came.

Two years ago my father and mother celebrated their golden wedding anniversary.

I think now I have made it plain why I declare I did not go to sea because I was a wastrel without home, luxury or parental love. I had all three; few men have been so fortunate. And the deep religious atmosphere in which I lived with my mother and father might have been calculated to give the final touch to my mother's ambition that I should wear the cloth.

But against all visible there was dual influence ever at work beneath my boyish exterior: the blood in my healthy young veins and the unending stories of my seafaring relations, many of whom were then at the height of their splendid maritime careers, that fell upon my eager ears.

For instance, there was Uncle John, my father's brother, born in Brigus back in '48. In the beginning, Grandfather Abram felt that ship's dock was no place for Uncle John's education, so he was put to school at Harbour Grace, eighteen miles away. There his schoolmate was the Headmaster's son, who later became Sir Thomas Roddick, Canada's great surgeon.

When John Bartlett had finished his education Abram, as a matter of course, had built for him the fine brig *Henrietta Grieve.* It was quite the usual thing in those days in our country for well-to-do fathers to give their sons a brig, just as a wealthy boy gets a fine automobile today.

John Bartlett, though just a lad, went out as master of the *Henrietta.* Mostly this able brig carried flour from

Montreal to Baltimore, and herring from Labrador to Montreal. He traded, too; that is, sold his herring at the Canadian port, buying flour and selling it again at a profit in Baltimore, plus the freight. All through the Civil War he was busy at that.

Each spring the *Henrietta* nosed out in the ice, seal hunting the east of Newfoundland. On her last hunt the figures show that she brought in 10,000 young harp seals, something of a record. And a record price they brought him too, for Uncle John got forty-two shillings and sixpence a quintal of 112 pounds.

I used to love to hear my mother tell about Uncle John's first steamer, the *Panther*. She was owned by his father, and was built at Miramichi, NB. The young skipper, then but twenty years of age, drove her across under sail alone in thirteen days to the Clyde, where she was engined and returned to this side to follow up the seal fisheries. The *Panther* was about the first steamer owned in Newfoundland to go seal hunting; and her master, John Bartlett, among the very first Newfoundlanders to obtain a British Master Mariner's certificate. With him as mate went my Uncle Sam Bartlett; and as second mate my father, William Bartlett. Later Sam succeeded John as master of Peary's ships, and I in turn succeeded him.

All this time Captain John had been roaming around the Seven Seas and up in the ice sealing. In 1869, came his first real taste of the Arctic—the first Bartlett to get his nose away in beyond the Arctic Circle. Tales of his voyages among the ice laid the foundation for my own love of polar work on which I put so many years of my life.

Dr. Isaac I. Hayes had been surgeon on the Elisha Kent Kane Arctic Expedition, which searched for the lost Franklin Expedition. In 1869, Dr. Hayes organized an expedition of his own. On that trip, which continued as far north as the Devil's Thumb on the south side of Melville Bay, the old *Panther* under Uncle John nosed her way into almost every fjord along the Greenland coast from Cape Farewell to the Duck Islands. With him Dr. Hayes took the American artist, William A. Bradford, many of whose Arctic pictures are now hanging in the American Museum of Natural History in New York City, and in the Library at Stonington, Connecticut.

A martinet was Uncle John, a first-class navigator, and a great hand for carrying sail. And what a dandy he was! Always spic and span, his gear shining like a liner's brass fittings. If he so much as touched his hand to emptying coal into the stove, he'd first put on some gloves. "Gentleman John" some called him; a few, "Black Jack," but that behind his back, because of the dark strain in us.

Now John Bartlett has set sail on his last voyage, out on the untroubled sea beyond the horizon of this life. May his fine pioneer spirit sail free before fair winds.

Another Bartlett, an older one, figured in a great Arctic experience of those early days. That was Isaac, uncle to my father and John. Hall, in the *Polaris*, went north in 1872. The vessel was lost off Lyttleton Island in October of the next year. Some of the party took to the ice and became isolated on the polar pack. They drifted all through the long winter night, working slowly down into Baffin Bay and further south.

That spring Uncle Isaac in the *Tigress* was out seal hunting along the Labrador coast. He sighted the Tyson party from the *Polaris*. They had been drifting on the ice for more than 200 days. Miraculously, not one of them was lost; indeed, there was one more human being on the ice at the end of the long drift than when they had started. An Eskimo woman, Hannah, had given birth to a baby!

Another one of our Bartlett tribe came into the picture about then. This was Uncle Harry, John's youngest brother, and a particular favourite with my father. Harry had been north with Peary on the *Falcon* for several voyages in the '90s. In 1894, he brought back Commander Peary, his wife, and little Marie, to Philadelphia. Marie was born the year before up at Redcliff on Bowdoin Bay in the very shadow of the Pole, the most northerly born white child in the world. After landing the Pearys at Philadelphia, Harry started back home in the *Falcon* with a load of coal. He was never heard of again and the mystery of his disappearance never was solved.

So it went, over and over again; tale after tale of mystery and adventure, with always the blue sea and stout ships behind a list of splendid mariners that made one proud to claim a kinship with them. And so was woven about my youth an irresistible lure to follow where my father had gone, where his father, and his father's father.

As my mother said: "I never intended you to go to sea, boy. But if you persist in going, I cannot stop you."

The truth was, I could not stop myself.

CHAPTER V

MY FIRST SHIPWRECK

I didn't sign up on that first deep-sea voyage in the fall of 1893, without a good deal of thinking. For though I was eighteen and had discovered that I was good enough to handle my father's schooner, I well knew that putting off in a big ship was to be an entirely different kettle of fish. In the eyes of my friends and family, I was a seafaring man; in the eyes of the law I was nothing.

The law says that you have to do your apprenticeship first and according to figure. Four years must be spent to get a second mate's papers; another year for first mate and a sixth year for Master Mariner. And these years have to be real years. They don't count in-between times. You have actually got to be on a ship every one of the 365 days of them and see service on each day. There is no getting around the law on such matters.

One thing that made me think hard was the sight of my father busying himself with our little schooner, the *Osprey*, which lay at the dock unloading her fish and skins which we turned in for credit at St. John's; with this credit he would buy up supplies for our small store at Brigus. Father's hair was just beginning to turn white; and though he was still the hale and hearty skipper I had always known, I saw he no longer put his back into the heavy lifts and straps the way he had done a few years before. It was with a pang I thought of adding to his burden by going off and leaving him. But if I was to succeed him later on I must get my "papers." And to get them I must do more than seal and fish.

While our little vessel was lying alongside the dock, and after I had my invoices and other papers pretty well checked up, I took a walk out around the hills behind the town. I was thinking things over very seriously. I could see ahead a few years. What chance would I have along with the rest of the fellows if they had papers and I didn't? I mean the legal papers that made them Master Mariners according to law. What good would it be if I could handle a vessel better than they, or as well as they, if the law didn't have me down in its books?

After a few hours I came back to the dock. My mind was made up. For a while I was going to leave my friends and my family and all the Labrador fishing and sealing that I loved and go into merchant service. It was not a happy thought. We of the sealing fleet looked down on the merchant service. The big ships that took cargoes were to us what a baggage car, I suppose, is to a cowboy. They were just big carriers of freight. There was no particular excitement about them except that they went to interesting parts of the world.

But my mind was made up; I had to get ahead. So I set forth at once rummaging around the docks for a berth. There was one big freighter, the *Corisande*, a square-rigged ship of large tonnage and fine record. As luck would have it, I fell in with her skipper that very afternoon.

I can see him now. He was a little fellow, more like a vice-president of a bank than a commander of a big square-rigged vessel. He was small, dapper and had a well-groomed look that goes more with the commercial landsman than with the carefree sailor. I don't say that sailors are not clean. They are the cleanest people in the world. But Captain Hughes had that clean look which comes from getting scrubbed up every morning in a bathtub at home and not from being scrubbed down by the wind and brine over the side. He wore gloves and he carried a stick with a shining ivory knob on the end of it. Below the ivory the stick had his initials in gold letters. The captain wore a stiff shirt with studs in it and a navy blue suit that was perfectly pressed. He certainly was the picture of a man who not only took great pride in himself but wanted to show the world that the sea was the finest profession going. There was just one thing about him that worried me. That was a nervous way he had of looking about him every now and then as if he were afraid something was going to happen, he didn't know what.

"Good morning, lad," said he, waving his stick as a naval officer might salute with his sword.

"Good morning, sir."

"Fine morning," he went on.

My feet felt nailed to the dock planking. I wanted to ask him for a job on his ship. I didn't know how to begin. I had a desperate feeling that he was going to walk away if I didn't say something. Finally I came right out with it.

"I'd like to go to sea with you, sir."

He looked me up and down and just as if he had suddenly discovered my presence. I felt my face go red. I didn't look like a sailor especially, though I was a good hearty lad with a fine coat of sunburn from a summer down among the islands. I didn't even have any seagoing clothes on; just a cap and an old suit and an open-necked shirt that I guess was faded from scrubbing the fish oil out of it.

"What do you know about a ship?" said Captain Hughes.

"I just brought mine in," I told him. "Just a schooner, sir; but she's all right. I can steer and reef and I have been in the *Hope* and the *Panther*."

"Very well," said Captain Hughes briskly. "Be at the shipping office at three."

That's all there was to it.

Remember this was October, the time of the year when the summer hurricanes are over and the winter gales haven't started yet. It was the ideal season for a trip down the Atlantic. I was to be an ordinary seaman before the mast and I had shipped for the round trip. As this was to be my first voyage, my mouth watered for the experience. Little did I dream that it would end in tragedy.

I went aboard the afternoon before we sailed. My personal gear I carried in a canvas sea bag and a big handkerchief tied together at its corners. Besides what I had on I took an extra suit of woollen cloth for the cold trip back, a change of underwear, two towels, a big razor my father had given me, and a spare pair of heavy fishing boots. When I opened my bag in the forecastle I found also a fine knitted muffler my mother had put in. Wrapped inside it was a jar of her best blueberry jam which she knew was my favourite sweet.

We were towed out of the harbour at dawn next morning.

While I was busy about the pin-rails faking down the various ropes in neat coils I had a heavy depressed sort of feeling. Part of it was pure homesickness; but there was also a premonition of trouble lay ahead. I am not especially superstitious, but now I have learned to trust my hunches about the future.

That time on the *Corisande* I surely was right. Scarcely had we left the dock when a fight started on deck. One man knocked another unconscious with a blow of his fist. Of course many of the men had been drinking as they always do just before leaving port on a long cruise. I guess even the skipper had it a bit up his nose too.

It took us sixty-nine days to make Pernambuco. The usual run was about thirty days. And all the while it seemed as if the *Corisande* knew she was doomed. I suppose I am stretching my imagination to say such a thing; but the others felt it as well as I. There were times when she suddenly trembled from stem to stern for no reason at all. There was more minor sickness aboard than there should have been. The ship's company were quarrelsome and ill at ease. At times a strange silence descended on all hands and we looked curiously into one another's faces to see if anyone knew the answer. A ship's cat we had aboard disappeared for no reason at all one calm night.

Captain Hughes must also have felt the shadow over us. He was no longer the same smart sailor man I had signed on with. He stayed much in his cabin and when he came out he was irritable and captious.

About halfway down my watchmate got laid out with a bad cut over his eye. As a result I did double wheel tricks, which in turn led to a boil on my neck getting chafed by dirty oilskins I hardly ever took off in the long hard watches. Soon the boil turned into a carbuncle that tormented me day and night with pain. The skipper wanted to lance the carbuncle. He declared that was the only way to cure it. Nearly every day he came at me with a long, thin knife he'd got out of the ship's medicine chest. But in his peevishness at my timidity his hand shook so that I was afraid to let him try it. This made him madder than ever. It got so that I was afraid to turn in. I felt sure he'd operate on me while I slept. Anyway, the pain was too dreadful to let me sleep. What finally saved my life was a series of hot barley poultices the cook put on when the old man wasn't looking.

Incidentally, this cook, like many cooks on such a voyage, was a great friend of all us sailors. I never forgot how, on the first day out, the cook caught me washing my teeth with fresh water. He said I'd have to go without that much water for my coffee because fresh water was so scarce.

One day the captain had a regular forepeak row with this same cook. We had all been complaining about the beef being too salty and were tired of eating salt horse every meal. The cook usually took it out of the kegs and boiled it the same day. We had a big Swede who threatened to throw the fellow overboard if he didn't improve the grub. So the cook made a sort of crate that would hold about fifty pounds of salt horse. He spliced a rope to this crate and hung it from the jib-boom so it would trail in the water. He figured this would iron out some of the brine.

The captain saw this gadget one day and threw a fit. "What sort of river barge do you think I'm running?" he yelled at the cook.

Cookie shook in his shoes.

"Haul that truck aboard!" screamed the old man. "Don't you know that if we get our horse too fresh that gang of heathen down forward will eat too much of it?"

Finally we hit Pernambuco and beached the cargo. As we'd lost so much time, we took only ballast for the return. The weather was very bright with fresh wind night and day.

The *Corisande* now suddenly changed her ways. She began to make speed, as though, now that her death was getting close, she got sort of panicky and terrified. When the wind stiffened to half a gale she stood up straight and took it without a reef.

We raced another ship north. She had longer spars and carried more, but we left her hull down astern on the fourth day. Even this triumph didn't cheer us any.

The crew began to feel surer than ever something was coming. How did we know? We didn't. A man often feels that way on a ship that is making her last voyage.

"All dead below there?" sings out the mate one after-noon down the forecastle hatch. He'd never heard so much silence, he said. Nobody answered.

Off Cape Cod real cold hit us. The wind backed around into southeast by south. The sun faded out. Snow flurries came with every squall. The days were dark and overcast. The steady whine of the wind through the rigging never stopped.

The skipper had her laid dead for Cape Race. I guess the wind must have stiffened as we were logging over ten knots right along. This was too much for the old *Corisande*. The mate came and stood by me at the wheel one day. His face was dark as the sky. He shook his head and grumbled: "She can't stand this—she can't stand this—" twice over, like that.

By this time the mate wasn't on speaking terms with Captain Hughes. So he didn't say anything about what was on his mind to the old man.

Things began to get bad in the afternoon watch of the day before the final tragedy. A heavy sea was running. Twice the *Corisande* stuck her nose, bowsprit and all, clean under. Two hands were busy chopping ice off her standing rigging. A big water cask lashed abaft the mizzen got adrift and nearly killed the cook. Sounding fore and aft showed she was making water. The heavy rolling and pitching and strain of the big spread we carried were pulling her seams right open.

We were due to round Cape Race the following morning. I had the middle watch—midnight to four a.m. Along about two I said to the mate, "We're near land, sir."

"You're landstruck, young 'un!" he bawled back at me to make me hear above the racket of the wind.

It was as black as your hat. But I'd heard seabirds off the port bow. I knew that meant land.

At four a.m. I turned in "all standing"; that is, with boots and slicker on. I even kept the strap of my sou'wester around my neck. There's no use denying it now, I was scared. What I was scared of, I couldn't have said. But I knew that sure as sunrise something terrible was going to happen. And something did.

An awful crash that threw me out of my bunk waked me. I didn't need to be told what it was. The ship had struck.

I rushed to the topside. To my surprise, the storm had disappeared. But the faint light of dawn showed me where it had gone. Ahead was a vertical black wall that jumped right out of the sea.

The cliff towered three times as high as our masts. I recognized it at once as the Devil's Chimney, the most dangerous spot on the south shore of Newfoundland. Over its top the storm still roared. Long streamers of snow licked out toward our topmasts.

"We've got to work fast!" I heard the mate yell. His voice sounded high and sharp with excitement.

I knew what he meant; we all did. The will of God had put us into a lee that might last an hour or it might last ten minutes. With the storm centre so near and the wind shifting northward it would be in the west the minute the centre passed. Then our lee would be gone.

There was no confusion. We got our boats over the side. I ran below and put on all my best clothes under my oilskins. Just as we shoved off we got the first puff of wind from the northwest. It was like a knife. Minutes counted.

In the half light and drifting snow we felt our way in. The wind was coming in heavy blasts now. Surf was picking up. We could hear it booming against the cliffs to the westward. As I rowed I kept looking at the poor old *Corisande* standing there alone and helpless like a fat sheep surrounded by wolves with white teeth. If I hadn't been so scared, I'd have cried.

Just before the gale's fury came full in we found a narrow opening at the foot of which was a small sand spit. But before we could reach it the wind struck full force. The boat I was in swamped. We floundered around in the icy water and somehow dragged ourselves ashore. God, it was cold!

By a miracle we came through, all of us. We dragged our gear as far as we could above the seas that rolled higher every minute. As soon as we finished, I crawled around on the rocks to get a last look at the poor old *Corisande*. You see, I loved her. She was my first big ship. She had weathered the storm and brought us in safely. Now I knew there was no hope for her.

The most terrible thrill a seafaring man can ever feel comes when his ship goes down before his eyes. I shall never forget that thrill thirty years ago when the *Corisande* was being flung against the black south cliffs of Newfoundland.

I strained my eyes to get a last glimpse of the ship's top-gallant sails and royals as the huge combers sprang upon her with a smother of foam. Then a flurry of snow shut her all out. Big waves forty feet high were rolling in. They made a regular thunder when they struck. I climbed higher, but couldn't seem to get clear of their spray.

Then, of a sudden, the snow stopped. I stood looking down into a dreadful, foaming mess of sea, boiling like a gigantic pot. In the centre of it was the *Corisande*. Her masts were gone—just a tangle of spars and rigging hung over her port bow. Her hull had broken clean across the middle. While I looked, her after deckhouse went over the side. Then her whole stern slewed and lifted bodily over the fore wreckage.

I felt sick all over at the sight. I shut my eyes. When I opened them again the *Corisande* was gone.

That was my first shipwreck.

Cold and miserable I rejoined the others who were huddled in a cleft in the rocks. For a while it looked as if we should all be drowned by the surf that roared at our heels, or frozen to death by the zero wind that slashed down upon us from the cliffs. When I saw the sufferings of some of the men less hardy than I, I realized what it meant to have had my years training down the Labrador with my father who had always insisted on us boys doing our full share of the work.

Finally one of the men said he knew where a fishing hut was on the plateau above us. He worked his way slowly up the dizzy cliff against which we crouched and finally reached the top. Here he was nearly blown into the sea by the blast which struck him. But he groped his way through the drifting snow and a few hours later staggered into the house he was looking for, where some fishermen had gathered to wait out the storm. When he told his story of the wreck they all hurried back with ropes and warm clothing and handed us up more dead than alive.

I reached home several days later. My mother was frankly overjoyed to see me again. What she wanted was to have me back safe and sound. But my father wanted to hear more about the wreck. To my surprise I found I couldn't talk much about it. Since then I have learned that the loss of a ship affects a seafaring man much like the loss of a dear relative; and it pains him greatly to discuss the circumstances of the sorrow.

The voyage was not without its benefits. I had made a deep-sea voyage, and had taken the first step towards my master's papers which I knew I must have if I were to succeed in my chosen profession.

CHAPTER VI

I CARRY BANANAS

The wreck of the *Corisande* "brought me up with a round turn" in life. It sickened and depressed me. Had the vessel been one of the small craft I had been used to down the Labrador, or even one of our coastwise sealers, I don't think I should have been so distressed. But to end a long voyage on a splendid ship with such a catastrophe just before Christmas oppressed like death itself.

For days I just wanted to sit around our house in Brigus. Never had the front room with its red sofa and big family album looked so pleasant. Never had the evening lamp and books and the voices of my brothers and sisters seemed so warmly comforting. For the first time in my life I took satisfaction in just staying quiet and sensing the shelter of a home. I smile now to think of the lumbering hulk of me, me who had never known what quiet was, poking around home like a depressed old man.

I think Father understood how I felt. He didn't urge me to go right off to sea again. When sealing season came he tactfully suggested I might get a berth with him or with Captain Stern, a neighbour. But even that plan he made dependent on me. I doubt if anything he ever did for me in all the years since has meant so much as his attitude at this time.

In the end I went sealing. Luckily too; for the sea and the ice down the old familiar Newfoundland coast soon made me forget what I had been through; and sight of the iron skippers in their glory leading and driving their men to do great things reminded me full force that I still had a long road to travel before I could get my mate's and captain's papers.

How seriously youth takes life—sometimes.

When summer came I put to sea again on another freighter. This time I kept at it without unusual incident until I had the full four years of good service in that gave me papers for the rank of second mate. There followed an uneventful six months more, this time with my first authority, on the year I must serve before I could finish my first mate's trick.

Then I got into the West Indian fruit trade. And as a result, it hurts me to this day every time I eat a banana. I don't mean they disagree with me. I guess I could eat a whole bunch of bananas, the fine way my plumbing works. But every time I see one I still think of the days when I used to have to cart the wretched things up from the Caribbean.

I had been off with Father for a few months that summer looking over our fishing station at Turnavik, and was eager to take on those last six months I needed for my mate's papers. Unsuspecting what lay ahead of me I went around to Harvey's, the big shipping agents in St. John's, and asked the assistant manager how the land lay.

This gentleman was a tall pale man called "the

Professor" by those along the waterfront. He had a way of looking over his spectacles when he talked to you. Before he answered my inquiry he uncoiled in his chair and pawed over some papers on his desk. Presently his eye lit on one that made him stop and read. Then suddenly he peered over his glasses and said jerkily:

"Good chance for you, Bartlett. Right down in New York. Couldn't be better. Steamer, *Grand Lake*. She needs a second mate. Why don't you try her?"

"What does she do?" said I. A sailor is the most trusting man on earth. But I had learned a lesson or two in the *Corisande*.

"Oh, bananas," jerked the "Professor" in an offhand way.

I tried to remember something about bananas. I always liked them. They were nice sweet fruit and we always used to have them at Christmastime. But I couldn't recall anything about going to sea with them. That was my big mistake.

"Sign me on," I said without a thought of what I might be letting myself in for.

So I got my ticket to New York from the agency and went down the same day. I didn't want to lose any time. That's the way life is: a man's misfortunes are often right ahead of him and he can hardly wait to get to them. Of course he can't see them; which, I suppose, makes it better after all.

The *Grand Lake* was really the first of the newfangled sealers. Old sealers were built of wood because a wooden ship is elastic enough to stand ice pressure. My father and his friends always used to say that ice would knock a steel ship to pieces. "Too brittle," was the way they put it. The *Grand Lake* was a mixture; a steel skeleton with wood on the top of that. In her first springtime out of St. John's she went down north with the regular sealing fleet. To the surprise of all the old-timers her steel frame stood the gaff all right. Nowadays most of the outfit are steel.

Captain Major commanded her. He seemed very sour and didn't say much when I reported to him in New York. I didn't realize at the time what he had on his mind; I do now though. It was bananas.

He was a great big raw man with a threatening look in his eye. And he had that droop to one side of his mouth that a person with bad temper often has. As I was just a bit cocky about being a mate now after having been so long an ordinary sailor, it struck me that the captain might pass the time of day a little with me. But about all I could get out of him was a few grunts.

We got under way next morning and made Jamaica in ballast ten days later. There I got my first sight of bananas, a whole lot of bananas all at once. And I tell you it's a terrible sight if once you have realized what can happen to this fruit.

First of all you bring the bananas aboard green. They are all heavy and hard and stiff. They look so nice and firm that it seems as if they will last forever. But they don't last forever, not by a jugful. Right away they have to be stowed just right down below so they won't roll around and bang each other. Then the temperature has to be adjusted like that in an incubator. The game is to get the bananas to New York with just as few as possible of them damaged. Profit is a matter of how many bananas *don't* spoil.

The running time of our ship was figured out so that the fruit would ripen on the way north. Thus when it

reached New York or Providence—we made both ports—
the bananas would be ready for the market. The trouble
with this arrangement was that if the ship was delayed the
bananas would be ripe before she got into port. All in all the
voyage was just a race against nature.

As soon as we got out to sea I learned some more
unpleasant things about carrying bananas. You have to wet-
nurse them day and night. In fact it took nearly half the
crew just to run around decks and trim ventilators and
watch the thermometers. It was worse than caring for an old
man with chills.

We finally got into port with our first cargo. We were
on time and the cargo was ripe and nice for the market. I
felt pretty nearly as much relieved as the skipper did. But
my pleasure was ruined when I went over the side that day
for a taste of shore food and the first thing I saw on the bill
of fare was "Sliced Bananas."

The next trip wasn't so good. The old man and I had a
falling-out when we got down to Jamaica. It happened this
way. As we didn't have anybody aboard who could paint
decently, I took a pot and went over the quarter one morning
to touch up our name. While I was on the stage busy with my
art, down the dock came a young West Indian courtesan, one
of those nice shiny black women you see all through the
Islands. She was barefooted and had only one garment on, a
bright pink skirt of trader's cotton. She wasn't much in the
"map" but she had a fine figure and a friendly eye. I should
say she was eighteen or twenty. She came rambling along
looking for a sailor and the first one she spied was me. Not
thinking, I laid down my pot and brush and sized her up.

Of course I didn't have my mind on anything except what a fine figure of a human female she was.

Then all of a sudden from overhead came a noise like a lot of firecrackers going off. It was Captain Major who had spotted me in what he thought was a flirtation. When he got his breath he called me on board. He talked to me all the way up the bow at the top of his lungs. As a result the whole dock was laughing at me by the time I got over the side— me, a mate, mind you. I never was closer to murdering a man in my life. But I didn't answer him back; I was afraid to; not afraid of him, but of myself.

That was the beginning of distressful days.

On the way north we ran into headwinds. As the skipper was unusually glum I first thought he was worrying about the weather. So I piped up with something to him about the ship taking it easy with all the freeboard she had. But when he whirled around at my little remark and nearly blew me off the end of the bridge with the raft of language that shot out of his mouth I realized I had put my foot in it; I don't mean his mouth either. It was at once plain that what Captain Major was worried about was those doggoned bananas between decks. They were getting riper and riper every minute; and here our speed had gone down to a crawl of about five knots.

While the headwinds kept up, nature was working overtime between decks. We trimmed ventilators and monkeyed with the draft, but all to no purpose. The bananas kept right on ripening. By this time the sea had made considerably. I was running about taking a hand at the ventilator controls when the captain threw another fit. I thought for a minute he was going to have a stroke, he was so excited. (He did have a stroke afterwards, which shows what bananas can do to a man.)

He came down off the bridge, taking six steps of the ladder at a time and strode over to where I was puffing and panting over a cowl lever. He was so angry his face worked and his hands were making chopping movements in the air. After he sputtered around for a few minutes I gathered that he objected to me, a mate, working harder than the common sailors. He was right. But I must say that as I was younger and huskier and heavier than any sailor aboard it didn't seem quite right at the time not to give orders and execute them at one and the same time. I had yet to learn what it meant to be ship's officer.

There came a disagreeable experience the second night of the blow. In those days a mate didn't stay on the bridge all the time the way he has to now. Despite he wasn't supposed to do manual labour he really wasn't much better than a high-class sailor. About half way through the evening watch with a heavy sea coming up over the bow I was worrying about the salt water getting to our fruit. So I began to prowl around the well deck smelling down hatches and checking cowls with the wind. The first thing I knew I heard a commotion up on the bridge. It was the old man bawling again.

The first mate passed me just then and said: "Better go back, Bartlett. The old man sounds excited."

I hurried back up the ladder. Captain Major was standing by the binnacle. The helmsman was on the opposite side of the wheel from him sort of huddled down out of reach of the old man's fists.

"Look at her! *Just look at her!*" yelled the captain.

I ran over to the compass. The *Grand Lake* was four points off her course! We were headed for Atlantic City instead of Providence.

"Terrible, sir!" was all I could think to say.

"*Terrible!*" exclaimed the old man. "If I weren't short-handed I'd have you throw this fellow over the side and make you jump after him!"

He went on at a great rate for some time. I didn't blame him. With the scud overhead and thick weather coming on there was no telling how long it would be before we could get another sight. Also a zigzag course only delayed us that much more with the bananas ripening all the time.

The following night, I had the mid watch and the same helmsman who had got me in trouble was on at the wheel. I was afraid if I got into any more fracases I wouldn't make my mate's papers. So I didn't say anything but moved quietly off to the end of the bridge and put my eye on the fellow. Meanwhile the skipper slipped below to his room and turned in. I imagine he was exhausted with his worry over those bananas between decks.

By the binnacle light I could soon see the helmsman's head droop. In five minutes he had nodded clean over twice. The more I looked at him the madder I got. Then and there I saw how a ship's officer was at the mercy of one stupid sailor; and I, a good hard-working lad, with my finger on my number trying to get my papers. (Remember I was only twenty-three.)

Finally my feelings got the better of me. I went up to the helmsman and took him a sharp clip on his ear. He came to with a jerk. He was my weight. He let go of the wheel and swung a wallop for my chin. I let him miss and landed a clean one on his teeth. I felt my knuckles sting from the cutting they got. Then I lit into him in earnest. As we both had oilskins on we couldn't do very much damage. But I had him going from the start. I pounded him so hard that I actually tired myself out.

Meanwhile the ship was going around in circles. Luckily there weren't any other vessels in our neighbourhood. I guess this circling let the gale shoot water in the lee port over the captain's bunk. The first thing I knew he was standing at my elbow. But I was too busy to bother with him. With all the strength that I had left I hit my man half a dozen times more and then leaned against the rail out of breath and done in from exertion.

At the same time I braced myself for what the old man might say for half murdering his helmsman. I even thought he might turn on me himself. Imagine my surprise when he stuck his nose up in the air and said in a friendly way, "Well, Bartlett, how's the glass?"

Not a word about the piece of human wreckage in front of him or of my own unofficerlike behaviour.

I filled my lungs a couple of times before I answered. Then I said, not having seen the glass for an hour: "About the same, sir." That was all. Captain Major grunted and went below. As for the helmsman he snuffled a lot, but he kept the course the rest of the watch.

The next day, real tragedy began. When I went on deck at seven bells of the morning watch I stuck my head in one hatch and got a whiff of 10,000 dying bananas. It almost hurt to smell them. Without thinking I started forward to ask the captain about it. But when I saw him raving on the bridge again I knew it was no use. Five minutes later the order came down to jettison the cargo.

It was a horrible job. Nice firm bananas can be handled. But soft black squashy bananas are worse than melted butter. You can't pour them into anything and you can't hook anything into them. By the time the sun had crossed the meridian our ship's waist smelled as if one gigantic banana had been stepped on by a thousand men. It was awful. It was ten hours before we got them all over the side.

That wasn't the end of our troubles either. The day before we made landfall the boatswain came to me with a stowaway.

"I found this fellow in the after lazarette," he said.

"Well, what are you going to do with him?" I asked.

My idea was that the poor fellow, who looked starved and cold (he was dressed in a cotton shirt and breeches, nothing else), ought to be fed.

Just then the first mate came along and threw up his hands and shouted:

"A thousand dollars fine!"

We soon learned he was right. That sum would be the company's penalty for bringing him in. When the captain heard this latest news he almost had another fit of hysterics. With a lot of hard language he told us that a ship with a stowaway was fined just as if she were trying to smuggle in a man. In this way the law prevented any alibis.

Two days later we got to Providence. By this time Captain Major was limp. He could hardly talk. He had lost a lot of money and the owners would be terribly angry. And there was the stowaway: a thousand dollars fine on top of a ruined cargo. It was enough to make a man lose his mind.

"Put him in your room, Bartlett," said the old man, speaking of the West Indian.

So I took the poor devil down and locked him in. This meant Captain Major would turn him over to the immigration authorities. By making a clean breast of it and proving the fellow as his prisoner he might clear the company.

I went back on deck terribly depressed. To add to all our other misfortunes the chief engineer had just reported civil war in the fireroom. It seems that the owners had given orders that the fireroom force was to be all one nationality: all Germans, or all Italians, or all French, or whatever. The chief had been careless and as a result there were three Germans and three Irishmen. The two nationalities didn't seem to get along at all.

Just as we passed the bridge outside of Providence a great screeching came up from the engine-room hatch. About two seconds later three very dirty men tumbled out on deck. They were falling over one another in their anxiety to get out. They reached the port rail almost at the same time. One fell down in his haste. But he bobbed up again and reached the bulwarks just as the other two were climbing up.

At this moment three other men just as dirty and just as excited shot out of the same hatch. Apparently they were chasing the three clambering over the rail. But the funniest part of all was to see the old Scotch engineer with his white hair and red face come bobbing out of the after companionway. He let out a roar you could have heard clear to St. John's.

"*Stop them men! Stop them men!*"

But he was too late. The three at the rail plunged over the side. Not a yard behind them were their three pursuers.

The Scotch engineer threw up his hands. Then he turned on his assistant and his oiler who had come out to see the fun and yelled: "Go below, you loafers. You'll blow up the whole ship!"

Just then the skipper came along.

"What's all this, McDonough?" he asked.

McDonough gave a sort of a chuckle down in his throat that showed he was not without humour and said: "Captain, the Irish Army has just chased the German Army into the ocean!"

The last straw came when we tied up alongside the dock.

The captain sent for me and said: "Bartlett, the customs officers will be here in a minute. Go down and get that Jamaica louse," meaning the stowaway.

I went down to my stateroom and unlocked the door. To my astonishment the room was empty. I looked in every drawer and locker. But the man had vanished. I went to the port and looked out. Then I knew what had happened. On the brass rim of the little eight-inch circular opening was a brown gummy smear all the way round. On the deck below it was a little pile of dirty rags, a cotton shirt and cut-off breeches. That negro had stripped and soaped himself and gone over the side through the port while we were mooring!

Signing off I hurried away from the *Grand Lake* as soon as I could. For weeks I could smell bananas. But at that, I had my first mate's papers.

CHAPTER VII

"SWILES!"

"**S**wiles!" cries the Newfoundland masthead lookout when he spies seals ahead on the ice.

After my banana cruise I found myself yearning for the seal fishery, for a whiff of dank blubber and sharp bite of a north wind sweeping out of Baffin Bay across 1,000 miles of ice floe. I wanted to hear "*Swiles!*" yelled like a call to battle, and then get on the pack and fight for the season's catch with 100 of my Newfoundland brothers.

As I couldn't resist my desires I went home to Brigus and got a berth for the spring on one of our ships. In a few days I was in the ice having almost forgotten bananas and legal certificates. Of course Father was along in his own ship.

For fifty-four years now Father has commanded a Newfoundland sealing vessel. He has brought into our island over two million dollars' worth of codfish, cod oil, furs, and salmon. Today, at seventy-three, he is still hale and hearty and able to keep up his end of the plank.

Since Uncle John Bartlett died in Fredericton, NB, on April 4, 1927, my father, Captain William, is the last of the old-timers of our Arctic-faring family. Both have been pre-eminent sealers in their time.

Many people think of seals living mostly in the Aleutian Islands or in Hudson Bay. As a matter of fact there are about fifteen different kinds of seals and they are found in many parts of the world. Pacific seals breed up on the Aleutian Alaskan islands and range as far south as California. Atlantic seals cruise in a big circle from the upper end of Baffin Bay down to the Grand Banks. A goodly parcel of them goes into Hudson Bay; but the big crew runs down around Newfoundland. Every year they come south for the bearing of their young. This important event takes place in March and April on the rough icefields around Newfoundland.

Our sealing industry consists primarily of a fleet of ships going north each March from St. John's with large crews of hardy men who land on the ice and kill the seals by clubs and guns. Between bitter cold and wretched living conditions aboard crowded ships it is one of the toughest games in the world.

When a seal is killed its hide is cut off then and there and the carcass left for the gulls. The hide has the fat left on it. The fat is scraped off when the ship gets back to St. John's and refined into a beautiful clear white tasteless and odourless oil. Skins are made into boots and bags and other useful commercial articles. During ensuing months our same sealing vessels carry these products all over the world.

Spring sealing crews come down from all the outports and inland settlements early in March. They are advanced a few dollars for an outfit by the owners of the ships in which they are employed. A small ship not much bigger than an ocean tug takes a crew of 175 men. The more men the captain has the more seals he can kill. Sometimes as many as 50,000 sealskins are brought in at a load.

Getting a load usually takes about six weeks. You'd think this would bring a lot of money to the crew. It would if there weren't so many of them. But sometimes these fellows go out and suffer in terrible cold and risk their lives on the ice from March until June and come out with a net profit of $15! That sum is taken home for flour and molasses, tea, and salt, during the months that must pass before fish money comes in.

It's not always this bad. Once the *Wolf* went out and brought in 26,912 seals in eleven days. She had 255 men aboard who got $72 apiece. The biggest sum I ever heard of distributed gave each sealing man $303 for his season's work. But against this the *Seal* came in not long ago after a hard struggle and was able to give her crew only $15.57 apiece. That wouldn't buy block-grease for a deckhand.

Early records of the seal hunting have come down mostly by word of mouth. Logbooks and diaries were most often kept by the old sailing masters. Stories and counsels were handed down from father to son. Luckily there do exist a few authentic records which give us something to go on and serve to confirm the harrowing tales we hear from the old folks at home in Brigus.

It was not until the latter part of the eighteenth century that seal hunting in boats began to be practiced. At first it was done entirely by nets which were set in January when the seals migrated south and before heavy Arctic ice made its appearance on the coast. Once in a while the whelping ice drove right in on to the coast carrying with it a host of young ones. On such occasions men, women and children with dogs and sledges went after the seals and reaped a great harvest. One season in particular it is estimated that 120,000 seals were secured in this way

Such work was attended with great risk and in some years many lives were lost. However, success encouraged adventurous men to build larger boats and go offshore for longer distances. These craft were nothing but shallops decked in, fore and aft. The spaces in both ends of the boat were called "cuddies" and used for the men to sleep in. They were dark and always stank. Dead seals were stowed amidships, a space which had movable deck boards. Later larger boats or schooners, all decked over, caulked and pitched, with hatch coamings, hatches, and tarpaulins, came into use.

One of our best historians, Anspach, who lived down the coast of Newfoundland from 1800 to 1813, tells us that the whole plan of the seal fishing changed owing to the enterprise and industry of the inhabitants of Conception Bay, the chief village of which was Brigus. These people introduced larger and stronger vessels, building them so that they could withstand the ice pressure and other hard conditions to be met with. During the cod season, such vessels could be used for fishing as well.

Anspach vividly describes in his history the excitement of the seal hunt of those days as well as its attendant dangers. He says: "Add to this picture a rock-bursting frost, gales whistling and howling in huge uproar, drifting masses of snow and sleet or else thick fogs, freezing as they fell and covering everything with ice—the deck, the masts, rigging and clothes of the mariners." These were the days of iron men and wooden ships!

It was marvellous the way the early captains handled their sailing vessels going through ice. Manoeuvring was done with the square sails alone. Often the ship was tacked into a place only a little more than her own length. Not only did shoals or reefs make sealing dangerous, but icebergs were also a great menace. However, at times an island of ice can be of great service to a vessel. Take, for instance, a sealer endeavouring to get windward where a patch of seals is lying; the ice becomes tight and the ship is jammed. To leeward of her happens to be an iceberg aground. If she can only keep from being squeezed on the weather side and get in the wake near enough to grab it, she will be all right. For in that case by hanging on she can shift many miles of ice to windward; and perhaps in time the ice with seals upon it will drive along by the iceberg!

With a sailing vessel it's ticklish work; baffling winds render the approach to an iceberg very difficult; and there is always the danger of getting too near the weather edge. With a steamer it is much easier. If a steamer misses the berg she can always steam up under the lee side. It is not a pleasant feeling in fog or snow to be driving through a region where there may be hundreds of these huge derelicts of ice. Many a sealer has gone to her doom striking one.

Shipbuilding was a great industry in Newfoundland during the first half of the last century. Prior to 1840, nearly every vessel prosecuting the annual seal hunt was native-built; by that I mean literally homemade. The crews belonged to the same harbour and seal blubber was converted into oil at the same place. This oil was then shipped in casks and the skins sorted and both sent in bulk to London and Scotland. Thus the entire trade was kept localized.

During the winter season in those days, the seal fishery demanded continual work for ship carpenters, sail makers, blacksmiths and riggers. As a result every village was a hive of enterprise. Timber had to be cut and dragged in by the men, dogs and horses; then it was made into oars for hundreds of small boats or "punts." In addition every winter forty or so larger vessels had to be overhauled and one or two new ones built. It is easily seen how busy all hands in a village were.

Saint Stephen's Day, December 26, was the day on which the crews all gathered at the homes or offices of the captains to sign on for the coming spring hunt. At that time from 1,000 to 1,500 men seeking berths would come into the village of Brigus alone, sometimes from a distant port or farm which necessitated walking 100 miles for their jobs.

Early in February, the different crews would be engaged at hauling from the forests firewood and logs ready to be turned into the various spars and punts to be used on the vessels soon to leave for the ice. Each man had assigned to him some particular part of the work of fitting-out for the coming voyage. This labour was not paid for by the day or the hour but was considered as part of the season's duty. All the men got out of it was grub.

The crews were hired on shares. Each man's share amounted to half of his catch; so if there was a good season he could be sure of a pretty definite sum at the end of the voyage. I have already pointed out how small this sum usually was; but it meant a lot to the womenfolk waiting patiently at home.

Skippers began about February 25, to get things finally ready, putting stores on board and seeing that everything was in shipshape order. March first was sailing day.

At the first crack of dawn on that date windlasses were manned and sails hanging on the yards already to "sheet home" as soon as the anchor was hove short. Perhaps forty or fifty vessels were ready, each captain eager to be in the lead.

It often happened that the harbour was frozen over with from two to four feet of solid ice. In this case all the crews joined together and began sawing a channel to open water. They sang loud shanties as they worked. The harbour was from one to one and a quarter miles in length. The channel had to be the same length, and wide enough for one vessel. This meant a good deal of labour and occupied ten days or more to complete. As the blocks of ice were sawn they were sunk under the edges of the floes and the ships in order to be moved down the channel. As the channel lengthened the van ship was moved up until the whole number of ships formed a single line. With forty to sixty vessels and 1,600 men in the parade, it made a great sight.

It sometimes happened that when the mouth of the harbour was reached no open water was visible, the whole outer bay being frozen over. Then there was nothing else to do but wait for a swell to heave in from the Atlantic and break up the ice.

Yet it was astonishing how quickly this could take place. Without any warning old Neptune would become restless and in a few minutes a flat ground swell would accomplish what it would have taken 1,600 men ten days or more to do. Neither powder or dynamite was ever used; ice-cutting was all done by saws. Some unlucky years an entire month went by before the swell would heave in. During this time the vessels lay imprisoned, helpless to move, and with thirty to forty miles of unbroken ice before them. Such enforced idleness usually meant that the best time for sealing had passed. Often mutiny was at hand in these critical times due to skippers trying to save on food. Indeed hard feeling in the forecastle was not unusual in the best seasons because many of the sealing captains were martinets. No admiral in the British or American Navy required more homage from his men than did an early Newfoundland sealing skipper.

Great respect has always been shown in Newfoundland for the Sabbath. Some captains were strict "Sunday men." I knew captains in my time who never would kill seals on Sunday and some would not even move their ships unless in danger. Such righteousness exists to this day and pervades our shore work as well as fishing and sealing.

Most of the captains were far better mariners than they were men of business.

There was Old Bill Whelan, for instance, master and owner for many years of the brig *Hound*. In her he was exceptionally fortunate despite the fact that there was little or no bookkeeping in those days nor were there any banks to put money in. Most of the money belonging to the masters or owners was left in the care of the big merchants, where not many statements were asked for by the smaller men. A captain turned in his codfish and herring, sealskins and fat, all of which were valued at so many pounds per unit weight, and as a rule never bothered any more about them. When he needed money he got it in big or small amounts as the case might be. His provisions and clothing for his family he purchased in sufficient quantities to last him a year and never bothered to have any further account rendered. What was the use? He had all the money he wanted. There was more in the merchant's hands, so why bother?

However, when these same men began to slip back and their sailing vessels to give away to the steamers, they realized the tragedy of their mistake in not having accurate accounts and not knowing where they stood. There were many pitiful cases. Some, like my father, were still in middle life, with ships or money, and knew nothing but sealing. There were, and are, only a few steamers. Not nearly enough for the scores of the captains of the now obsolete sailing vessels. So it came to pass that many of our finest masters just wilted away and died in poverty.

On the other hand there was Captain Bill Whelan, of whom I was just speaking, who was not a "Sunday man," but was very fortunate. A berth on his vessel, the *Hound*, was as they said, "as good as a cheque on the bank." Some declared that he, like Faust, had sold himself to the devil; anyway his Baccalaureate sermon on getting his crew on board before sailing was:

"Now men, remember there are seven working days in my week and also the *Hound* is no Meeting House; neither is she a nunnery. Any man doesn't like that—get on shore!"

It is said that the old man seldom swore but when he did use strong language it was no profanity of the pierhead, but a private brand all his own. He never started anything unless he finished it. He always began his day with a toddy of rum; every half watch he had another or so. Blow high or blow low, rain, snow or frost and from dawn until dark, he kept on deck. When he went below at night he had his skin filled with good old Jamaica or Santa Croix. But the next morning he was back again at dawn, as fresh as a rose. He always carried a boy whose job it was to keep the small copper kettle filled with hot water so that he could have his hot grog on short notice.

Bill Whelan had a good ship and a smart crew; it was no use for a slacker to go with him. His officers were as hard as nails, and the whole man was iron. Nothing could escape his hawk eyes. With the crew and ship and the constant driving of her, he always got the seals.

In those days, "the good old days" as they were called, seals brought forty-two shillings a quintal (112 pounds) and it was considered a poor voyage if an owner or captain didn't make $2,000 in a season's cruise between March and June.

It is said that when Captain Whelan died he left $250,000; too much for a seafaring man to possess with peace of mind.

When steam was introduced in Newfoundland the sailing vessels were doomed. In a few years hardly a vessel was left where once had been a fleet of 400 craft, total crews of 13,000 men and a gross tonnage of 30,000 with a net revenue of over $1,250,000 seals per season. The present industry yields a revenue of around $200,000. Year by year the catch has dwindled until it is but a shadow of what it used to be.

To give you an idea of what I mean, here are some of the figures on the number of seals that have been killed in one year by our fleet:

Year	Number of Seals Killed
1830	558,942
1840	631,375
1858	507,624
1906	341,836
1923	101,770

That dwindling column on the right tells the whole story of Newfoundland's terrible and downgrade slide in the last 100 years; it explains the poverty of her people and the misery of some of the finest mariners that ever sailed the sea.

The New Englanders were wiser. When they saw their whale fishery slowly going to pot the shipowners began to quit it and invested their money in other things, such as cotton, woollens, boot and shoe factories, and so forth. Also they hove around to their big grants of land. Being near the cities where railroad and all sorts of buildings were being erected they jumped from whaling to real estate and became woollen merchants, copper and steel magnates. Yet the nucleus of their fortunes had been originally in whales and seal blubber.

I sometimes visit Salem, Newburyport, New Bedford, New London and Stonington. Notwithstanding the great changes which have taken place I can still see identically the same types of homes, furniture, etc., as those in

Newfoundland, even to the china, old four posters, rugs, pictures, front doors and brass knockers. For the same sort of men who manned and owned the New Bedford and Nantucket whalers manned and owned the sealing vessels of old times in Newfoundland. But I also see fine houses on splendid estates which prove my point that the Yankee mariners knew how to change trade when forced to.

We Bartletts of the present generation feel the change keenly because we have endured its worst phase. My own father had thousands of acres of land. Today it isn't worth the space it would occupy on a blueprint. This same property in New Bedford would make it possible for me to own a yacht with brass rails from now until I die and still have plenty to spare to give a good deal of pleasure to my friends along the beach.

Be that as it may, sealing was a great game; it still is. And there were fine men in it and fine ships. But my prophecy is that sealing will go just as whaling has gone. A few years hence and artificial products will take the place of the skins and oil won at such terrific cost from the ice and sea. Then Newfoundland must turn to other occupations. She may lose some of her picturesqueness in so doing; but she will never lose her courage and fine spirit.

CHAPTER VIII

DOWN TO THE BANKS

I took the summer off and fished before I went back to the long drudge of winning my papers.

The sealing season ended on May 1. As usual it brought enough money to start the family through the summer. Summer was fishing season. "Slave in the summer, sleep in the winter," was the saying; meaning the more fish one brings back, the bigger the bank account against winter hardships.

In a sense the fishing is more of a slavery than sealing. It takes longer time and you have to stick right at it, to say nothing of the unending toil involved. There are two kinds of fishing: that down the Labrador, and that out on the Grand Banks; but both are for mostly the same kind of fish, and both mean exposure, hard work and small profit.

I was very young when I first went to Labrador. Sometimes my whole family would go in the summer. Father would bring Mother and two or three of us children. We lived at his fishing station well up the coast at Turnavik. It was a huge holiday for us all. At Turnavik many of the Eskimos from the Moravian mission at Hopedale would visit us to exchange skins and furs for tea, biscuit, flour and sugar. Sometimes the Nauscopee Indians from the interior would come out to trade. As a boy I used to take trips up to the head of the bay, where a man named Perrault lived. Perrault was a leathery old fellow who at one time was in shrewd service of the Hudson's Bay Company. Now he did quite a bit of trading with the Nauscopee Indians. He was an expert fisherman who every season would secure many tierces of salmon and trout.[1] From him I learned much fish lore that has served me ever since.

Salmon were plentiful in those days. The fish were taken in spawning season by nets laid across the rivers from shore to shore. Staples were driven in to keep the bottom of the net from rising with the tide. Few salmon could escape such a trap. As a result the fish soon became more and more scarce. Since one female salmon carries many thousands of eggs it is not surprising that the breed fell off. When I was a boy many hundred tierces of salmon were secured at each of the Labrador ports; but now only a few tierces are obtained along the whole coast.

In the bays we got the wood with which to build our fishing stages, houses, and stores. We sometimes used the local timber for building boats; but it was not so good as that of Newfoundland. Spruce was especially brittle, and lacked the strength of the spruce at home. You could find trees from fifty to sixty feet high, though the trunk was only thirty inches in diameter at the bottom. The wood line ran close to the water, but ended a few miles back in the wilderness where the barrens of muskeg began. Trees ended alto-

---

1. A tierce of salmon weighs 303 pounds.

gether at Okkak which is a few miles west of Cape Mugford.

Cod-fishing was the principal industry along this coast. My father employed about 150 men, women, boys, and girls catching and curing the cod. My first job as a lad was going in the large trap boat with the trap crew.

In earlier life I was frail and not at all strong. Father said that enough linseed poultices were used on me every winter to stock a drugstore or two a year. I mention this because I now weigh over 200 pounds and am very hardy. Outdoor exercise and hard work toughened and gave me the vigour that comes only from a fisherman's life. It was hard work and the hours were long. Often I would wish that I had taken my mother's advice and become a clergy-man, especially after a tough day's work when I would reach the station late at night with aching arms and hands sore from dragging ropes and stiff tarry twine. I was shown no favours but had to do my share. I was crazy for this work and therefore got all that was coming to me.

Once I overheard my mother remonstrate with Father over the large number of traps I had to tend.

"The boy'll have his hard years soon enough," she said.

But my father only shook his head and replied: "You can't temper steel in a cool fire."

Little by little I learned to make the gear a fisherman uses: kegs, floats, nets, traps. The cod trap is woven from either cotton or hempen twine. It is knitted by machinery or by hand in rows or "leaves" with meshes from three to five inches square. The length varies according to the size of trap desired. When set in water the trap is a square pound sixty fathoms more or less on the ground; that is to say, fifteen fathoms on each side. I have seen a black bear walk down to a salmon net at low water and steal the salmon and trout out of it.

To keep the heads or top rim from sinking cork is strung on a rope laced into the top rim. To keep the trap in position requires from five to seven heavily anchored moorings. Large kegs or buoys are fixed on each corner and side and in the middle of the outside rim, for in many spots strong tides run and gales of wind rise so that without moorings the traps would go adrift. Handling moorings in cold raw Labrador weather with a sea running is one of the nastiest jobs I know.

From the shore to the middle of the trap is a leader, a straight piece of net exactly the same as the rim of the trap and of the same depth. When fish swim between trap and shore they strike the leader and follow its trend into doorways at the mouth of the trap.

It is a wonderful sight to see thousands of fish swimming side by side in the pound. To empty or haul it, a corner of the trap is lifted with a boathook, getting leverage from a crutch resting on a strip of wood on the inside of the boat. A man then dips the fish into the boat with a long-handled net, or into a bag which is strung alongside. The boat brings the fish to the shore stage and from there they are thrown up by pitchforks on to the stagehead, thence to a table where they are cleaned, and put in salt bulk for a few days. They are then washed out in tubs of water, and carried to a flake or a bald rock, where they are piled in bulk, so that the salt and pickle can be squeezed out. Twenty hours afterwards, they are spread on the flake to dry. Finally they are heaped into big piles and allowed to remain for a day or two, before they are shipped to market. Our salt-cured fish generally go to Portugal, Spain, Italy, and Greece.

One raw night I went out to the drying stage, to find my knife which I had dropped. As rain was driving in from the east I wrapped a bit of white sackcloth about me. Just as I reached the stage my lantern blew out. A few minutes later one of the men from a nearby schooner came by and caught sight of me.

"Whoopee!" he let out a terrific yell and lit out down the beach screaming.

I thought the fellow had lost his mind until next morning I heard that a ghost had been seen on the stage the night before. No amount of explaining on my part could shake the fisherman's belief in the vision.

Another time I was horrified to find a dead body washed up on the beach, fully visible in the moonlight. I was not yet twenty and thoroughly believed in spirits. After some hesitation I nerved myself to move up and lean over the remains. I nearly had heart failure when with a loud splash the "body" rolled over into the sea and swam away. It was a seal!

Labrador fish are also caught with hook and line from small boats, two men to a boat. Some work all summer catching cod in this fashion, whilst others take it up only after the trapping season is over. It is a slow business at any time. The fish generally strike the land in June and early July, time of their coming depending on the temperature of the water. If there is much ice around, the surface of the sea is too cold and they remain in deeper water. When the ice moves off they come to the land. Preceding them are millions of little five- to ten-inch fish called "capelin," which come to the land to spawn and incidentally provide the codfish a means of sustenance. They are the advance guard of the cod.

Should the "capelin" come to land and spawn before the cod, chances are great that the latter will stay to feed on the spawn, giving us fishermen a better and longer opportunity to secure a big catch. Later on, when the fish leave the shallow waters for deeper, fishermen use herring for bait. Fish obtained by herring are much larger as a rule than those obtained in the traps or hook and line posts earlier in the season.

Large cod seines are sometimes used. They are stowed in the after end of the seine boat, which has a crew of from six to eight men. In the bottom of the boat is a glass window through which a man looks as the boat is rowed along. In this way he can tell when there is a large school of fish below. If he thinks it worthwhile he gives the order to throw out the seine, which is from eighty to 120 fathoms long. As the net goes overboard the boat is rowed in a circle until all is out.

The first end or arm of the seine that goes overboard is the cast-arm. In the olden days, when rum was plentiful, a keg was thrown over the net to keep it from sinking and make it easy to pick up. When everything was hauled in, including the keg, all hands had a stiff drink. When the other end or arm is all overboard, the boat keeps rowing for twenty or thirty fathoms farther paying out a single rope attached to a grapnel which anchors the seine. The boat is then hauled back and the two arms of the seine are taken up to the head and stern so that the boat is placed across the two ends of the seine. One man stands in the middle of the boat with a long boathook which he uses to keep the fish from getting out under the foot of the net. Meanwhile, the men in the boat haul in simultaneously until they reach the bunt. The fish are turned into cod bags which are laced on the rim of the seine. As it is emptied the seine is dragged aft into the stern sheets and is soon ready to be thrown out.

Fish aren't the only thing that come in with a net. One summer we had a pet black cat aboard our schooner. When the weather continued foul our men began to blame it on the cat. In a few days the cat disappeared. On the quiet I learned that an old man named Tom Barb had flung the animal into the sea because he believed it to be a witch. At once the weather cleared and Tom's seine brought in the body of the cat. He cursed loudly. "Came back to haunt me!" he shouted. That summer Tom died and all hands swear to this day it was the cat's revenge.

Both capelin and herring are caught in a small mesh seine. At one time on the Labrador coast the herring industry was carried on with as great success as the mackerel industry today in the United States. But at present the herring are very scarce and often the fishermen cannot even get enough for bait. In the fall, thousands of barrels of salted Labrador herring used to find their way down to Boston, New York, and Canadian markets in brigs which brought back flour, lumber, and other imports to Newfoundland. Perhaps if the day ever comes when Newfoundland gets reciprocity with the United States the herring will return to their old haunts on the Labrador.

Besides the squatters who still go to Labrador to catch cod as we used to go, there is another class of fishermen known as floaters, who remain on the schooners all summer long. As they can cruise in and out of scores of harbours along the coast, they have a far better chance than the squatters, until they find good fishing grounds.

At times we met with heavy losses owing to heavy gales of wind and sea, or to the drift ice which carried away our traps. Now and then large icebergs floated in and took traps, moorings, and all away with them. Or again a berg would sail in when the fish were plentiful and the traps full, and plant itself near the traps, lying aground for days. This meant an irreparable loss, unless we used dynamite and blew the berg to pieces. I have spent many hours, day and night, towing pieces of ice from the traps. Sometimes the pack ice that is late in drifting from the north will come to land. Should the fish be in the vicinity, they will go far up the bays and deep inlets to escape the cold water in the neighbourhood of the ice. This keeps the fish longer inshore. The fishermen follow them in such cases, and invariably succeed in getting a good voyage.

My destination toward the end of the summer I took to the open sea for my fish, was 100 miles or so to the east and south of Newfoundland where lies the immense submarine plateau known as the Grand Banks, millions of acres in extent, but only a few hundred feet below the surface. It is a kind of enormous submerged island, entirely surrounded by deep water. This vast area of comparatively shallow

ocean is literally swarming with cod; and such is the pro-
lificness of the fish and the size of the Banks that the commercial fishing of the last 400 years has not appreciably
diminished the supply.

Nature has lavished every resource to make the Grand
Banks the greatest home of codfish in the world. The cod is
not a true deep-sea fish; he cannot withstand the tremen-
dous pressures of really deep water. But his chief food consists of smaller fish which live upon sediment and low forms
of life collected on the ocean floor, so that the cod must stay
near the bottom or else starve to death. Moreover, the cod
must have cold water. He cannot thrive when the temperature is much above the freezing point.

From the point of view of the intelligent cod, little
could be done toward improving the Grand Banks as a
place to live. There he finds a huge expanse of water not too
deep for comfort, a constant supply of palatable food flow-
ing in with the great Arctic current, a water cold and
healthful—and all this within easy reach of a great continental mainland where he may spawn. The only snake in
the garden is the presence of the fishing fleets; and they
probably bother the cod very little until he is actually
hooked.

Every summer the fleets assemble on the Grand Banks
and stay until September. Most of the fishing is done from
small boats which put off from the ships early each morning and return laden with their catch in the evening. This
hook-and-line fishing is old-fashioned and inefficient; but
improved equipment is expensive and fishermen are poor.
Other and better methods are being slowly introduced, but

it will probably be long before their use becomes extensive. My own gear in the summer I speak of was only hook and line, but I came out with some profit at that.

Catching the cod is only a small part of the fisherman's job. Cleaning and packing processes are far more arduous than the fishing itself. When dories return in the evening, the ship presents a scene of great activity. Fish are pitched one by one into the ship from the boats in the water; on deck they are seized and cleaned then and there. No part of the cod is valueless, livers, tongues, bones, and carcass all have to be packed separately.

The "cut-throat" takes the cod first. With one stroke he severs the attachment between the gill-covering and the belly; inserting his knife in the opening thus made he slits the abdomen. He then passes the fish to the "header," who extracts the liver and drops it into a cask by his side, the contents of which are to be converted into cod liver oil. Next with a wrench he tears off the head and removes the viscera, which are preserved for fertilizer. The fish then passes on to the "splitter," whose business it is to remove the backbone. Finally, the "salter" gets the fish carcass, salts it, and packs it away in the hold.

Value of the products from the cod fishing industry in Newfoundland is four times as great as that of all the other fishing industries combined. Seals, salmon, herring, mackerel—these riches of the ocean are insignificant compared with the cod. The average value of the cod fishery exceeds $7,000,000 a year, and the number of fish taken out of the sea is annually something like 80,000,000.

But while the aggregate statistics are impressive you

will have a false notion if you suppose that anyone is growing rich beyond the dreams of avarice by fishing cod. The $7,000,000 has to be distributed as the major support of about 150,000 persons—less than $500 a year apiece. The number of men actually engaged in catching and curing fish is about 60,000 but this figure is more than doubled when we include their dependants.

Of course few men rely entirely upon cod fishing for a livelihood. The same men who go north with the sealing fleet in early spring go out again after cod when the summer comes on; and in the autumn and winter they fish for mackerel and herring. But cod fishing is the grand staple; the other products are side issues.

My summer's cruise along the coast fishing again was a pleasant break in my years of service I had to do to get my master's papers. But when it ended I couldn't rest. Off to sea again I went, this time to meet what in many ways was the most extraordinary and disturbing experience of my whole life.

CHAPTER IX

I FALL IN LOVE

Right bang in the middle of my first mate's cruise the worst happened. I fell in love.

You may not believe it, but she was certainly a beautiful girl. I cannot tell you her name. And I don't dare describe her because she is alive today and going strong. In fact she is, if possible, more beautiful than ever. But she is not my wife; she is another's.

It happened like this. I guess I got in a sort of daze over the studying I did while off watch. I found meteorology especially hard. I went ashore one day in a foreign port to walk some of it off and air out my brain. The first thing I knew I banged head-on into a young lady. As I stepped on her I apologized and took off my hat and bowed. But she didn't seem angry. She looked at me and smiled the most fetching smile I had ever looked at. She said in good English: "I always did think a sailor ought to walk in the road where he has more room."

"How did you know I was sailor?" said I. Somehow it didn't seem strange to talk to her; she was so nice and friendly.

Well, in about three minutes I was walking down the

road with that young lady, passing the time of day with her and not realizing a woman had hooked me at last. I could see by her trimmings and the way she talked that she was a nice girl.

Pretty soon we came to a neat little cottage with a red tile roof and roses growing in the front garden. She said: "Won't you come in and have a cup of tea?"

I was about to say "Yes" when the door opened and a woman the size of the captain's hatch stepped out and said: "*Mary!*" (I'll call her that for the present).

We both looked around and the girl gave a little exclamation.

The big woman in the door took a big breath and let go this time with a real yell: "*MARY!*"

I figured that I was headed for the wrong berth and had better be under way. So I took my hat and started off. But before I could escape the girl had me by the arm and up the front walk and was introducing me to "Mother."

Mother turned out not to be so bad after all. She gave us some tea and some cake but I could see she was studying me all the time. She asked about where I came from and what ship I was attached to and said her husband was also a seafaring man. She interlarded her talk with a good many remarks about the dangers of a young girl associating with sailors. I blushed every time she got off one of these aspersions on my profession.

Things went from bad to worse. I liked the mother and I fell in love with the girl. At least I imagined I did, though I had never been in love before. I had every reason to believe that the girl fell in love with me. But, on the whole, it wasn't as simple as it sounds. In between visits I tried to get my mind back on meteorology again and I couldn't. Another thing, the ship was going to sail back to America. I was confused and worried at the situation.

I got into a terrible state. I couldn't sleep and I couldn't study and the captain said I was getting absent-minded in my work. But when I start a thing I like to go through with it. So finally I went to the young lady one day when I knew her mother was to be away and asked her if she would marry me. Talk about your master's examinations. I never shook in the examination room the way I shook that day while I was proposing. To cap the climax she accepted me. That is, she said we could get married "week after next when Uncle Tim gets home."

"But I can't do that," I told her. "I have to go back to America and get my master's papers. I want to support you properly. I won't have enough money as things stand now."

Well, I was young and she was young and we neither of us knew very much about life yet. So right then and there our beautiful bark of happiness went to smash on the rocks. We argued maybe five minutes. As a matter of fact we didn't argue. She was hurt because I didn't want to get married right away. And I was hurt because she couldn't see my side of things, and that was the end of it. I went back to the ship and sat down and opened my book on meteorology and swore I'd never say another word to another woman in my life.

Thus ended my love story, except that years afterwards I was lecturing on the Arctic one night in Canada when all of a sudden I felt a cold chill come over me. Right down in front of me in the audience sat my sweetheart of bygone days, the one I had asked to marry me. My tongue froze between my teeth. I forgot what I was saying. Rapidly I was drifting on a lee shore. I tried desperately to remember if she had any lien on me. Only with the most violent effort did I pull up and come about. When the lecture was over she came up and shook hands with me. To my relief it turned out she had married a fine man, much finer than I, and she had several splendid children. I said: "Mary, just think what it would have been if you had married a poor sailor!"

But she was not stumped by my question. She laughed and replied: "And think what you might be like if you had to support a family." Whereupon she stepped aside and introduced me to her husband, a small thin man with a bald head. But I saw the twinkle in her eye and sized up the father of her children as a fine earnest citizen.

While I am on the subject of women I may as well speak of other avenues of sin and troubles. There is liquor, for instance. I am a teetotaller and always have been. I expect to be buried as a teetotaller. I wouldn't mind if they put it on my gravestone because I am proud of it.

Yet strange to say, I know a lot about liquor. I am not hitting at my friends when I say that many of them drink. I have discovered that the right sort of man can drink and not have it hurt him. I don't say it doesn't damage his health to some extent. But I do say I have known some fine men who thought differently about liquor from what I do. A seafaring man gets all sides of a question while cruising in all parts of the world.

One acquaintance of mine was talking to me on the subject and said: "You miss a lot out of life by not drinking, Captain."

"I suppose I do," I said.

"Then why don't you drink?"

"Because God gave me my body and I propose to take care of it."

"But you drag your body all around and put it out in the cold and get it wet and do a lot of other things that damage it more than liquor would."

"But every time I have a good reason to do so."

"So have I when I take a drink. It's the finest feeling in the world, Captain, to be drunk. You forget your troubles and you look forward to success and you are a pleasure to be with."

"A healthy man is all of that," I told him.

But he retorted: "A healthy man often has a grouch. And a healthy man usually cannot think of anything but business. He sits around and plans his next job if he isn't already at it. A healthy man is often a curse to everybody in sight."

I opened my mouth to tell him how weak his arguments were. But just then in his excitement he came close to me and I smelled his breath. He had been drinking. Then I knew there couldn't be any real logic in what he said.

I said I know a good deal about liquor. Every Newfoundlander does. This is because our big fish cargoes and our oil and skins are often sent to countries where the main industry is winemaking. For many years our sailing ships took fish to Portugal. In my tramp ship life I sailed with many a load of cod and seal oil and brought back many casks of wine in return.

Probably as fine wine as was ever made was bottled right in St. John's, Newfoundland. Our sailing ships used always to put a few casks of Portuguese ferment in their holds and carry it back and forth for voyage after voyage. Rolling and pitching of the ship worked the wine around in the casks, making it mellower and mellower. Sometimes this process went on for years. Then the wine was put away in the great vaults of Harbour Breton.

The wine expert will know that rolling the cask by hand, turning over the bottles and that kind of thing is considered a great help to the wine in aging it. Imagine what our old sailing ships did to that fine Portuguese liquor when their voyages often lasted over 100 days. A ship rolls several times a minute from side to side. Multiply that by hours and days and then compare it with turning wine over once or twice a month by hand. Why one voyage of a sailing ship would do more for a cask of wine than fifty years of human handling!

Newman's port wine has for two generations been a great tonic. How many men and woman will remember the name. It was bottled in St. John's from that Harbour Breton stock and sold all over the world. I have gone down into the famous old rathskeller, Dewey's, in New York and heard its merits heatedly debated, each speaker trying to outdo the other in praising it. There was scarcely a London public house that did not consider it among its best stock. Dropping in one day at the exclusive St. Botolph Club in Boston, I overheard one man say to another: "Will you have some Newman's port wine?"

If I had been a hard drinker and just come out of the desert I couldn't have stopped quicker or cocked my ears more sharply.

There at the table was the chief justice of Newfoundland. At once I went up and told him who I was. We had a great reunion. For the moment I was almost sorry I was a teetotaller.

Sometimes the wine casks taken back and forth across the ocean got down in among the general cargo of fish and occasionally got lost or one was sent out that hadn't been fully emptied. As a result the wine would go bobbing around inside the cask not for a matter of days for but for a matter of years. A cask was turned up not so long ago that had been undergoing this process for more than a generation. The wine inside of it had worked into the wood and possibly evaporated through the microscopic fabric of the cellulose. All that was left was a thick liqueur, the very essence of the original wine. I happened to see a man who knew wine taste this nectar. When his tongue dipped in the glass there came over his face an expression as if he had caught a glimpse of Paradise. Little times like that make you realize why some really good men are willing to put the stuff in their stomachs.

Prohibition was started in Newfoundland by my father among other men. He was a teetotaller, too. He not only felt the way I did about his body, but he had years and years of experience with drunken crews coming aboard his sailing vessel just when he wanted to put to sea. This was a cause of great sorrow to him because many of the boys were sons of his neighbours and best friends; and also there was always great peril to a ship manned by men, many of whom were not altogether in command of their senses.

Some of the leading citizens of Newfoundland got together a few years ago and put prohibition into effect. They scouted around along the families of the sailor men and among those most interested in the cargoes brought back by sealing and fishing vessels. There was a great wave of fine feeling and the country voted Dry. Of course many of the voters were at sea on their ships.

But those of us who went on voyages to Europe and the West Indies and other parts of the world where our fish and oil were taken, secretly realized there would be trouble. For, after all, sea trade is just about in the state that trade among primitive races was. That is to say, it is a matter of barter. Money isn't so important in big commercial exchange. A country produces fish and oil the way Newfoundland does and barters that to a country like Portugal for what she can produce. If a lot of clerical help in offices mixes in money with the transaction that is of no great consequence to the seafaring men or to the actual trade. It is value for value that counts. And this holds as true as ever between Europe and America today. It is a fact that should not be lost sight of by citizens interested in the standing of their country in the eyes of the world.

When prohibition came to Newfoundland, we who went to sea saw at once that it would disturb trade relations. And it did. A ship couldn't take a cargo of fish to a wine country like Spain or Portugal and come back empty. That would mean half her running time would be lost. A ship doesn't have a taximeter stuck on it rigged out to take account of return trips. (I didn't know this until I took a taxi one day out in the country and had to go without lunch for about three days afterwards.) No, a ship has to take a cargo out and she also has to bring a cargo back. A ship runs in ballast only when a cargo is so valuable and profitable that she can afford to lose half the time of the round trip. This is not the case with fish.

So our Portuguese traders and others got very angry when we went Dry and decided they had to protect their own interests by trading elsewhere. The same thing happened last year with Norway. She lost her big fish trade when she went Dry and was boycotted by other nations.

The whole thing was brought to a head when a big deficit turned up in our annual budget. Jack Crosby was Receiver General at the time. Jack was a boyhood friend of mine. He is just my age and we grew up together. He is a fine citizen too. But he is out to protect Newfoundland against herself. So Jack got busy and showed everybody that there was an $800,000 deficit in our country's finances. There was one quick way to cure this. That was to go Wet again. Now Newfoundland is Wet; also she is solvent. We have Jack Crosby and the laws of trade to thank for both. Norway is Wet again too, and for the same reason.

CHAPTER X

SKIPPER AT LAST

I was now approaching a crisis in my life. One who has not gone through years of struggle and anxiety to secure the papers of a Master Mariner cannot realize what it means to a seafaring man as he finally approaches the fateful day on which he is to come up for his skipper's examinations.

My six years were almost up. For six years I had wandered around the globe on all kinds of ships carrying all kinds of cargoes. Besides my coal and banana cruises, I had a good deal of voyaging with dried fish, seal oil, lumber, slate and many kinds of general cargo. I was delighted particularly with Europe; and I like South America. I never fell in love with the tropics; too hot and too many snakes, bugs, bad water, and fever.

In the old days, there was so much smallpox and yellow fever that I have seen times when half a dozen ships would be lying behind the reef in Pernambuco with not a man on aboard; every man jack of them on his back in the hospital ashore, dead or only half alive.

"You want to watch yourself, Bob," said a friend of mine to me on one of my many cruises there. "If you get ill don't close your eyes if you can help it. Just as like as not, if you do, they'll have you in a box with quicklime on you before you can open your mouth to holler 'Help!'"

Acting on this advice I watched until I got in such a state that when I saw a fellow with a wheelbarrow of quicklime coming down the street I went around the other side of the block to avoid him.

But what I started to say was that in all these years of cruising I was headed for just one thing: that was my master's papers. If I could only carry my certificate back home my biggest ambition would be realized. For a long time I had worked and studied, and now I felt that I deserved the honour. But I wasn't sure. I heard many tales of the stiffness of the examinations and the severity of the high officials who gave them.

As the time drew nigh I applied myself even more industriously to my studies. I mastered navigation so that I could almost navigate backwards. I had learned all the practical seamanship a man need have in my early cruises with my father. I now began to learn it out of a book so I would know the high-class words that are used by the examination board. I studied up on compasses and piloting and rules of the road and a lot of other technical details. I didn't think I had it in me to be such a student.

As I look back it seems to me that I can remember plugging away at a book about this time much better than I can remember some of the interesting countries I visited. Down at Cadiz I was working on adjusting a compass. Up at Grangemouth I was studying seamanship. At Leghorn I was prowling through a book on oceanography. I was investigating meteorology twice while crossing the equator. At the rate I was going I certainly would have been a professor in a year or two if I had kept on.

One of the last cruises I made as mate was on the SS *Strathavon*, a big steel cargo ship with huge open holds for taking ore and coal. She had always tramped around a good deal and sometimes took mixed cargo. But her trips over to Cape Breton Islands after coal and ore, and across to Cardiff, Newcastle, and Ardrossan after Scotch coal, kept her on the high seas most of the time.

Captain William Cross of the *Strathavon* was one of the best Newfoundland skippers that ever passed the Narrows. He was a sailor from the word go and a seafarer of the old school. He had commanded his own ship, a big square-rigger, in his teens.

Bill Cross had Spanish blood in him and I suspect he had a Spanish grandee for a great-great-grandfather. He was tall and slender and he had that graceful erectness to his shoulders when he walked that goes with the gallant knight. His bearing towards ladies marked him out ashore beyond other men. And he was a fine dresser to go with his courtly manners.

One thing that struck me as a lad about Captain Cross were his beautiful hands, an unusual possession for a man of the sea. His were the tapering fingers of an artist. And he could wear rings too; fine big heavy gold rings and rings with stones in them.

I mention these personal items about the man because the next thing I say about him might not seem to fit. Captain Bill Cross was one of the greatest fighters I ever knew. I don't mean by word of mouth or in getting around people by strategy. I mean in stand-up hand-to-hand fighting. One day a six-foot-two Irishman with pretty nearly twice Captain Bill's tonnage came aboard tipsy. He got fresh with the old man. I was sort of standing between the two expecting trouble. Suddenly, faster than my eyes could follow, the captain had sprung into the air, turned over with bent body and landed on his hands. His heels flew out and up like a donkey's. It was a strange manoeuvre. I didn't realize at the time it was the way French boxers fight. Anyway the drive of the captain's heels struck the Irishman a crashing blow about the middle of his chest, knocking him flat and stunned to the deck.

Another time when I had to shift the *Strathavon* down dock because a sudden storm came over the south hills of the harbour, the captain happened to be up at a place named Strange's with some friends.

Hearing his ship was in the manoeuvre he came aboard. At that moment some of the men down forward were feeling their oats. In high spirits one of the gang began playing with the *Strathavon*'s bell. Now the bell aboard ship is sacred. It is used to strike the hours so a man can tell when to go off watch and when to eat; and is used for fire, funeral, and as a fog signal. Its use for any other purpose is considered a sacrilege.

Captain Cross came striding up the deck with those fine hands of his doubled up into hard knots. One of the firemen was standing by the bell. The old man promptly knocked him flat as a deadlight. Just then he heard the rumpus down in the forecastle. In one jump he was down the ladder. As an officer I had to follow. It was a fine fight.

The captain had three of the crew on their backs before I got into it. In five minutes that forecastle was like a Quaker meeting. And not all of those present were sitting up and reflecting on their sins. Some were lying down.

A few days later we went over to the Sydney mines for cargo and it wasn't long before I got to know coal pretty nearly as well as I got to know bananas. You never find bananas in your coffee. But you do find coal there. On the other hand coal doesn't show in things like boiled prunes, one of a sailor's chief articles of diet. It's pretty plain, though, in mashed potatoes and hominy. The worst of carrying coal is when you come to go ashore to see some of your lady friends. You take a clean shirt out and polish your face off with a razor. But by the time you have got your shirt on, your face is all smudged and the shirt has an ornamental design on it never put there by the manufacturer.

I went ashore at Sydney to take a look at the coal mine. I think it is part of a seafaring man's duty to investigate places he visits. That's part of his education. I made friends with the manager of the mine and he said, "How would you like to go down for a look?"

"Is it safe?" I asked him.

"Probably not, mate," he said without smiling. "Coal mining is one of the most dangerous occupations in the world. They blow up every day or so. Look at this." He showed me a paper with an account of a big explosion in Pennsylvania where 150 men were killed. But he couldn't get my goat.

I went in a sort of elevator which was really only a cage on the end of a wire cable and was lowered down what seemed a million feet into the mine. They had Newfoundland ponies down there pulling small cars around and the miners wore lamps in their hats. It was a dark, damp, unpleasant sort of place and I didn't stay down there long.

One of the things that most impressed me was fossils I saw down there in the main coal vein. For the first time I had before my eyes proof of the great age of the earth. Millions and millions of years before I stood there trees grew and flowers bloomed.

"Very fine," said I to the manager, "but today is Solomon Goss's birthday and we have duff for dinner. So I must leave your fossils and go." I went back to the old ship which had looked a dirty dump when I left her. Now she looked sweet as a bride's home. That's the effect that a coal mine had on me.

A few months later I got a look at another side of the mining business when we carried dirty iron ore instead of coal. Just below my home on the east coast of Newfoundland is one of the largest iron mines in the world. Captain Cross took the *Strathavon* in there for a cargo that was to be brought down to Sydney where the big smelters are of the Nova Scotia Steel Company. In some ways iron ore is worse than coal. It does not get in your coffee but it gets into the compass. With a cargo of ore below hatches the compass acts like a woman in love. It doesn't know which way to turn and ends up by running in circles.

I really oughtn't to run down the old *Strathavon*. She was the first ship where I was a real official. Although I was second mate on that banana boat I was really only a better sailor than the rest of the gang. Now on the *Strathavon* I had a boy come around in the morning and give me coffee and I lived in a stateroom and I had a radiator alongside the bulkhead to dry my clothes on.

That radiator was a big step forward in my life. For years I had been going down to Labrador on ships that didn't have any heat except in one little cabin stove. This stove was a hot box when it was working; but when the vessel was close hauled with main boom amidships the wind would pour down the smokepipe and keep the cabin smoky and cold. Also there never was room enough for us to dry our wet garments, which finally became mildewed and ill-smelling.

Now here on the *Strathavon* I was shipmates with a fine fat radiator in my own room. In our first blow on a run to Liverpool I got wet to the skinny as usual. No amount of oilskins can keep the salt water out when you are climbing up and down ladders, trimming ventilators, and so on in a January North Atlantic gale. Had I been down sealing I should have simply looked forward to putting on damp gear in the morning. But on this mate's cruise of mine I skinned off my woollen socks and my shirt and mittens and wrapped them around the radiator by my bunk. I sat back and felt like a millionaire on his first yacht. I had reached the pinnacle of comfort in my sea life. Of course the radiator looked as if it had a sore throat from one end to the other. I sat back and smoked my pipe and thought how fast I was getting along in the world. (Remember, I was only twenty-four.) I fell asleep. The first thing I knew I heard a loud banging on my door. It was the chief officer.

"Hey, Bartlett," he yelled. "Are you frying fish in there?"

I came to with a jump. I had been dreaming I was home in the try house where they steam the fat out of the seal hides. I opened the door.

"How's that?" said I.

"I said are you frying fish?" he repeated. He put his hand over his nose and stepped back.

Then I realized what was wrong. The radiator was so hot and my wet clothing so drenched with brine that the odour was terrific. I felt a little logy myself.

It wasn't all a bed of roses on the *Strathavon*, however, even if we were officers. When heavy weather came and the wind was ahead, the main deck used to be thoroughly danger-ous. The bridgeworks were forward and the living quarters aft. Between them stretched a long space which the steward had to cross every time he brought dinner back to us. If a big sea caught him while he was on the way the dinner as likely as not would float over the side. Often the basket in which he carried it must have gone under because I recall that the meat and potatoes were usually flavoured with salt water.

Time passed rapidly and there were no important adventures to break it. So finally I landed back in New York with my six years' service on my master's papers all in. My great day was at hand. I could now go to Halifax and pres-ent myself for examination. I was walking on air.

I didn't have very much money. The company had paid me $36 a month and found as mate on the ship I just quit-ted. I couldn't put by much out of this although I led a very temperate life. I mention the fact only because it has a bear-ing on my troubles ahead.

I thought I could save a few dollars by not getting a

berth on the train down to Halifax. So I sat up all the way up the coast and down the peninsula. This was in a day coach. It was cold as blazes. And there was a pretty rough crowd there with me. When we got close to the lines we learned there had been a smallpox epidemic and a medical inspector came aboard. He went through the aisle checking up on vaccinations.

Suddenly I realized what I was up against. I hadn't been vaccinated recently. Either I must be vaccinated now or they would not let me into Canada. As I was a British subject at the time I had to get into Canada to take my examinations. A moment later the inspector was at the seat in front of mine. I heard him say: "Right arm, boys."

There was some argument but he insisted on the right arm. Remember I was young then. I wasn't sure of myself enough to argue with a medical inspector. If he told me I had to be vaccinated on my right arm I knew I would sputter and get mad and he would end up by doing it. But a lame right arm might have meant postponing my examinations which had to be written. And I couldn't afford to do that. Suppose my money ran out.

I thought fast. It was like being caught at the wheel when she starts to gybe. There was not much to do but duck. I ducked. I hurried up to the end of the train. We were just arriving at a station so I had a chance to hop off and get aboard again at the opposite end of the car. For a few minutes it looked as if I had outflanked my enemy. But I hadn't.

The inspector had seen me. He came out on the platform and was pretty sore that I had tried to escape him. He told me to roll up my sleeve. I didn't want to be in jail so I took off my coat without trying to argue. But before I could get my sleeve rolled up something diverted the attention of the inspector. That gave me my chance. I glanced down and saw a pin I had stuck in my lapel on my coat. I snatched it out, jumped into the washroom at the end of the train and vaccinated myself with the pin! That's about as close to committing suicide as I guess I will ever come. What a chance I took! But I didn't have sense enough to realize it at the time.

I got out before the inspector came back. He found me rolling down my sleeve. I showed him my right arm. There it was, scratched and bloody. He looked at it, then at me. Probably he thought his memory was getting bad because he couldn't recall having vaccinated me. But there was the vaccination big as life, a dozen bloody crisscross scratches. So he checked me off and I got through. I guess I had some pretty clean fluid running through my flesh because the scratches I had made with the pin healed right up and never troubled me at all.

On reaching Halifax my first move was to go to the nautical academy. That is the school where a seafaring man applying to the board of trade for his papers gets his final brushing-up. I inquired for my old friend Captain Matson who I knew would put me through if anybody could. I was saddened to learn that he had died. With heavy heart I enrolled, determined to do my best anyway.

Five weeks of hell, that's what it was. Day and night, with scarcely time out for eating and sleeping, I struggled over my books and papers. I didn't dare take any chances.

For six years I had been working up to this point. If I slipped, it would be six months before I could take another examination. And my failure would certainly count against me in the minds of the examiners. A second failure was fatal.

Finally, the day came. The first man I went up before was Captain Smith. He was a Royal Naval man and at one time commodore-captain of the Allan line. He was a very distinguished-looking officer and very plainly a mariner. He was big, ruddy and square-jawed; and he swung a pair of hands that must have laid many a time on the shrouds. He had piercing black eyes and a close cropped moustache which, with his hair, was white as snow. He was very erect and talked in sentences clipped like his moustache.

I was soon at work. The examination lasted three days, each day beginning at eight and ending at four. They were held on the top floor of the customs building in a room that reminded one of a ship's main deck.

There were elaborate precautions against any sort of favouritism being shown to candidates. Questions were sealed up in London and mailed to the officer in charge. Not until he opened the envelope before the candidate was it known by either officer or man what the questions were going to be.

My eye caught a familiar question right off the bat. That gave me new courage. I wrote all morning. I went out for lunch but I couldn't eat. My mind was working too hard. I wrote all afternoon. When four o'clock came, the other candidates and I went slowly down the street. There was no gaiety left in us. I felt terrible depressed although I knew I had gotten along all right. It was the mental exhaustion, I suppose, after the terrific effort I had made.

My first impulse was to go back to my room and get busy at my books again. But somehow I couldn't stomach the thought. Instead I wandered up the street, up the hill, up through the municipal gardens and finally reached the graveyard. Somehow there was something soothing in the thought that all these people under the stones had reached a point where there could be no more examinations in their lives. Here nobody would bother me; nobody would speak to me; and the inscriptions on the stones were so much more entertaining to me just at that moment than the examination questions I had been looking at all day that I read them avidly.

The second day was even more of a terror than the first. I came then to the practical examination which was mostly compass work. This was held by Captain Tingling, R.N.

I want to say a word here about the fine system the admiralty has for determining whether a man should hold his master's papers. The safety of a ship depends more on a compass than any other thing aboard her. For if a master does not go too fast and keeps his head he will hardly ever get into trouble so long as his compass is right. Therefore it is a fine practice to have the biggest thing in a master's examinations for the candidate to prove that he knows how to make a compass right and keep it so.

Up there in the examination room they had an imitation ship. This is the way it was: You know a compass is acted on not only by the earth's magnetism but by the magnetism of all the metal of the vessel on which it stands. So when I say an imitation ship I mean they had a compass stuck up there on a sort of deck at one end of the room and around that compass were metal smokestacks, davits and beams all to represent the same articles on board a ship. Of course it wasn't a full-size smokestack and the beams consisted of several long iron pipes instead of the scores of beams that constitute a ship's frame. But the effect on the compass standing in their midst was as if it had been aboard ship.

Captain Tingling led me into this curious device and said:

"Now, Mr. Bartlett, I am going to put you here aboard a brand new ship."

He pointed out that the smokestack and davits and beams were movable so that I would not likely get the same combination that any other candidate had.

"I want you to install the compass," he went on. "Consider she is lying at the dock now. When you get the compass fixed up I want you to take her down the harbour and swing her for deviation and heeling error of the compass."

For the reader's sake I won't go into all the technical details of this compass business. But, take my word for it, it is one of the most involved things in the world. Magnetism is so peculiar that the effect of all the metal massed around a compass is one thing when the ship is on one heading and quite a different thing when it is on another. And when she goes up on her nose in the trough of the sea it is still another thing. So there is an endless variety of forces pulling away at the compass needle and doing their best to make the helmsman steer his vessel on the rocks.

It was Captain Tingling's fetish to see that the men he passed really knew how to adjust a compass. Believe me, when I placed the athwartships and fore and aft "compensating" magnets he watched every move I made. And as I shifted them up and down until the needle hung right between the big iron correcting balls on either side you would have thought he would have exploded if I hadn't done it right, so intense was his interest.

But my preparation had been sound. For years I had been waiting for this moment. For months I had been studying day and night and at the school my coach had been one of the best. So even though I was tremendously disturbed by Captain Tingling's presence, and not a little embarrassed, I did it right. I stepped back and let him have a final look.

He turned held out his hand and snapped out: "I congratulate you, Mr. Bartlett, you have passed. I wish you success. I hope no red ink ever mars your certificate. I hope you will always keep up the fine traditions of the sea, especially those of the British merchant service."

I was a Master Mariner at last.

CHAPTER XI

POLAR POISON

When an explorer climbs a hill or rounds a headland he is always stuck with surprise at what he finds on the other side. What he sees is never quite what he expected.

That's what it was like when I "circled the hatch" for the right to be called "Captain" aboard my own ship. My master's certificate was a landfall in life I'd been looking forward to for years. And I expected it to mean just one thing: I'd go to sea with a cargo of freight and slide around the oceans over which for so long I'd done my tricks as second and first mate. But, as so often happens, fate had an altogether different course laid for me to steer.

Instead of going into the merchant service I got started on Arctic voyaging. And this strange work was to continue intermittently for more than twenty years; indeed at this writing it is still going on.

Uncle John Bartlett was in command of Peary's exploring ship the *Windward*, at the time, 1898.

"Why don't you come along as mate, Bob?" he asked me.

I didn't answer this question. Instead I put another question to him: "What sort of man is Peary?"

Uncle Harry scratched his head. Then he said: "He's

like a T-square, Bob. He thinks in a straight line. And you can't bend him any more than you can steel."

"Does he know his business?"

"He's the kind that doesn't make it his business unless he does know it."

"Is he a rough handler?"

"Not by our way of thinking. He doesn't ask a man to go where he wouldn't go himself."

I haven't forgotten those words because my twenty years of work with Admiral Peary confirmed every one of them over and over again. Moreover, as Uncle John went on and told me what the great explorer was trying to do and how he was using the Eskimos to help him succeed where others had failed, I found myself becoming so eager to know the man that my mind was soon made up without my knowing it.

When I asked my father's advice he pointed out that for a young man the exploring business was a good way to get ahead. He said that if I could become attached to the staff of a man like Peary it would no doubt help me later on to land a ship of my own.

I had no fancy dreams about exploration. I had no scientific education or training beyond the limited navigation and other nautical knowledge required by my mate's and master's papers. I didn't want to become a professional explorer. I had sense enough to realize my limitations in attempting any scientific work. But it was in my blood to keep to the sea and to push out into the wild spaces of the earth.

I went north in the *Windward* in the summer of 1898. Lord Northcliffe had presented her to the American polar expert. Peary had finished his work over the Greenland ice cap the year before. Two crossings of that ice desert had shown him that it was not a practical route to the Pole. He was now determined to work up the east coast of Ellesmere Land as far as he could go and then travel by the polar ice to the top of the world. The *Windward* was to return that year, but she got caught and had to winter in a small bay just north of Cape Sabine where Greely's party died only a few years before. From our deck we could see Greenland only about thirty miles east across Smith Sound.

I want to throw a little light on this part of Peary's work because it had such a powerful bearing on his later success. People never did realize what he did in the hard years before he finally reached the Pole. Even so-called "polar experts" think that he was just a strong man physically who by sheer force of muscle and willpower finally drove himself out to his goal.

It wasn't that at all. Peary reached the Pole mostly because he spent nearly twenty-five years of eliminating the obstacles that had prevented other explorers for four centuries from doing what he was trying to do. I think the main thing that made possible the discovery of the Pole was the placing of a ship at the north end of Grant Land on the shores of the Polar Sea. In this way, both dogs and men could set out early in spring of the year and travel directly across the polar ice, without any preliminary struggle. Peary achieved this by studying ice conditions from Cape Sabine north to Cape Sheridan, a stretch of several hundred miles along the Ellesmere coast and Grinnell Land. If you look at the chart you will see that this stretch includes Kane Basin and Kennedy and Robeson Channels, bottlelike sounds between Greenland and Ellesmere Land. Both are practically always choked with ice.

I cannot say always because about twice a generation Kane Basin seems to be free. That's what got Greely into trouble. His ship steamed right up to Lady Franklin Bay without meeting any serious ice and Lieutenant, afterward General, Garlington, later Commander of the Relief Expedition, thought that conditions were like that every year. The next year he found himself a prisoner of the pack and finally had to retreat with disastrous results.

Now that it seems to be no trick to fly to the North Pole these details appear unimportant. They are as regards modern Arctic travel which is done by air. But they are worth citing because they show how slow methodical progress is the best way to success. The system behind Peary's success may well be applied in only slightly different form to air explorations of the future.

Beginning with the summer I went up on the *Windward* Peary struggled up and down the Ellesmere Land coast for four years. He learned every inch of the ice foot and he saw at all seasons of the year the exact conditions of ice and sea. He discovered that in August the choked passages between him and Greenland loosened up as a result of tide and moderate temperature. This loosening was accelerated along the shore by melted ice and snow running into the sea. In consequence there was a lane of open water a few feet wide near both shores. Due either to prevailing winds or, as some scientific men have pointed out, to the rotation of the earth, the main pack shifted eastward during early September and left a narrow but navigable lane along the Ellesmere Land side. This lane was by no means always open. In fact when he went up with *Roosevelt* in 1909 we got jammed right in the middle of the pack in Robeson Channel. But by that time Peary knew more about navigating that important stretch of pack ice than any man who had ever lived. He had learned to use open leads close to land formed by ebb and flow of current tide.

Peary was pretty much of an Eskimo even in those days of the *Windward*. He could dress and eat and travel like a native. He used to disappear with a few sledges and stay away for many weeks. He didn't mind rotten meat or low temperatures. And he could out-walk the best hunter in the tribe.

On our way to our base we picked up about a dozen families of the Smith Sound group. Although I had seen Eskimos down the Labrador, I was not prepared for this most northern people on the globe. I had looked forward to a lot of dirty, stupid people. I thought that they would be half animals. And from what I had read and heard among whalers I was apprehensive about their being bloodthirsty, treacherous, and thieving.

Imagine my surprise when I discovered the Eskimos to be a reasonably clean and very intelligent lot of people. They were fun to have around. The men were hard workers without any vices; and the women were good wives and mothers. The children were the prettiest little tots I have ever seen.

We couldn't talk Eskimo. Peary never really pretended he could talk Eskimo. I know he says in his book that it is easy to pick up the language. It was easy to pick up enough words for us to get along. But we never talked more than a jargon—just rough grouping of nouns and verbs and adjectives without any attempt at grammar.

It may sound impossible that we could get along with so little speech. But don't forget that in the north you get down to brass tacks. You are there to travel. To travel you have to have food. And the food isn't successful unless there is shelter behind which to eat. So if you know some words covering sledge work, a few names of game animals, and the general details of igloos and the places best to build them, you can travel all over the north. We did. As time went on we learned more. But essential words were always the most in use.

I remember going out the first autumn to lay down some supplies by sledge for Peary. A good Eskimo named Sipsu and two other hunters accompanied me. Although I knew only about six words of the language I got on famously.

For instance we got caught in a bad blizzard the second afternoon out. Sipsu said in Eskimo:

"Big wind. Very cold. Igloo."

I nodded assent and the boys built a snow igloo. We had supper. After we ate we sang songs. First I'd sing one then they'd sing one. They liked "O Susanna" best though I wasn't exactly a nightingale.

The following morning, Sipsu stuck his head out of the igloo. He jerked it back quickly and said: "Big wind. Very cold. Igloo."

I nodded assent and we sang songs all day.

The next morning, he pulled his "Big wind" line again but this time the weather didn't seem so bad. So I said, pointing outdoors: "Big wind," and nodded. Then I stuck out my chest and pointed to myself and said in Eskimo: "Big man." I pointed to each of the others and Sipsu, saying

"Big man" each time. I ended by saying all at once: "Big wind. Yes. Big man. Yes. We go."

The Eskimos finally got the point and laughed and went out and packed up their sledges. You don't need much of a vocabulary to travel with these type of people so long as you can pay them and they are willing to go.

I watched Peary closely all the time because I knew he was already the greatest Arctic traveller alive. I noted that he handled his Eskimos with a firm hand; yet he was kindly towards them and joked with them and helped them out in their family troubles.

I remember one day he was making an inspection around the ship. He came to where our native women were sewing. He lifted up the face of one by her chin. She had been crying and her face was streaked with tears.

"What is it, Alakasina?" he asked.

She shook her head.

"Come on tell me what the trouble is, I won't let you work until you do."

Then she told him that her baby in her shirt-hood was ill and that her husband had beaten her for letting the little thing suffer; which, of course, she hadn't.

Peary took the whole family into his cabin and played with the baby and talked with the father and mother and soon had the trouble straightened out. After that there wasn't anything those two Eskimos wouldn't do for him.

All that winter in which Peary struggled hard to get his supplies to Fort Conger he sent party after party from the ship in wind and cold and darkness. He was always with one or another of them. He wanted to be in a position to work out over the Polar Sea as soon as light came. His first out-base was about 200 miles from the ship at Fort Conger, where Greely had been. By December the thermometer was fifty degrees below zero and the wind worse than ever. But when the moon rose on December 30, he started off with four teams and four Eskimos, all disappearing in a smother of snow. We didn't see him again until late in February.

While he was gone, we kept the ship as clean as we could and did odd jobs of repairing. But the darkness and inactivity got on the men's nerves a lot.

One morning Captain John sent me down in the fore hold after some line. I was surprised to find the hatch unbolted and the cover half off. But there was no light to show anyone was down there. I was about to yell down and ask when I heard what sounded like a groan. I grabbed my lantern and hurried down the ladder. There amongst the gear I found two men rolling and tearing at each other in a murderous fury. Both were bleeding and one had the other by the throat and appeared about to kill him. I tore them apart and tried to find out what it was all about. Finally I gathered that they had gone down there to fight out a private grudge they had been nursing for months. That's what the Arctic night does to men unless they can be kept busy.

We got very anxious about Peary after a month passed and he didn't show up. He was to be back in January. What had happened was that he got caught in the darkness on his way to Fort Conger. Two of his Eskimos gave up in the middle of a blizzard. When the other two went ahead Peary realized the two men behind might be lost. So he turned around and went back after them. That is the kind he was. He found the poor devils huddled in a snowdrift ready to die. He cheered them up and got them started towards Conger. In the meantime, he became so exhausted himself that when he finally reached the place both his legs were frozen to the knee.

He stayed there in a little wooden shack for nearly two months while his toes sloughed off from dry gangrene. It is difficult to believe that any man could have stood the agony of what he went through. When the moon came back on February 14, 1899, he had himself lashed on a sledge and started back for the ship.

How he ever endured the bumping over that rough ice with his gangrenous feet is beyond me. Only those who have gone over similar roads can realize the suffering that he must have stood. On the ship we knew there was something wrong with him, but had no idea it was so serious. He had sent ahead a team of dogs with Eskimos and a note to the captain telling us that he was a little bit under the weather. He always minimized his personal ills.

I was at the sea end of the road leading through the ice foot when I heard the homecoming dogs in the distance. I waited on the ice until the party came along. When Peary's sledge passed by, to my surprise he was lying on it. He greeted me in such a way that I felt everything must be all right. Yet why should he, our champion walker, be riding? I got hold of the upstanders of one of the sledges and trotted along with it to the ship. Then I saw that there was something seriously wrong because Uncle John had the sledge carried up the gangway with Peary on it. We soon had in laconic form the gruesome story of what he had been through.

On March 13, Peary's toes were amputated. After a short time he began to hobble around on crutches, much against the wishes of the surgeon who did his best to persuade him to rest a while longer. But early in May the cripple left his ship, going up Princess Marie Bay over the ice and onto the Grinnell Land ice cap, crossing it to the west side. Having failed in his winter effort, he was determined to see if there was a better way west.

We did not see him again until August. By this time his feet were in terrible condition. Flesh over the bones on his feet was raw and bleeding. At this season of the year the surface of the ice was shorn of all snow, leaving no cushion and nothing but the bare granulated ice to walk upon. Further, he had to walk through pools and streams of icy water, which, of course, rendered his footgear soft as pulp. One can imagine with feet in that condition the terrible time he had had. I asked him how he could stand it, but he only said: "One can get used to anything, Bartlett."

I don't pretend to tell the story of those four terrible years we spent in Ellesmere Land. I mean they were terrible for Peary who kept right on banging away up the coast. At that time I was purely a mariner and I did not attempt to explore, although I went out sledging sometimes with the Eskimos. Peary, however, continued his trips poleward until 1902 when want of food and fuel forced him to return to America. He finally got around to the top edge of Grant Land and made a northing of 84° 17' on April 21, 1902. This was small compensation for the punishment the man had taken.

All the time I was soaking in more Eskimo lore. I learned how to take care of myself in cold weather. Sipsu showed me how to fix my boots with grass in them, form-ing a pad under the stockings to prevent the soles of my feet from freezing. I learned that I must keep my clothes as dry as possible; wet boots meant frozen feet every time. I found out that sleeves of skin shirts should come down over my knuckles to keep my wrists warm.

I was used to seal meat already. But now I learned to eat it raw and sometimes decayed. I found out how to mix blubber with my diet so that I could stand the cold better. I learned to do long tricks behind a dog team forty, fifty, and sixty miles a day at a stretch. I learned to struggle over steep rocky hillsides and glacier crevasses without knocking my footgear to pieces or breaking my legs. I learned where to look for avalanches and how unsafe the rubber ice was and how to find my way through drifting snow.

I learned more and more about the Eskimos them-selves. This knowledge came in handy later on when I had to go out on the Polar Sea. I found the natives were a hard-working crowd. They had been brought up on work. At the same time I found they were like children and had to be kept cheerful.

As a sample of the way their minds worked I remember once when Peary asked Pooadloona what he was thinking about.

"I am not thinking," laughed the hunter. "I don't have to think. I have plenty of meat."

That's the way it was. So long as they had enough to eat they didn't worry. None of them ever laid any sort of valu-ables aside.

They didn't have any in fact, except meat and skins and

babies. The wives didn't count very much. This same improvidence is often found among our fishermen.

One of the things that struck me about them was the fact that they had no written language. There was no way for one Eskimo to send a message to another. Sometimes this was important, especially in our Polar Sea work and in long traverses over the land ice. The way they'd mark a cache would be to stick up two or three rocks or small bones in a line in the direction of the cache. The smallest stick or bone would be the closest to the cache. You don't realize how important this sort of thing is until you come struggling in over rough ice and deep snow with men and dogs half starving. It surprised me too, that Eskimos sometimes got lost just like white. But they'd laugh about it and not worry.

I always say a good word for the Eskimos when I get a chance. Few white men have as fine characters. The Eskimo is honest. He says, "What is the use of telling a lie except as a joke? The truth always comes out sooner or later." In emergency, however, they get excited and sometimes panicky.

They don't seem to have any morals such as we have. They trade wives around without ceremony; and sometimes there is doubt about who is the father of a child. But they are certainly careful about their taboos and beliefs. Breaking a taboo is their idea of real sin. In this way they are as moral and religious as we are, if not more so. The only great spirit they seem to be afraid of is the Almighty Devil. They don't take his name in vain. The Devil resides in everything: wind, bergs, rocks, darkness, etc.

People often ask me about how we were able to keep

clean up north. I think we were cleaner on Peary's trips than we ever were down sealing. An Eskimo knows pretty well how to clean skins and Peary always kept the ship in good shape. You cannot do that on a sealer loaded up with fat. Also there wasn't any dust such as we have at home.

We were nearly always lousy. But that is true of over sixty per cent of the white race. Newfoundland sailor men say that lice won't go to an unhealthy person. For this reason I have never minded being lousy when away on a long cruise. In the north, we always had women pick up our shirts when we returned from a field trip. Even the Eskimos take their igloo skins out every few days and bang them in the cold air. As a result the lice get numb and can then be knocked off easily with a stick.

It sounds like a rough life. But it wasn't. Peary had a neat ship with plenty of books aboard and always some form of music. In later years he kept us busy, too. That was his cure for Arctic depression. The reason the old expeditions had so much scurvy I think was that they used to have so much trouble finding something to do in the winter. Peary's system which he developed was for his men to travel all winter long while there was no moonlight. In this way health and spirits did not relapse into Arctic melancholy so fatal to the success of an expedition.

When I got back home in 1902, I realized that I was committed to Arctic work. I had got the poison in my veins. I knew I would have to keep at it. I told my father how I felt.

He said, "My boy, there's no money in it unless you have your own expedition."

"But I don't want my own expedition," I told him, "as long as I can go with Peary." That was the grip the man's personality got on me.

CHAPTER XII

A NARROW ESCAPE

Now came the hardest year of my life. Certainly I suffered more mental anguish in it, and endured more physical hardship than at any other time. Also I had some very close shaves. This was the year 1905-6.

Peary then was forty-nine and a failure. He had laboured hard and accomplished practically nothing. It was a wonder he was alive after the Ellesmere Land adventures. But he was alive, still determined to reach the Pole; and he knew more about Arctic work than any other man living. For fifteen years he had been studying Eskimos and polar conditions. Luckily a small group of public-spirited men at home believed in him; they made possible the building of the *Roosevelt*. The rest of the public looked on him as a misguided zealot.

But Peary went through some terrible disappointments about this time. The Navy Department tried to order him to the Pacific coast; in fact, did order him; but he got out of it. The Peary Arctic Club was formed to get money; but it failed. The *Roosevelt* was planned and partly built when the money gave out. It looked as if he had suffered all for nothing.

Finally Morris K. Jesup and General Thomas Hubbard each gave $50,000 for the steamer *Roosevelt*, provided Peary could raise the money for the expedition. This he set about to do by writing and lecturing. It made me laugh when people said he hoarded his money. As a matter of fact he gave everything he had and pawned Mrs. Peary's possessions as well. He was always mortgaged up to the hilt for his next polar voyage.

We sailed from New York with the little *Roosevelt* in July 1905. Peary was very frank with me.

"We are going to put her right out into the Polar Sea," he declared. And I knew by the way he set his jaws that he would do it.

I remember shaking my head.

"It might be done some years, Commander," I answered, "but we cannot be sure. You know what that ice is."

His lips tightened into a hard line. "We are going to do it this year, Bob," he said.

Well, we did it all right, just as he said we would. We jammed her right up through the heavy ice of Kane Basin, Robeson and Kennedy Channels, solid floes miles in extent and ten to forty feet thick. We had a lot of Eskimos on board for use as dog drivers on the Polar Sea. They were so scared they wanted to jump off and run home. Twice they tried to desert with dogs and sledges. But Peary managed to hold them.

It was a terrific fight. Day after day we thought the ice was going to crush the ship. But we finally won, thanks to Peary's courage and tenacity. And when we laid her up there in the Polar Sea pack for the winter Peary went down to his little cabin and wrote in his diary:

"With my feelings of relief came a glow of satisfaction that by a hard-fought struggle we had successfully negotiated the narrow, ice-encumbered waters which form the American gateway, and route to the Pole; had distanced our predecessors; and had substantiated my prophecy to the Club (Peary Arctic) that with a suitable ship, the attainment of a base on the north shore of Grant Land was feasible almost every year."

In his book he has told his story of that spring's heartbreaking effort to reach the Pole; how he and his Eskimos were caught out on the Polar Sea and nearly starved to death. I went with him a good deal of the ways out, being out on the ice in all 121 days. He sent me back with one of the supporting parties. The big lead, one of those open lanes that form by movements of the ice, was what cut him off from going further. On April 21, he reached 87° 6' North, only 174 miles from the Pole. Here again he wrote a paragraph in his little greasy diary that I think is classic. It reads:

"As I looked at the drawn faces of my comrades, the skeleton figures of my few remaining dogs, at my nearly empty sledges, and remembered the drifting ice over which we had come, and unknown quantity of the 'Big Lead' between us and the nearest land, I felt that I had cut the margin as narrow as could reasonably be expected. I told my men we should turn back from here."

When I got back to the ship I found Peary waiting impatiently for my party to return. He was much worried.

Conditions had been very bad out on the ice. Now Peary went west to explore the unknown coast beyond Grant Land. My troubles began then. If he did get back from this new trip I wasn't sure we could ever get the ship out. She was wedged in against the land by enormous floes that must have weighed millions of tons.

Already our voyage had been a chapter of misfortunes. Right outside Sydney on the way up two of our Almy boilers had blown up. Only by luck nobody was killed. Only the Scotch boiler was left. We didn't dare delay because the season was so late.

By the time we reached Etah, a North Greenland Eskimo village, the rotten whale meat we had taken on down the Labrador had seeped into the vessel's timbers all along the main deck. Then one of our Eskimos knocked out his pipe and the first thing we knew the ship was afire. It was bad enough to have her burning up but the smell of the smoldering whale blubber was enough to asphyxiate one. After a fight we got it out.

As soon as I had got back from the Polar Sea, after leaving Peary on his way northward, I saw the *Roosevelt* was in a bad way. She was pinched up against the land by the main pack. To save her from destruction by the June tide I had to use dynamite. In my excitement I used too much. I not only broke the ice but I damaged the ship.

Scarcely had we got out of this pinch than another one began. This went on for several months. When real summer came it was worse than ever. It was July and the main polar pack was getting loose. This made me terribly worried about Peary who was not back from the West yet. There was no telling how he would get along the coast with so much open water among the floes. Three days later the ship got an awful wallop from one of the big sheets. It hove her stern right out of the water and jammed her hard against the solid land ice. It sheered two blades off her propeller and ripped the skeg and rudder post from their fastenings.

I hopped down the after hatch and dived into the lazarette. There I found a big hole in the ship's bottom. I could see the ice right through it; in fact it was big enough for a small boy to crawl through. All this time the pressure was enormous and held us fifteen minutes before it released, the ice crashing and popping all the time and the poor old ship groaning as if she were a human being in pain. Then it suddenly let up. The rupture in the overhang closed a little bit but it was still there when the ice slacked away.

We worked all day and all night landing provisions in case we had to abandon ship. We kept the pumps going steadily. As the pressure released the ship went down into the water and began to leak badly. We piled waste and oakum and cement into the wound. This saved us for the time being.

As soon as we were afloat again (we had been jammed up in the shallower water by the pressure) I had the engine started to see if we could back clear. I didn't know two of our propeller blades were broken. One of them jammed. We nearly cracked the shaft in half. So I had to stop the engine.

Right in the middle of all this party it began to blow and snow. We had a regular blizzard from the north. But we didn't dare stop work. If the ship were lost we had to have enough food so we could work back to Etah. Forty-eight hours later wind and pressure fell. We had saved the ship, but all the hands were exhausted.

Through it all I kept wondering where on earth Peary and his Eskimos were.

A few days later I happened to be on deck and saw a black figure in the west coming slowly over the ice. It turned out to be one of the Eskimos. The poor fellow could hardly walk, between sore feet and exhaustion. Peary came alone behind him.

I didn't bother Peary with much of a description of our troubles. He was too much all in at the time. After a brief exchange he went below for food and rest. We went right ahead on deck meanwhile making a new rudder and trying to keep the ship afloat. The next day, the leader came up to help me. He said:

"We have got to get her back, Captain. We are going to come again next year."

I should have thought he wouldn't have wanted to ever to see that place again. But it was like him when he was lowest to be still planning for the future. Already he was thinking of his next attack on the Pole.

We shifted all our coal forward. This lifted the ship's stern out of the water and let us cut away what was left of the crushed rudder and the post. We finally forced a makeshift rudder down into place so that we could steer if we ever got free from the murderous ice.

During the first week of August, a southwest gale blew up and loosened the main pack. I took a climb up on the high hill inshore of us to see how far the water extended. It looked as if a winding lane of clean sea ran some miles to the east. I hurried back. By this time the wind was blowing a gale. When I left we had been moored to a floe. Now we had to anchor to keep from being carried into the pack again. In getting the anchor up one of our men fell overboard and was nearly drowned. He couldn't swim an inch. We managed to hook him out with a grapnel.

We got steam on the boiler and were under way in a few hours. To add to our troubles the boiler was leaking and showed suspicious signs of blowing up also. As our makeshift rudder was small we couldn't steer very well. The remaining propeller blades gave us only about five knots. But we limped along as best we could and made about five miles east, thankful to be escaping at last from the clutches of the polar pack.

At Wrangel Bay we picked up a family of natives we had left there for hunting. They had come up two days before from Fort Conger. On the way the woman had given birth to a baby which complicated matters somewhat. But we managed to get them aboard our wreck and were soon off again. A few babies or dogs more or less in the bedlam aboard made little difference.

We were headed at last through Kennedy Channel south towards Kane Basin. But here the channel was choked with heavy ice. All we could do was to drift helplessly and wait. We were under pressure most of the time. It looked as if our last two remaining propeller blades would be nipped off. The ice kept jamming the cement and oakum out of the hole we had in our bottom, each time threatening to sink us with the water that poured in. Only by keeping men stationed at the hole did we save ourselves when this happened.

It began to look as if we might have to winter in the north whether we lost the ship or not. The season was now seriously late. Already it was August 26. On that day Peary came to me and said:

"Captain, I give us three days more. By that time either the ship will be out or have to winter here."

"Well," I said, "if we stay up here we ought to get some muskox. You know how good they taste."

He worked out a complete plan for what we should do if we wintered. We had very little food left. The doctor and Marvin and I were to go with the Eskimos in three different directions inland and collect meat. This would keep us from starving, our first consideration. But once more just when we were all ready to go ashore hunting for winter meat the ice loosened up and we began to move south again.

My diary is full of details about this time. I used to go up on deck and decide that we would sink in a few minutes and then go down and make a last entry in my diary. Then I'd come up again and we'd still be afloat and I'd try to explain how it was possible for a wreck like ours not to sink. It went on like this for two whole weeks. It was an awful strain. All the time the jury rudder we had rigged was being punished worse and worse and the bottom was getting more holes punched in it. Most of our men had given up hope long ago. Only Peary was at all optimistic.

A big sheet pushed us over to Cape Sabine on September 14. We kept the engine running so as to avoid being taken ashore. Finally on September 16, with the engine going at full speed and all our canvas spread, we escaped. For seventy-five days we had been battling our way in a sinking ship from Cape Sheridan southwards. I say we escaped, though our troubles had really just begun.

We escaped over to Etah, across Smith Sound. This tiny Eskimo settlement lies in latitude 78° 50' and consists of only three igloos. We managed to enter the fjord there, and took the ship three miles up towards the glacier and put her aground. We wanted to patch her bottom up for the long trip south. Peary was feverishly anxious to get home that winter because he wanted to come north again the following summer. Also we were out of food and the Eskimos hadn't been able to gather much meat for the dark months just ahead, unless we could recover our cache of a year's provisions left on Bache Peninsula. (Later we gave this to the Eskimos.)

We beached the *Roosevelt* stern first at high tide. When the tide went down we certainly saw a mess. Our stern was ground almost to pieces. Our jury rudder was in kindling wood; and the propeller blades, such as were left, were twisted and cracked. The hole in the bottom looked as though it could never be repaired. Not only was it a big gaping wound, but the timbers all around it were crushed and splintered. I must say I would just as soon have walked home as to have tried to put to sea in the *Roosevelt* at that time.

Peary sent for me and said briefly:

"Captain, we've got to hurry now. The nights are getting dark."

I almost laughed in his face. It did sound funny for him to be so sure that we could sail home. Yet from the way he said it I knew we would. I even had a feeling that I might spend Christmas in the south.

"All right, Commander," said I, "all sleep is cut out until we fix her." I turned all hands to at once, and gave orders the work would not stop until finished.

We tightened up the nuts on the propeller and straightened the plates as best we could with mauls. We packed a lot more stuff into the holes in the bottom and nailed canvas over them all. On the next tide we floated, though we were in some doubt as to how long.

We steamed down to our coal depot near the entrance of the fjord. This fuel had been left on our way north. Ordinarily we should have gone right up to the shore and brought it aboard in wheelbarrows. Now our bottom was so fragile we didn't dare touch the rocks. So we lashed several boats together and brought the coal out on a sort of raft. All went well until a blizzard came up in the middle of the party and we lost a good deal of coal, nearly swamping the boats and drowning some of our men. Incidentally, the coal was lying out in the open and was all frozen together. We had to use dynamite to loosen it, dangerous work in the cold and drifting snow.

On the evening of September 20, we steamed out of Etah. The nights were now getting very dark and young ice was forming right along. I had never cruised around up there so late. The landmarks all looked queer in the strange light. Less than four weeks more and sun would be gone for good, not to return until the following March. Ordinarily we wouldn't have dared to have steamed in those waters at this advanced date. But we were racing for our lives.

Down at Kookan, another Eskimo settlement, we got caught in ice and darkness and tide all at one time and to our dismay ran aground again. That's the end of us, I thought. Our bottom would certainly cave in. By a miracle there was no sea running and no wind blowing. When daylight came we got out our kedge and hauled ourselves off.

As a matter of fact this grounding turned out to be a blessing in disguise. For when the tide went down and left us high and dry we discovered that the bolts and nuts on our last remaining propeller blade were loose. Had they dropped out and the blade come off we should have been helpless because we couldn't sail in the ice; there wasn't room to navigate. All hands got overboard in the icy muck and managed to tighten up the bolts. Also we put a little more patchwork on our rudder and bottom.

Down in Parker Snow Bay we got in close enough to send ashore the last of our few Eskimos. They were glad enough to leave us as they were sure the ship was soon going to sink. We had persuaded them to stay aboard so long because we were short-handed. The *Roosevelt* seemed very empty without them and their 150 dogs. They left their trace, however, in the stench which hung for weeks between decks.

On September 26, in a blinding snowstorm we headed out from Cape York across Melville Bay for home. We had almost no coal left and were down to rock bottom on our provisions. The *Roosevelt* was a cripple and her boilers ready to go to pieces at any moment. Not much of a bump was necessary to injure her weakened bottom. It wasn't a nice feeling there in the driving snow and the darkness. But

Peary was not at all dejected and continued to talk about his plans for the next voyage.

This blizzard wasn't a circumstance to what we ran into next day. It is often said there are no real storms in the Arctic. This is true in the sense that, while the wind may blow fifty miles an hour up there, the hurricane rarely gets into high latitudes. But this time our glass began to fall rapidly and there were unmistakable sighs of the approach of a powerful circular storm.

Next day it came. And it was a humdinger. When we began to ship seas regularly we hove to. Ashes in our stokehold clogged our bilge pumps. The water rose rapidly. Soon our fires were put out. This was serious because it meant we would sink if we couldn't use the pumps. We saved ourselves by hacking a hole through the after bulkhead of the main hold adjoining the engine room. This bulkhead was seven inches of pitch pine, both vertical and thwartship layers with iron fastenings. The hole we cut let the water go through to our main pumps.

We weathered this gale only to run into another on October 3. Now we were using our canvas and making nearly eight knots. The trouble was that our makeshift rudder wasn't broad enough to steer properly with. We had to do a good deal of our steering with our sails. Remember, we were using our third rudder now. It carried away on October 4 at four a.m.

We now hove to under our foresail, and began getting another beam out of the hold to make a rudder post with. When the wind dropped we unrigged the mizzen boom and got it out over a crutch lashed to the taffrail. The foretopmast carried away with a crash during operations. Luckily no one was hurt. On the outboard end of the mizzen boom we hung a small kedge anchor to weigh it down to work like a blade. Also we attached a hawser which led back about twenty feet from the sea end of the boom. There we lashed and middled it; that is, made two ends. One end we passed through a quarter chock on the port side and the other on the starboard side. These lines became our tiller ropes, the weighted boom our rudder. We led the lines to the winches, forward and aft. For a while we steered fairly well with this improvised steering gear.

The next day, a heavy sea was running with strong northeast wind and blinding snow. We had to heave to again. In doing so we discontinued using our boom rig. Although hove to, we finally finished the new rudder and hung it. This made our fourth rudder.

Twenty-four hours later all hands turned to, to get another beam from between decks. With the ship standing on her nose every few seconds and our tackle limited we had a great job getting up the heavy timber. But by dark we had the beam in readiness. It took the combined force of all the men and all available tools before we finally fastened to this beam a rudder blade made up of a lot of planks bolted together. By means of sheer-legs over the stern we got this new rudder in place. It was ticklish work with the ship dancing around like a chip on the surface of the water. But we finally succeeded. We were exhausted by the job.

We now cleared away for the Labrador coast a little south of Cape Chidley. Even under favourable conditions this part of the Labrador is an ugly place. But we could not afford to pick and choose. We were afraid our rudder would carry away again. We had very little water left for drinking purposes. We had practically no coal left; in fact the firemen were sweeping the bunkers to fill shovels. We began cutting away beams and loose timbers for fuel.

Two days later, we limped into Hebron where the Moravian mission station is. But victory turned to disappointment when we found we could get only wood and blubber for our furnaces. However, we were all so relieved at escaping into the safety of a fairly landlocked harbour that we didn't worry much. When the missionary asked Peary to dinner, the commander had to refuse because he had no trousers. The missionary sent out a pair of moleskin breeches from the trading post so we had the banquet after all.

As the season was getting later and more dangerous all the time we hove up anchor the next day. We were now burning wood and seal oil and blubber to make steam with. The wood was green but with the blubber it served us well. We ran about 100 miles; then had to stop in again and get some more wood. Also we chopped some out of the between-deck passages of the ship.

A curious accident happened near Hopedale. I thought everything had happened that possibly could to delay our getting home. But another gale broke as we were about to enter Windy Tickle. I had only one chart of the place. A terrific gust of wind struck us just as I was trying to pick out my landmark from the sheet and swept it overboard. I stopped the ship and lowered a boat. It was a case of life and death. Without the chart it would have been very easy to lose the ship then and there. We could see the white paper floating for some minutes. But just before the boat got to it, it sank. There was only one thing to do; we went on without a chart. Providence guided us into Hopedale.

At Hopedale we got some more wood and blubber. I wish I could repeat some of the things that our engineer said about keeping up steam with that kind of fuel. But I am afraid this printed page would go up in smoke if I did.

We reached Battle Harbour on November 22. Ordinarily we should have passed this point in September. The nights were pitch-dark and the weather almost continuously bad. There was always something coming down out of the sky, either rain or sleet or snow. There are no more dangerous waters in the world to navigate in bad weather than those of the Labrador. At Battle Harbour our anchor carried away owing to the heavy strain put on it by the gale. Luckily the agent there had loaned us some chain which we ran out to the rocks. Once more we were saved by pure luck.

There is a lot more to tell of the same sort of misery. It was one storm after another, and always the terrible anxiety of our fifth rudder which we kept on patching up; not to speak of the wretched condition of the *Roosevelt's* bottom. But there is no use prolonging the yarn because it was all exactly the same; just one narrow shave after another, and interminable hours of hard labour.

At Sydney we finally got some coal. We took on 250 tons. It began to look now as if our troubles were over. But going through St. Peter Canal in thick weather I ran the *Roosevelt* into a fence which was built down into the water, and jammed her nose hard and fast into the bank. This happened because our rudder could not operate fast enough to let us manoeuvre in narrow waters. I remember a girl was milking a cow behind the fence. When she saw the *Roosevelt* headed straight for her she grabbed the stool on which she was sitting and dashed screaming up the hill. The cow galloped after her. The poor old *Roosevelt*, as well as ourselves, was ready for the insane asylum or the dump heap.

On Christmas Eve at six p.m. we finally anchored in the North River. As the chain rattled over the side Peary turned and silently gripped my hand. We were too numb from all our experiences really to appreciate our escape. I just went down and climbed in my bunk and passed off into beautiful unconsciousness. The following morning, Mr. Herbert Bridgman came aboard early and shouted down the hatch: "Merry Christmas, Bob."

After Mr. Bridgman came aboard we called on Mr. Jesup at his home in Madison Avenue. When we got up to go he placed a $20 gold piece in my hand. I looked on this as a token of good luck since we had just escaped from a long series of perils. So I have kept that $20 gold piece ever since, though many a time it would have bought me a good meal when I needed one.

CHAPTER XIII

TO THE NORTH POLE

After a man has been through great strain there is always reaction, both mental and physical. The fearful strain of our hard 1906 trip back to New York in the *Roosevelt* had been just as much on our nerves as on our bodies. Now both demanded a change.

Had I not been a teetotaller I suppose I should have gone on some sort of drinking spree. As it was, my spree took the form of eating and sleeping. For many weeks I had been conscious of a powerful hankering for steak smothered in onions, with hot strong coffee on the side. Now that I was back in civilization I sneaked off every time I could and ordered a big thick steak piled up with fine greasy fried onions. I confess I did this even when I had dined with some friend at his home. Indeed, I found myself holding back amidst luxurious food, biding my time until I could furtively slip away to some restaurant and indulge my fantastic craving for meat.

Also I seemed to be sleepy all the time. Of course I had lost a lot of sleep on the ship; but being in fine fettle, I soon made it up on arrival. Despite this my body kept urging me to take more hours lying around in bed and "corking it off," as the sailor calls sleeping soundly. By the end of a week my steak-onion diet plus about fourteen hours of sleep a day had me so groggy that it took strong effort of will to break loose and buy a ticket for Newfoundland where my family were awaiting a sight of me.

I reached Brigus early in January. My father at once proved the most interested listener to my fabulous tale of our escape from the North. I suppose his years amongst the ice made him see more clearly what we had been through. After I had sat up half the first night reciting our adventures he shook his head and said: "It is God's will, boy, that you are back with us." I think he was right.

When it came time for spring sealing I wrote to Peary asking leave of absence. I knew he planned to go north again early in the following summer, and he had already asked me to be master of the *Roosevelt* once more. I was glad when he replied that he did not need me in New York until May; so I at once got a berth to go down sealing with my father. We had a good trip and returned with a profitable cargo of skins and blubber the first week in April.

A few days later, I received a wire from Peary telling me that the *Roosevelt* was being fixed up in New York and that he wanted me to supervise the work. So I hurried down and went right aboard. We were to get away from New York early in June but the boilermakers were slow.

All was excitement on the dock where the vessel was tied up. Once more I could feel the suspense and eagerness that goes before departure on an Arctic expedition. Peary scarcely slept; and his face looked drawn and tired. I could see that he was worried more than usual. Without the knowledge of the rest of us, he was deeply anxious about his finances.

He had published his book, *Nearest the Pole*, in the winter. He had been counting on royalties from this volume to help with his bills. But, like his attempt at the Pole, the book was a failure. Somehow people weren't interested in reading about hardships that didn't get the explorer to his goal. I realize now that the world prefers to read about success. Of course Peary could have put together a fine ornamental story on his 1906 debacle; but he was not a man to embellish the truth. In writing to a friend about his disappointment in the book he said: "Fortunately I did not know that Fate was even then clenching her fist for yet another and more crushing blow."

This blow was the death of Mr. Morris K. Jesup, Peary's chief financial backer. Peary knew that if he couldn't get money at once he would have to give up his plan to attack the Pole again that year.

I joined in his battle for more money. I knocked at the doors of political leaders and millionaires. I was rebuffed, laughed at, offered jobs, sympathized with and in a hundred ways resisted. But I kept on. I didn't understand these men and they didn't understand me. It was a glorious fight; but we failed—that year, at least.

There was nothing for me to do but go back home again and make what money I could at sealing. I spent the winter (1907-08) at Brigus and St. John's, Newfoundland. Rarely have I been so depressed as I was in those months. In March I joined the sealing fleet and again went down into the ice. But I had a tough time. Instead of fattening my bank account I got few seals and in the end went through a tragedy that no ship's captain can forget. My vessel, *The Leopard,* was crushed in the ice and I lost her. Luckily I got my men out alive. I shall describe this catastrophe in a future chapter.

Early in June I left with my crew to join the *Roosevelt* in New York again. We had to work day and night in the boiling heat to get our supplies aboard and place the vessel in a seaworthy condition. Certainly by this time the *Roosevelt* should have been ready for sea. But she wasn't. Lack of money was the reason. People will never know how poverty stricken Peary was despite the wonderful aid he got. All his money went into equipment which he did not dare economize on. But at the last minute General Thomas H. Hubbard saved the day with a big cheque; and Zenas Crane topped the fine gift off with $10,000 more.

We cast off on July 6, 1908. On the Recreation Pier at 26th Street, East River, were gathered thousands of men, women and children. Their cheers and the chorus of whistles that rose as we backed out made us feel better after all our setbacks. The next day, we stopped at Oyster Bay for a couple of hours, where we dressed ship and welcomed Theodore Roosevelt aboard. He came with Mrs. Roosevelt, Secretary Loeb and Theodore, Jr. Kermit, a small lad then, was with them, too. He looked up with glistening teeth and squinting eyes as he came alongside.

The first thing T. R. said when he came aboard was: "*Bully!*" in a loud voice. Then he walked around and let nothing escape his piercing eyes. He went into the lower hold and into the engine room. He inspected Peary's quarters and the living spaces of the sailors. Just before leaving he said he would like to shake hands with each member of the crew; not satisfied with that, he demanded to know the names of every one of us. I soon realized that his reputation was well-founded. He took a deep and personal interest in important matters, but he did not forget to note the details about him. And he had a mind that could hold them.

We stopped at New Bedford and picked up some whale boats, strong wide and deep. Harry Whitney joined us there to go up for some summer hunting. Remembering our terrible 1906 experience, we picked up a spare rudder at Portland. At Sydney the *Erik* joined us with about 800 tons of coal. This was a great luxury, since it meant we would not have to face a dangerous shortage of fuel in case we got caught in the north. At Turnavik on the Labrador we made another stop at the fishing station owned and managed by my father. Here we found about fifty pairs of sealskin boots waiting for us. We took on ten tons of whale meat at Cape Charles. We loaded the whale meat in our well deck. It had already begun to decay. After a few days of sunny weather the odour of it was overpowering, even to our Newfoundland sailor men, who were used to pretty strong stenches on our sealing ships. But we had to stand it a good many weeks before we got it ashore at Cape Sheridan. The meat was meant to feed our dogs.

Our journey to Cape York up the Greenland coast was uneventful. At the cape we were met by the Eskimos and a blizzard, fitting forms of Arctic hospitality. Right away we began picking up hunters and dogs. The natives were over-joyed to see Peary again. Each time I went north it was a revelation to me how they loved the big white man who came to them year after year, treating them like a father and always leaving them with gifts of priceless value.

At Etah we dropped off Boatswain Murphy, Billy Pritchard and Harry Whitney with coal and supplies. Peary left orders for them to help out Dr. Cook who had gone northwest the year before and had not yet shown up. We were afraid Cook was in trouble. We all knew he didn't have enough food for a polar trip. Whitney has written feelingly of subsequent events. Dr. Cook had left his one miserable companion there. This fellow was suffering from scurvy. Peary gave him passage back to the States in the *Erik*.

We now were on the home stretch north. We left Etah about four p.m., August 14, 1908, with 550 tons of coal on deck. Mixed up with the coal were seventy tons of whale meat and 246 dogs, all fighting and screaming; the dogs, I mean. In addition we had forty-nine Eskimos and the blubber of fifty walruses. To get some idea of what this meant you must remember that the *Roosevelt* was not any bigger than the average tug. She was already weighted down with a heavy cargo of supplies and equipment for at least a year in the Far North. To my dying day I shall never forget the frightful noise, the choking stench and the terrible confusion that reigned aboard her as we steamed slowly down Foulke Fjord and swung around into the pack of Kane Basin. We had some canned peaches that night for supper; but the odour about us was so powerful that the peaches simply felt wet and cold on one's tongue, having no fruit flavour whatsoever.

Now came once more the long fight through the ice

from Etah to Cape Sheridan north through Kane Basin and Kennedy and Robeson Channels. We had fought the same battle before in 1905. It was mostly a grim struggle to save the ship while forging ahead by inches. Yet Peary never was perturbed; I was the one who got excited. But it took a good deal of excitement on the pilot's part to make noise enough to reach our helmsman through the uproar of dogs and Eskimos.

On September 5, we made our last lap. At 7:15 on that morning we were up to our 1906 winter quarters. Cape Sheridan, low and bleak, was just to port. Open water ran a little beyond the Cape, 'twixt ice and shore. In order to beat our former record we steamed to the end of the land and came back. On September 5, 1905, three years before, we had steamed hopefully into our winter quarters. Now with even higher hopes we began hurrying our provisions to the beach. We had to put everything ashore in case the ice crushed us or fire broke out. By September 7, we had everything over the side and our boilers blown down.

Now began the task of sledging supplies to Cape Columbia ninety miles to the west. This Cape was to be our hop-off point to the Pole. We had seven white men, nineteen Eskimos, 146 dogs and twenty sledges in our field parties. Peary planned to break a trail and by constant travelling keep this trail open all winter long. Then he could start at the first coming of light in early February and hop off fresh and fully equipped for the Pole itself.

Most people picture a winter in the long Arctic night as a terrible nightmare. It surely used to be with the old expeditions. They would coop themselves up in their ship and have theatricals and other entertainments. They read a lot and talked a good deal more. Such a thing as travel in the darkness and cold was absolutely taboo. It wasn't good for their health or their dispositions.

Peary's plan was just the opposite. He kept all hands busy day in day out, on board and ashore. You know the monthly moon rises in the Arctic above the horizon and does not set again for ten or twelve days. It goes around in a big spiral until it reaches its point of maximum declination. This takes about a week. Then it starts down again. This takes nearly another week. So every month there is a lot more moonlight than we have down here. In this moonlight Peary kept all hands sledging and hunting. During the dark days, we had all we could do to get our gear cleared up and in shape before the next moon came. Naturally with such a routine the winter flew by. The men kept in fine physical shape and spirits and we gathered more and more fresh meat and skins for the stiff spring dash to the North.

At ten o'clock in the morning of Washington's Birthday, February 22, 1909, Peary left the *Roosevelt* for the North Pole. It was blowing a half gale. The temperature was about thirty below zero with a blinding smother of fine snow. It was ten o'clock in the morning before we could see to travel.

In other expeditions the leader's departure from his base meant as a rule that the main effort was just beginning. Peary's plan was much more complicated. In the first place he was preceded by a hard winter of sledging supplies westward to Cape Columbia. Every one of us white men was a leader of a unit, consisting of three or four natives, each with a dog team. Each sledge carried an average load of about 650 pounds.

As a seafaring man I always admired Peary's sledges. He realized that no manufacturer at home could picture Polar Sea ice. So he brought planks and runners north and let his Eskimos build the sledges. Peary designed them after the native sledge. But he kept on where the native left off. For instance, lack of material prevented the native from building a long sledge though a long sledge distributed a heavy load better. Also the native couldn't put rocker runners on or wide shoes on his sledge uprights. Peary provided both. As a result the Eskimos were delighted. Throughout the winter they spent the dark weeks in fashioning the sledges that were to carry fuel and provisions northward when the sun returned.

As I said, each sledge carried about 650 pounds. With ten dogs in a team, 500 pounds of the load had to be dog pemmican so that each animal could have a pound a day. Then there were fifty pounds of biscuit and fifty pounds of man pemmican for the driver. Also each man had a little stove with some alcohol for fuel. These items with a few pounds extra of tea and clothing completed the load. We used no sleeping bags but slept on our snowshoes covered by a piece of skin.

Peary had long ago learned that the size of a unit should be three men because a snow igloo can just comfortably hold three men. Also three men can just about handle a 700-pound sledge mass over the rough ice we often met in the shape of mountainous pressure ridges. At such times we would get one sledge through the barrier and then go back and get the others, one at a time.

My own departure from the ship on the western lap to the hop-off point had been January 31. As it was moonlight we made good time. I had with me eight sledges and fifty-six dogs, carrying 140 tins of pemmican to the base camp at Cape Columbia. In the meantime, Marvin and Borup were also working back and forth to the Cape, piling up grub for the big effort. After a few days of blizzard I returned to the ship for another load. I left again on February 15, making the first final unit to get away from the *Roosevelt* bound for the North Pole.

On February 22, the day Peary left, my party reached Stubbs Point. Here my hunters took a look around for muskoxen; but a blinding drift and a temperature down past fifty below made hunting practically impossible.

On February 26, Peary came in to my camp at Columbia. He and I climbed the hill behind our igloos to see how the sea ice looked. We were pleased not to make out any water and the pressure ice didn't seem very bad. Peary said little. I think he knew this was his last try, after a lifetime spent on his fight for the Pole.

A few days later we were all at Cape Columbia: Peary, the doctor, Marvin, MacMillan, Borup, Henson, and myself, each one at the head of his own division of Eskimos. Before we set out northward MacMillan, Borup, Marvin and I got together in a little council of war in my igloo. In short words we talked over the coming trip. Marvin and I were old hands at the game and felt optimistic. The others were game, but a little doubtful. I had my kerosene oil stove going full blast and the igloo was warm to cheer us all up. We expanded over our plans. After a fine talk I suggested each man sing a college song. Marvin from Cornell, Borup from Yale and MacMillan from Bowdoin. After this we all joined hands and each fellow gave his college cheer. Honestly I began to be sorry I hadn't gone to college when I heard the way those fellows could yell. I could make as much noise but somehow it wasn't organized when it came out of my throat. I must add that the natives thought we had all got so scared we had gone "Pibloctoq" or crazy.

We pledged each other that we would fight to the bitter end and do all in our power to help Peary plant the Stars and Stripes at the Pole. I remember Marvin was especially moved; little did we think he would soon be taken from us. But what is to be will be. I believe that when a man's time has come he will die and that it is useless for us to worry about the future.

Our Eskimos were also in fine spirits. They weren't giving any college yells or singing any college songs, but they were making their own particular kind of barbarous noise which the nearly 200 dogs joined in.

The next morning, Sunday, February 28, I left the land with three Eskimos and dogs. We were the pioneer party. Our work was to set the course, break the trail, and gauge the distance for the main party. About two hours after I left Borup followed in my trail with four sledges and three Eskimo dog drivers. In the early stages with our heaviest loads, we had orders from Peary to make short marches of not over ten miles. The going was fair but our heavy loads had to be watched carefully through the rough inshore ice.

There now followed a month of terrible labour for all

hands. Each unit had the task of working out and back over a broken trail and keeping Peary with his best dogs and Eskimos fairly well in the rear. This put the leader in touch with units that had gone back to the land for more supplies and also with units ahead of him who were breaking trail. You don't have to travel along the Polar Sea to realize how important this keeping-in-touch business is. Eskimos get discouraged, sledges break down, fuel tins leak, dogs die, leads break the trail, and there are the thousand and one minor delays and difficulties which complicate the whole problem. I suppose now that men fly over the Pole most people will view with scorn the struggles and hardships of us who plodded out and back behind our dogs. But I think the details of sledge travel ought to be recorded in the history of polar exploration because the sledge is to the Arctic what the covered wagon was to the West: it represents a period in history full of human drama.

So many other writers have told the story of our trip over the ice there is no use in going into it now. Many still declare that Peary didn't get to the Pole and that we faked our diaries and figures. But I think any man who has been through a polar trip would only laugh at such accusations. Navigational observations in latitude over the Polar Sea are about as easy to take as they are on any other portion of the globe. The observer lies down on a warm muskox fur and measures the altitude of the sun above the horizon with his sextant. This takes only a few moments. Usually (Peary and I always did) he makes half a dozen such measurements to be sure he is on the right track. These he averages up. To get the latitude it is necessary only to correct this altitude with a few simple figures. The whole computation can be finished in a minute or so by any mariner with his master's papers. There is nothing very complicated or obscure about it. I don't know how many thousands of times I have done the same thing. Marvin, of course, was a mathematician and an engineer; so he was even more apt than I. Peary had been taking sights all his life. It seems quite inconceivable to me that anyone with a knowledge of human nature could study our hard trip over the ice and our simple observations and think for a moment that Peary's record could possibly be anything but what he claimed it to be.

I admit he didn't say much about his sufferings and his discouragements. Heaven knows, we had our share. On March 7, Pooadloona, my best man, sulkily said he was ill and was going back to the ship. The next day, Panikpah wanted to go back. Both these natives finally deserted. This was very demoralizing to the other Eskimos but Peary managed to keep them in line, one minute by being fatherly and the next minute being firm.

Our alcohol leaked out until it looked as if we should have no more hot tea. The ice floes faulted and broke the trail day after day. The weather was fearfully cold; never warmer than fifty below zero with cutting wind. Open water held us up until I thought we'd go crazy. But through it all Peary never lost his head, his temper or his nerve. In times of stress he usually became very stern. But unexpected little flashes of humour would creep through and then we'd feel all right again.

One by one the boys turned back. Marvin's last march

took him to 86° 38', or four miles beyond the Italian record. I kept on until 87° 48'.

On the first of April I left the igloo at five in the morning. It was cold and a sharp wind nipped me. A white uneven desert surrounded the spot on which I stood. I wanted to pass the 88th parallel. In fact Peary urged me to; his feeling was that he wanted me to go as far north as possible. I mention this because people think I ought to have kept on with Peary to the Pole. The American public has held it against Peary for not taking me. They say that he should have taken me instead of Henson. I suppose if he had I could later have made a lot of money out of lectures; and I don't deny that it would have been a great thrill to have stood at the peak of our globe. But don't forget that Henson was a better dog driver than I. So I think Peary's reasoning was sound; and I have never held it against him.

I walked more than five miles beyond the camp; but when I came back the observation I had taken showed us 87° 47'. The drift of the ice to the south had robbed me of my record. It was a tough blow to my pride, but made no real difference.

Peary was in fine condition. He had with him forty dogs, all prime. For over a month he had been picking the best dogs and keeping them with light loads. He had four undamaged sledges and four Eskimos beside Henson. He had full rations for sixty days.

His sledges were not loaded heavily and ice ahead was improving all the time.

Before I pulled out for the south I went in to Peary's igloo and told him goodbye.

"Goodbye, Captain," he said. "Take care of yourself. Watch out for young ice. Clean up the ship when you get back. Don't worry about me; I'll be back."

I tried to thank him for what he had done for me in taking me this far. It was an honour that he had chosen to bestow upon me. I told him something of this.

"It's all in the game," he said. "And you've been at it long enough to know how hard a game it is."

He gave me more directions about the ship and about our supplies. He wasn't heartless; he was just businesslike. He was always that way.

"Goodbye, sir," I said again.

"Goodbye, Captain," he said. "If we get there it will be the South Pole next and you as leader."

I went right out and started south with my party. I didn't make much of a march; there was no longer the incentive to go fast. Our dogs went well with their light sledges but I didn't want to hurry. I felt like lingering a little in case anything happened to those north of me.

At this point, I must chuckle again when I think of people saying that Peary didn't go to the Pole. There he was only a few days' march from it with good going and the pick of the whole Eskimo tribe, both in dogs and men. He was past fifty; but he had the physique of a man under forty. There was no point in his falsifying his position even if he had been that sort of man. It was an easy jaunt to the Pole from where I left him, and conditions were improving right along. Anyway, the Eskimos never keep a secret. And they knew well in which direction I was going. Had he not gone on those extra marches to his destination, that fact would have been the first thing the natives would have told us about when they got back.

I had a rough time before I reached the land. We lost the trail in drifting snow and I fell through young ice and nearly drowned. It was about thirty-two degrees below zero. The natives hauled me out and rolled me up in a muskox robe. I was almost paralyzed with cold before I got dry garments on. Luckily we were near an igloo. So I came out of the jam without serious damage.

On April 17, I reached Cape Nares. There we ran across sledge tracks. I figured this must be Marvin's trail. I couldn't understand why there were only two sets of footprints when he had two Eskimos with him. I had decided that Marvin must have his feet so badly frozen that he was riding on his sledge.

When I got to Cape Columbia I looked all around for the note Marvin had promised to leave for me. There was no sign of it. I figured this meant he must be ill. After thirty-six hours of rest and sleep at the Cape we got under way and on April 23, reached the ship. About a half-mile from the *Roosevelt* I met one of the firemen. He told me Marvin had fallen through a lead on the way home and drowned. The rest of the crowd were very uneasy. Since Marvin's death they had feared for the rest of us. It was not until the summer of 1926, that I learned that Marvin had not fallen through the ice, as the Eskimos reported, but had been shot by Kudlooktoo.

Peary reached the ship on April 27. I happened to be up on deck when the Eskimos shouted that he was coming. I ran out on the ice to meet him. He looked haggard but not weak. He grasped my outstretched hand while I exclaimed: "*I congratulate you, sir, on the discovery of the Pole!*"

"How did you guess it?" he asked, laughing at my excitement.

Then I told him the news of Marvin's death. He was stunned. He had always prided himself on getting through expeditions without hairbreadth escapes and tragedies that had marked so many other expeditions. He little knew the greatest tragedy of his whole life was soon to confront him.

Late in August we broke out and started south. After our 1906 trip we were prepared for anything. But this time we escaped as if by magic. The Arctic is like that. We dropped our Eskimos at their homes, worked down through the icefields for Kane Basin and emerged early in September. We heaved a sigh of relief to be out, never imagining that our real troubles were just about to begin.

Captain Bob Bartlett on the SS *Roosevelt*.
Courtesy of the Peary/MacMillan Arctic Museum and the Historic Sites
Association of Newfoundland and Labrador.

SS *Panther* (Bartlett Sealer). Courtesy of the Historic Sites Association of Newfoundland and Labrador.

Captain Bob Bartlett and Robert Peary hosting a crowd on board the SS *Roosevelt*. Courtesy of the Historic Sites Association of Newfoundland and Labrador.

Captain Bob Bartlett, Peary Expedition, 1909.
Courtesy of the Peary/MacMillan Arctic Museum and the Historic Sites
Association of Newfoundland and Labrador.

1909 Peary Polar Expedition.
L-R: Panikapak, Harrigan, Ooqueah, and Bartlett. Courtesy of the
National Geographic Society and the Historic Sites Association of
Newfoundland and Labrador.

Explorers Club dinner at the Astor, 1915. Courtesy of the Historic Sites
Association of Newfoundland and Labrador.

Silhouette shot of Bob with iceberg. Courtesy of the Historic Sites Association of Newfoundland and Labrador.

Karluk crew in Victoria before departing. Courtesy of the National Archives of Canada (PA74066) and the Historic Sites Association of Newfoundland and Labrador.

Kuraluk and Kiruk (Auntie), with their two childred Helen and Mugpi. They were hired to hunt and sew winter clothes for the *Karluk* expedition crew. Courtesy of the National Archives of Canada (C70806) and the Historic Sites Association of Newfoundland and Labrador.

William McKinlay relaxing on deck of the *Karluk*. Courtesy of the National Archives of Canada (PA74058) and the Historic Sites Association of Newfoundland and Labrador.

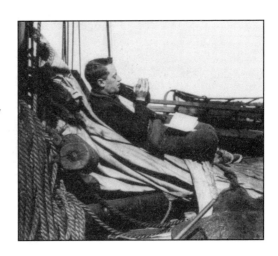

The *Karluk* cutting a path through the ice in August 1913. Courtesy of the National Archives of Canada (PA74047) and the Historic Sites Association of Newfoundland and Labrador.

The crew unloading supplies from the *Karluk* upon realizing they were trapped in the ice. Courtesy of the National Archives of Canada (PA74047) and the Historic Sites Association of Newfoundland and Labrador.

Photo of Wrangel Island located 100 miles off the coast of Siberia. This is where the *Karluk* suvivors were rescued. Courtesy of the National Archives of Canada (C70808) and the Historic Sites Association of Newfoundland and Labrador.

Bob and Katiktovick driving through pack ice on their way to Siberia.
Courtesy of the National Archives of Canada (PA74027) and the
Historic Sites Association of Newfoundland and Labrador.

The survivors of the SS *Karluk* of the Canadian Arctic Expedition. L-R
John Munro (back), Robert Templeton, Robert Williamson, John Hadley,
Captain Bob Bartlett, Auntie, Mugpi, Helen, William McKinlay, Kuraluk
(front), Ernest Chafe, "Clam" Williams, and Fred Maurer. Courtesy of
the National Archives of Canada (PA105130) and the Historic Sites
Association of Newfoundland and Labrador.

After the *Karluk*, Captain Bob Bartlett gazing out to sea. Courtesy of the Historic Sites Association of Newfoundland and Labrador.

CHAPTER XIV

A WORLD OF LUNATICS

My friends say it is dangerous to get me started on the Cook-Peary polar controversy. I do get excited sometimes when I think of how unnecessary it was for Peary to have suffered the way he did. But I want to make my own position clear. The important thing that should stand out from that whole terrible row is the tragic figure of a man who had struggled his life through to achieve something; and who then, just when he won, was nearly crushed by a contemptible hoax.

Naturally I am prejudiced in favour of Peary. No man could serve for years with a leader like him and not feel a deep loyalty and respect. But had I never faced Peary or taken his hand in mine I should still feel a deep and natural compassion for the anguish the good Lord saw fit to impose on him. In the afternoon of my own career, I think of him not as a party to a controversy that shook the world; but as a brave adventurer who set out in his youth to do a task of great scientific value to mankind; who finally succeeded, and at the very moment of his success was kicked in the face by his own countrymen. That may exaggerate the picture a little bit in the eyes of many. But it's the honest reaction of a seafaring man to a clear-cut human tragedy.

It is easy to be bitter; I could almost say it is natural to be bitter when one is sure an injustice has been done. And when one has a chance to publish one's thoughts and experiences one has also a chance to be vindictive. Now that sledge travel is a matter of history, and nearly twenty years have passed, I want to avoid both bitterness and vindictiveness. I want just to tell a few of the facts of that interesting polar controversy in 1909 as they came into my life. Surely, from the public to the principals there has seldom been so unique an illustration of human frailty.

In 1907, I sat at dinner in Dr. Cook's house in Brooklyn. He was going north on what he termed a "hunting expedition." I had come to know him through our mutual friends, General Brainard, the hero of the Lady Franklin Bay expedition, and Mr. Herbert Bridgman, business manager of the *Brooklyn Standard Union* and close friend of Admiral Peary's. The doctor was a suave, affable man, with a ready smile and an air of pleasant humility. If he had a shifty eye, as some say, I did not note it then.

I can see him now with a spoonful of soup halfway to his mouth peering over it at me and asking eagerly as a child:

"Will we get bears in Ellesmere Land, Bartlett?"

"In the summertime," I told him.

Down went the spoon. Not a word to me did he say suggesting the true purpose of the expedition he was planning.

A few weeks later at his instance I went to Gloucester to look over a ship he and his backer, the millionaire John

Bradley, were picking out to go north in. I wanted to help them. I had learned from Peary a spirit of generosity towards Arctic travellers. When we got back from Gloucester after choosing the ship, Dr. Cook put his hand in his pocket and said:

"How much do I owe you, Bartlett?" I don't know to this day whether the pocket was empty or not.

"Forget it, Doctor," said I. "We are all friends, and you are friends of my friends. Later on you can help us out by taking lumber and coal to Etah and telling the Eskimos that we are coming." You see he was headed for the same neck of the woods we were, though for an avowedly different purpose. You must remember that at that time the *Roosevelt* was slowly being put into shape for what was to be her final voyage north. But things looked dark for getting away that summer (1907). However, the friendly attitude Dr. Cook adopted every time I saw him made me feel that his proffered assistance might be valuable. If we had to wait a year he could lay down some supplies for us in North Greenland.

He now clapped his hand on my shoulder and exclaimed:

"Of course I'll help you out!"

After that every time I met Dr. Cook he inquired solicitously about our plans and the details of our preparations. It was more than pleasing to find a man so interested because many Americans habitually sneered at our polar efforts. I expanded under the Doctor's amenities and like a fat fool told him everything. No wonder the trusting sailor man gets into hot water ashore!

Another thing: Peary had so little money at that time that I was paying my own salary and that of our crew out of some money I had in the bank in St. John's. To ease the strain, and with Peary's permission I acceded to the request of Dr. Cook to let his schooner have some of the men we were holding for the *Roosevelt*. These were picked sailors used to ice navigation.

Not long after this—it was already late spring, 1907—I had a last dinner with Dr. Cook. As usual he was most entertaining and made a lot more specific inquires about our chances of getting away. Once more I told him everything I could. It was like pulling a boat plug at the davits, the way I went on. A few days later he sailed away on his hunting trip and we who knew him all hoped he would have a pleasant and successful cruise. I warmed to the idea of this friend paving the way toward our arrival next year.

Imagine my consternation after a hard summer's work with the *Roosevelt* added to her failure to leave, when I was called on the phone by Mr. Bridgman who said:

"Did you know that Bradley was back with the schooner and that Dr. Cook has been left north to go to the Pole?"

"*What!*" I yelled.

"Exactly that," said Mr. Bridgman.

"But how on earth can he make it without equipment or ship?" I could feel all my confidences with Dr. Cook burning into my brain.

"He can't," said Mr. Bridgman with finality and hung up.

I was stunned, but felt Dr. Cook's daring could only be rewarded with complete failure.

Next June, we set out in the *Roosevelt*, reached Cape Sheridan on the shores of the Polar Sea and wintered. I have already told of our long hard journey out across the ice toward the Pole and back. We escaped from winter quarters in late summer and reached Battle Harbour, Labrador, in early September. MacMillan and George Borup were among the first to go ashore. Both boys returned in a state of ill-controlled excitement.

"They say Dr. Cook claims he got to the Pole!" exclaimed Borup.

Quickly the meagre details came out and in a few minutes the whole ship was buzzing with the astounding news. It was good to find Peary was not especially concerned. He and I with our years of Arctic experience knew how utterly impossible it was for Cook to have crossed 1,000 miles of Polar Sea ice without supporting parties; especially since he had taken the Ellesmere Land route, which meant hundreds of miles of stiff travel before he even set foot on the Polar Sea. Goodness knows we had had a tough enough time doing the job with all our strong supporting parties lugging food and fuel back and forth, breaking trail, and hopping off right at the edge of the Polar Sea.

"He's handed them a gold brick!" George Borup burst out in the heat of our excitement. The phrase began to rattle around our main deck. At the moment Peary was writing a telegraphic reply to one of the New York papers who made inquiry about his reaction to the Cook story.

I remember he looked up sharply from the little cabin table where he sat. "Isn't there a better word than gold brick?" he asked.

As none of us could suggest one, he wired back to New York that Cook had handed the American public a gold brick. This was the origin of that famous message.

Peary was later criticized for lingering in Battle Harbour. I want to say right here that he was chafing at the bit to get home. I did my best to detain him as long as possible. Our ship was worse than a Chinese stinkpot. Think of it: for nearly twelve months she had harboured seventy-seven Eskimos, men, woman and children—who had never had a bath since their birth—not to mention 200 dogs and fifty tons of rotten whale meat and blubber. If we had entered New York Harbour at the time, I think the Board of Health would have rushed out and sprinkled us with lime and sent us to sea again.

The next thing that blew in was a chartered boatload of newspapermen. They wanted to climb aboard and know the "inside" of the row with Cook.

"What row?" asked Peary angrily.

But the only sensible thing to do was for him to give all of the journalists a fair hearing. So he called a conference in the twine loft of the little Labrador trading station ashore. It was a great sight: Peary, battered and brown from his great fight on the Polar Sea, surrounded by a group of eager, excited and very intelligent young men—the cream of the newspaper world—striving to satisfy their frantic editors at home. The trouble was that neither Peary nor any of the rest realized how frantic the editors were. Even then we couldn't believe that Dr. Cook had made any public impression with this story. It never remotely occurred to us that even the man in the street who is almost ignorant of Arctic affairs could picture an explorer doing right off the bat and with no equipment what Peary had done only after a lifetime of effort and with the finest equipment money could buy, not counting the help of a whole tribe of Eskimos!

The writers had hundreds of questions they wanted to put to our leader. But he forestalled them by simple account of what had gone on, of our voyage and of our ice travel. He conceded nothing. He made his statement and it was put on the wires. I can hear him now:

"We had eighteen dog teams. Advance parties went ahead of us from Columbia. They broke the trail. Supporting parties followed. They improved the trail. My best party and I came last. We went fast and easily. When we made the final dash we were strong and fresh. The going improved . . ."

It was such a simple story. Yet I could see it didn't make an impression. The trouble was Peary didn't put in enough harrowing details. I didn't know that fine writers all over the world were laying it on thick about Arctic hardships and complications and a lot of other things which filled up space and confused the minds of the public. When Peary left such things out his story sounded fishy.

One thing that dispelled the idea of controversy for the time being was that telegrams from Arctic experts came flooding in bearing congratulatory messages. I remember among these were some fine words from Fridtjof Nansen, Admiral Sir George Nares, Admiral Sir Lewis Beaumont, Admiral Cagni, H.R.H. the Duke d'Abruzzi and many others.

After a few days we escaped from considerable of our odour and most of the journalists. We got under way and went on to Sydney. Here again the noise of welcome and admiration far exceeded the rumblings of the distant controversy of which we as yet knew dangerously little. All of us were making quite unguarded statements that were soon to be twisted into grotesque untruths. The populace turned out en masse. Flags decorated every building. The harbour was full of yachts darting to and fro. You couldn't spit without hitting a silk hat. It was a great show. It made us very happy, especially because we felt it was the tribute that belonged to our leader because he had at last succeeded.

Still there was but slight warning of what lay ahead.

We went on down to Peary's Eagle Island in Casco Bay. As we had no wireless we were deaf to the swelling chorus of controversy. Peary thought he had scotched the Cook lie in the beginning. At Eagle Island we unloaded our small cargo of equipment and completed our polishing for the great welcome we knew must come on our next stop, New York.

We reached New York about a week later, early October, 1909. The Hudson-Fulton celebration had brought warships from all nations into the North River. I remember standing on deck and thinking how fortunate a man was who had gone out from a great country like America and done something of which all Americans could be proud. How I envied Peary!

And how, only a few hours later, I shrank from what he had to face.

I wish I could tell clearly what happened next. As I look back on it I feel as if I'd been through the French

Revolution, or something just as rough and noisy and horrible. It was all very confused; and there was a lot of anger in it, as well as poisonous bitterness and recrimination. It seemed to me bad enough to have had a scientific debate; but to have almost a public riot over the question of who reached the Pole was pretty low. The papers kept the pot boiling furiously. I guess they didn't have any good murders just then.

Naturally I came in for a lot of pestering. Peary was a storm centre; Cook wasn't. Cook cleverly chose the role of conciliator. He could afford to be courteous and unctuous. Peary, a stern facer of facts all his life, was willing to face the facts now. He did it with a courage that was not new to me.

I wasn't allowed to eat my meals or get unbroken sleep. News gatherers and cranks were after me all the time. Yet there wasn't anything for me to tell. I had been a navigator for half a lifetime. If I hadn't known enough navigation to reach the pole I would have been shipwrecked hundreds of times. So far as food and dogs and ice went that was a simple arithmetical problem that any schoolchild could see. As for Peary, he was a trained engineer, twice my worth in fine sights.

But the reporters wouldn't let it end there.

"Were you afraid you'd never get back?" they'd insist.

"I wasn't thinking about that."

"How many times did you freeze your feet?"

"I didn't freeze my feet."

I could hear my teeth snap when I slammed my mouth shut after each of these foolish questions.

"Did you see any polar bears or walrus at the North Pole?"

"I didn't go to the North Pole."

"Is Dr. Cook a liar?"

"Answer it yourself."

"What is the sense of going to the Pole?"

I tell you after three or four days of this sort of thing I was in a state of mind where I wanted to kill the next man that came to me with a piece of paper and a pencil. I think if my own mother had asked me anything about the North Pole I should have growled at her. As a matter of fact she did write me a letter. She said:

```
Dear Bob:
    We have heard a lot of racket up here about
your trip and I am beginning to thing that
somebody ought to be spanked. Send me a letter
and let me know whether it's you or not.
```

One funny result of it all was the offers I had. Sometimes I think Babe Ruth and Gene Tunney haven't got anything on me. I was urged to write books, magazine articles, go on the lecture stage, appear in vaudeville and preach sermons. I often think what I would have been like if I had accepted some of these offers. Surely I'd have fattened my bank account. However, though I may know something about ships, when it comes to orating or acting I'm a ship without a rudder.

One bright spot in all this wretchedness was when the National Geographic Society gave me the Hubbard gold medal for "attaining the Farthest North, 87° 48', March 31, 1909." It was a fine big banquet with Willis L. Moore as toastmaster. Ambassador James Bryce from Great Britain made the presentation speech and handed me the medal at the end of it. After all the things he said I was pretty well down by the head. But I had taken the precaution to write a speech that morning so I didn't blow up. I tell you it is worth any price to stand in a company like that, with an organization like the National Geographic Society behind you, and men like Bryce Moore, Grosvenor and others in front of you, and hear words of praise.

I felt it all so strongly that I ate only one thing that night, a big piece of fish. It tasted like codfish and looked like codfish and I am not a man ever to turn down an old friend—especially the cod.

In the meantime, the main row went on. The papers had no mercy on any of us. In despair I went over and stayed with a friend of mine, Tom Foley, in Brooklyn, hoping to escape the buzzards who were after me. Tom and I had been schoolboys and grew up together, and the idea of spending a few quiet days with him was most attractive. Two days later poor Tom was on the verge of a nervous breakdown trying to stave off the gang that were after me. I must say that if I hadn't had a strong constitution I never would stood those few weeks. They were far harder than the polar trip.

The climax came when I went down to Washington as guest of the Press Club, at their annual gathering of the brightest newspapermen in the country. They are a live crowd, too. Naturally with the controversy going strong I was a person of great interest. The newspapers had had many thousands of columns out of the row.

When I got up to speak I felt the pressure of a critical stare from 1,000 eyes. There was a dead silence. I could see men all over the hall leaning forward. Most of the faces wore a cynical expression. It was just as if their owners were all ready to say, "Now, you son of a——, tell us the truth and stop just trying to back up Peary because he is your boss."

I tell you I felt it. It was like a man standing in front of you had told you he is going to shoot you if you move and you are not so sure what's the best thing to say to him.

Luck saved me.

Some fellow who couldn't stand the strain sprang up and yelled out so you could hear him all over the place:

"Captain Bartlett, how did you know when you got to the Pole?"

I didn't figure out my answer. I was in no mood to debate. I turned on him as if he had called me a liar; and I yelled right back at him just as loud and I could yell:

"Did you ever cross the Equator, sir?"

"Yes," he shot back at me.

"*Well, did you feel the keel of the ship bump when she went over?*"

That broke the spell. A roar of applause rose up like an explosion. The relief was general. I think every man there felt that the Press Club as well as I was well out of a disagreeable situation.

——

PUBLISHER'S NOTE

The publishers feel that the presentation of the Hubbard Medal by the National Geographic Society to Captain

Bartlett was so important a distinction that it is worthwhile to introduce here the exchange of speeches upon that occasion. The Hubbard Medal had to date been given only to Rear Admiral Robert E. Peary, Captain Roald Amundsen, Captain Robert A. Bartlett, Dr. Grove Clark Gilbert, Sir Ernest Shackleton, Vilhjalmur Stefansson, Commander Richard E. Byrd, and Colonel Charles A. Lindbergh.

In opening the Toastmaster, Willis L. Moore, spoke as follows:

"The Board of Managers of the National Geographic Society has voted to Captain Robert A. Bartlett a Hubbard Gold Medal, and I shall introduce the Ambassador from Great Britain, one whom we all love so much and who has been with us before, to present to Captain Bartlett, one of his own countrymen, the medal, for twice commanding the *Roosevelt*, and for being one of those heroic characters that have done so much to bring honour to our nation and honour to that great nation of Great Britain."

The Ambassador from Great Britain, Honourable James Bryce, replied as follows:

"Mr. Toastmaster, ladies and gentlemen: It was a graceful and charming thought on your part, gentlemen of the National Geographic Society, that you should present this medal to Captain Bartlett, and I can assure you that it will be heartily appreciated in the good country to which Captain Bartlett belongs, and by those who, in other lands, on the shores of many seas, live under the British Crown. I thank you and the National Geographic Society for it. But you have already had an acknowledgement by cable from the President of the Royal Geographical Society—one who bears an honoured name, for he is the son of the great Charles Darwin—of the pleasure which it has given to the oldest of the Geographical Societies of the world.

"Now, Captain Bartlett belongs to an ancient and famous line of Arctic explorers who have sailed under the flag of England. That line begins with the ever-to-be-honoured name of Henry Hudson, who perished in the great bay that he discovered. And it is illuminated by many an illustrious name thereafter, among whom perhaps the most famous is Sir Edward Parry, who made his wonderful advance toward the Pole, far outstripping any who had gone before him; Sir John Franklin, Captain Ross, and McClure, and McClintock, and many another whom time would fail me to tell, dauntless spirits who have bent their strength and their powers to the work of Polar and Arctic exploration.

"I remember seeing, long ago, at meetings of the British Association, and of the Royal Geographical Society in Britain, some of these ancient weather-beaten veterans of Polar exploration, and I know how it would rejoice them now to think that that for which they laboured had at last been achieved. And if you want to know that the gallantry which animated those men and which made them bear cold and hunger and ill health, and face all the perils of snowy wastes and floating ice in pursuit of discovery, if you want to know that that spirit lives still with undiminished force in men of British stock, you have only to read the lately published narrative of the gallant effort to reach the South Pole made by Lieutenant Shackleton and his comrades, which brought them within ninety-seven miles of the remote and perilous goal. This was done by the courage and hardihood of Lieutenant Shackleton.

"Ladies and gentlemen, we are proud to think that the United States and Great Britain have been partners in this splendid work of Arctic exploration. The United States took up the work some forty years ago, and the names of Kane and Greely and others, above all of Commander Peary himself, show with what energy and spirit and courage and skill and perseverance you have pursued it.

"But do not let us forget, in the pride which we feel in the achievement of the stock to which we both belong, what has been done by the other great nations of the world, to some of whose members reference has already been made, more particularly to the Duke of the Abruzzi, whose representative is present here tonight. Barentz must be remembered, and Weyprecht and Nordenskjold. And there is another man whose wonderful feat of launching himself out upon the Arctic Sea and voyaging for many hundreds of miles upon ice floes is perhaps without parallel in history of its daring, and ought to be remembered in the presence of the Minister from Norway—I mean Dr. Fridtjof Nansen.

"Now, ladies and gentlemen, I have the great honour of being asked to present this medal of your Society to Captain Bartlett. You, Captain Bartlett, belong to a calling which has always been able to boast of a host of hardy and adventurous seamen. You have been, on your own grim, tempestuous coast of Newfoundland, accustomed to all the perils of storm and iceberg, and it is in the line of your calling to know how to deal not only with the dangers that icebergs threaten, but with all the other terrors that the Northern sea contain. You belong to a family which has signalized itself even in your land by the number of gallant seamen it has produced. I may state that there are so many Bartletts who have made distinguished and successful voyages on the North Atlantic coasts that this one who we see here tonight is familiarly known by his Christian name. He stands out from the other Bartletts as Captain Bob. He has had ten years' experience sailing with Commander Peary as the captain of his ships in various expeditions. And I want to tell you that in those years that Captain Bartlett was sailing there never was a man lost upon those ships in those expeditions.

"Captain Bartlett, I have the honour to present to you this medal. Brave men are always generous, and Commander Peary, with characteristic generosity, has acknowledged how much he owes you. Your name will go down with his in connection with the discovery of the North Pole, and you have in this medal a trophy which you can pass on to those who come after you as a memorial of the honour, the well-earned honour, which the National Geographic Society has paid you.

"Ladies and gentlemen, I rejoice to think that Great Britain and the United States are associated on this occasion. And as we congratulate you, Captain Bartlett, so I venture, on behalf of my country, to congratulate you, Commander Peary, and you, citizens of the United States, upon this splendid achievement—an achievement which will stand alone to the end of time."

To which Captain Bartlett responded:

"Mr. President, ladies and gentlemen: I would ask you just to bear with me for about three minutes. I am afraid to trust myself in speaking, but I have few words jotted down here that if you will not mind I will read off.

"I have the medal that you have been kind enough to bestow upon me, and I thank you in my heart. To be thus decorated by so eminent a body as the National Geographic Society is an honour of which any man can justly feel proud. To say, however, that the notice which you have taken of me affords me pleasure of the most genuine sort would be to state only part of the truth. I am more than pleased. I am deeply moved at your distinguished consideration. My happiness in receiving this honour at your hands is increased by the fact that I never expected it. It is as unexpected as it is pleasant. It may be also that my appreciation of this medal is enhanced by the knowledge that its like can never be conferred again. It was struck off to memorialize a complete work, a work that is done, and well done. Commander Peary, with the pleasure that comes to me as I find myself in the midst of these honours, there comes the solid satisfaction feeling that I have been of some assistance to a man of such sterling worth as Commander Peary (and I can look you straight in the eye, Sir, and say that), a man whose heroic character and high aims make him quite worthy of the great fame that has come to him.

"For the very great honour that you have shown me on account of my humble aid in the great work, I once again return my heartiest thanks."

—

EDITOR'S NOTE

Captain Bartlett was elected an Honorary Corresponding Member of the American Geographical Society. In 1926, he addressed the Society on the subject of Hair-Seal Hunting off the Labrador Coast.

CHAPTER XV

FACE TO FACE WITH A KING

It took nearly a year for the controversy to simmer down. Then in the spring of 1910, I went to Europe with Peary and walked around arm and arm with a real king. I even paid my own way. I remember the ticket cost me $137.

I am going to tell how this trip began; it shows how complicated life is. Two years before when we were starting out for the Pole we hung up at Oyster Bay because we needed some more money. Peary had a good friend, William Reick, a newspaperman whom he thoroughly trusted. He preferred to deal through an individual than through a big piece of newspaper machinery. So when Mr. Reick was able to send him a personal cheque for $4,000 as an advance payment on exclusive rights to his polar story it not only meant we could at last be free to sail, but that the placing of the news rights was completed.

Now follow me closely; this yarn proves how careful you have to be with business deals even though your important job is one of fighting ice and snow and cold and starvation. In the days of Peary, it was not customary for an explorer to have a business agent at home. Anyway, Peary was too poor to afford one. Nowadays, Byrd, Amudsen, Wilkens, and the rest of them have their business affairs handled by an office at New York and London. They have a fine lot of machinery, much of which I can't even understand.

Now Mr. Reick was attached to the New York *Herald* as one of the editors. If you remember, James Gordon Bennett owned the *Herald* and was out to be a top-notcher all the time. Naturally when Peary got back in touch with civilization he at once shot his report through to Mr. Reick. He was trying to keep a personal and business obligation for which he had been paid. At the same time he thought of course that he was sending his message to the New York *Herald* to which Mr. Reick was attached. He had no way of telling his friend had changed jobs. Imagine his surprise when he learned that Mr. Reick was on the *Times,* which therefore got his exclusive story instead of Mr. Bennett's *Herald.*

James Gordon Bennett felt that since Reick had been on the *Herald* when the cheque for $4,000 was given Peary, the polar story should have come to the *Herald.* As a result, Mr. Bennett, a rich friend, was antagonized. No doubt some of Mr. Bennet's annoyance was really tied up with his loss of an editor. Nevertheless, Peary thus became a victim of circumstances beyond his control; and much of the spleen vented on him by the *Herald* in the Cook-Peary matter surely sprang from this unfortunate incident. And since the *Herald's* stories were widely distributed Peary's public standing suffered terribly.

What I started out to say was that the $4,000 cheque was indirectly the cause of my going to Europe. When we got back from the Pole, the *Times,* now our proprietary newspaper, gave an honorary dinner to Peary. Lord

Northcliffe was one of the many distinguished guests. Mr. Ochs, owner of the *Times*, was host.

I came to like both these men a lot. Both were examples of the axiom that greatness rises above race or colour. One didn't think of Ochs as a Yankee or Northcliffe as a Britisher. Both men were somewhat silent, astute, alert executives who, when they said anything, made you feel right away that that thing should be believed or done. There was a prodigious conviction in their words.

Lord Northcliffe owned the big pulp mills in northern Newfoundland. After dinner he took me aside and surprised me by saying:

"Captain Bartlett, I have a special interest and friendship for you outside your polar work. You know I am in the newspaper business. A lot of my paper comes from your home country."

I looked into his fine face and saw that he meant the friendship he was trying to show to me.

"Thank you, sir," I said.

He went on. "I want to give a little dinner up at the Plaza Hotel for you. There will just be a few of us with Lady Northcliffe. Will you come?"

For a moment I hung in irons at this unexpected honour. Then I heartily accepted though with some doubts as to my social competence. The closer I got to the party the more nervous I became. It was set early the following week. As a friend had put me up at the Union League Club, I got the valet there to help me out with my duds about two hours before the time set for dinner. I wanted to be on the safe side. As I wasn't very skilful yet with evening clothes, he got my studs into the shirt and fixed my bow for me. I noticed he looked admiringly at my hands while he did so. I was pretty proud of them. For the first time in my life I had had a manicure.

That afternoon I had happened to look at them myself. Thirty years of seafaring life does things to your hands that are hard to undo. With a good deal of embarrassment I decided I would go to a manicure. I had never tried one before, and had always shrunk from the idea of such a performance. Well, I felt pretty sorry for the girl. She certainly worked hard over my paws before she made any progress. She must have done at least five dollars' worth of work before she gave up. I handed her five dollars anyway and told her to keep the change. An hour or so later I was admiring what she had done when I suddenly realized that the job was still unfinished. So I hunted up another manicurist. The poor girl did her best and finally I didn't recognize my hands. I can't say they looked beautiful, but they certainly looked funny.

I got to the Plaza on time feeling as if I had a suit of armor on. I was told that Lady Northcliffe would go in to dinner on my arm. She soon appeared with a train about twenty-five fathoms long. At sight of it I lost my head completely. For five miserable minutes I was like a fellow on a bicycle trying to dodge a pig in the road. Everywhere I stepped that train was there ahead of me. Before long sweat began bursting out of my face. I am sorry to say that I so far forgot myself that I began to sputter out some words I hadn't meant to. Suddenly Lady Northcliffe smiled, turned around and began petting my hand and said:

"It's all right, Captain Bartlett."

Somehow her quiet words soothed me. I guess she was so used to bringing British admirals in to dinner on her arm that it wasn't hard to take care of me. Right off she saw my difficulty lay with the train. So she took half a dozen round turns of it over her arm and away we went four bells and a jingle.

Over our coffee Lord Northcliffe asked me to come to England and be his guest. I couldn't accept because Peary had already got leave for a trip abroad and I had promised to join him. He had many invitations to accept honours and medals at the hands of the presidents of the great geographical societies of Europe and knew that he should now take proper notice of them in person. I told Lord Northcliffe how grateful I was for his invitation but that I felt I belonged with my leader. I didn't add what was in my mind, that I wanted people to see that Peary was still my best friend, though the press had tried to split us.

We sailed on April 22. It was a nice feeling to be a passenger. I could sit around all I wanted to and not have any responsibility as to whether the helmsman was on his course. He could steer in circles for all I cared. But they didn't serve cod brewis (boiled cod with biscuit soaked overnight and hot pork fat poured over it) very often.

"The more rain, the more rest," is an old Newfoundland proverb. However, this was one time when it didn't rain and yet I had rest enough to last me several years—that is, until I got to Europe. Then I was busy enough.

The first thing we did we went up to London. King Edward VII had died that week. So a good many of the special festivities for Peary were called off. But at that we had a great time.

One thing that engrossed us both was that we found Captain Scott preparing to go south. He was destined on this expedition to reach the Pole but never to return. By special invitation we went down to the London docks and saw Scott's ship, the *Terra Nova*. While we were aboard Lady Markham presented the brave leader with the Royal Standard which was hoisted to the vessel's masthead.

Two things especially struck me about what I saw: the attitude of the country and the kind of equipment.

England really felt this was her own expedition. The First Lord of the admiralty was aboard and a lot of other lords. There were gold lace and cocked hats and dignitaries enough to run a Navy. I couldn't help comparing all this formality with the shoddy almost sneering attitude of the American public towards Peary's efforts. It is only necessary to compare press notices of Peary's sailing with those of the sailing of Captain Scott to see how differently a seafaring country like Britain felt toward an Arctic expedition.

The reason I felt so was probably because the basis of all Peary's work was application of Eskimo methods to the white man's problem. The Eskimo for many centuries has learned to clothe himself properly. He has contrived to build a sledge that will stand rough ice and his blubbery diet is suited to continual cold weather. One of the first things Peary always did when he took a party north was to insist that his men learn how the natives lived. He used to get his tenderfeet to go and stay a few days with an Eskimo family in an igloo or tupik. In this way the amateur would learn to take care of his footgear and to get used to native diet. Little tricks about following the ice in bad weather and keeping warm in the bitter cold were thus absorbed almost automatically.

In contrast to this, the British worked out their own theories. The old English explorers proved on paper that it wasn't worthwhile to use dogs. Dogs, they stated, ate up more food than they could drag along. Peary, on the other hand, concluded that if Eskimos had been using dogs for a good many centuries there was reason to believe that they were the proper draft animals.

Scott's men pulled their sledges to the South Pole. They suffered terribly from frozen feet and wet garments. Despite the windproof fabric of their outer shirts the cold sapped their energy until, in a pinch, they perished.

I thought of these things as I looked at the fine woollen clothing, the specially designed (in England) sledges, and the other gear. None of it looked like the Eskimo stuff that we were used to. It wasn't many months afterwards that the suffering and death of the men who used them confirmed my thoughts.

It may seem silly in these days of Byrd and Lindbergh to be talking dogs and sledges for polar travel. But the subject is surely of historic interest; and we mustn't forget that the trans-polar flier must be prepared to walk home over the ice if he comes to grief. His emergency equipment will be evolved from that of the old explorers.

In the Royal Albert Memorial Hall, Peary received the gold medal of the Royal Geographical Society. President Darwin (son of the great Charles Darwin) of the Society handed it to him. I had to come next as they were kind enough to give me the silver medal of the Royal Geographical Society, a duplicate of Peary's. Peary's medal was a special one designed to commemorate the discovery of the Pole. Mine was struck off from the same mould. It was designed by Lady Scott, wife of Captain Scott who died on his way back from the South Pole.

I had known for some days ahead of time that I would have to speak a piece before the King. Unless you have been up against a thing like that you don't know the sinking feeling that grips you. I thought for a long time about what I was going to say. Then I tried to write something. But somehow it all fell flat when I tried it alone behind the locked door of my room. So I paid a man £2 to prepare a speech for me. I think he did about $25 worth of writing before he had it right; anyway I felt much relieved when I saw his fine long sentences and expensive words.

Through the chairman's introduction and other formalities I sat nervously awaiting my turn. Peary got up and in his fine direct way told the story of reaching the Pole. He was roundly applauded. I think the Englishmen more than the Americans appreciated what Peary had done. For so many generations English seafarers had sought the Northwest Passage and the Pole.

My turn was next. To be on the safe side I had kept my speech in my hand through it all. I looked out over the sea of faces in front of us. As I remember, there were over 10,000 people in the Hall. There was standing room only. The galleries were packed. And when Peary spoke you could hear a pin drop. I don't think I ever felt a strain quite so much. And now I had to get up to speak.

"Thank God," I thought. "I have a speech all ready and don't have to worry."

The Chairman turned to me and bowed. Applause broke out. It was an hospitable audience. On wooden legs I stood up and moved forward as in a dream. In my hand I gripped the paper that was my speech. I reached the edge of the platform. Imagine my horror on looking down to discover that in my nervousness I had torn my £2 piece to bits!

I had to speak. Somehow I got through it. But what I said is lost to posterity so far as I am concerned because I don't remember a word of it. However, the crowd seemed to like it. Not only did people clap, but they cheered.

Owing to the fact that the English court was in mourning and the Pearys had pressing engagements they crossed the Channel and went down through Europe. I lingered in London. I wanted to see the funeral of a King. A kind Englishman secured a fine seat for me in the window of one of the clubs. I sat up there on a high-priced thwart and saw the great procession pass. There were Roosevelt and the Kaiser and King Alphonso of Spain; hundreds of fine officers and thousands of fine troops. But I think the thing that impressed me most was a little brown dog that trotted along under the hearse. He had been a special pet of the King, and in all that long procession he was the only living creature that seemed to be thinking about the dead King more than about the people who were looking at him.

The funeral depressed me. I packed up and crossed to Paris. To my surprise and disappointment the atmosphere of mourning seemed to be deeper there than in London. But I was well taken care of. A friend had written to a lady, a beautiful girl, who took care of me while I was there. She knew Paris like a book. She showed me the Church of the Madelon, the art galleries, the palace at Versailles. I even went up on the Montmartre, for a look at high life. But I must have been a wet blanket as I wasn't a drinker. However, I had what was a giddy time for me. My companion didn't drink either. But she was gay and I was gay because we were happy. I even stayed up all night and saw the sun rise over Paris. I went to Maxime's and watched the girls dance on the tables. I guess their names were Margot and Jo Jo out of the old song. "If only some of our Polar Sea boys, Inughitog and Itukershuk, could see those fireworks," I thought to myself.

I dallied as long as I dared. There were engagements ahead of me I dare not break. Finally I pulled away and went on down to Rome to join the Pearys. On the way I stopped over a day and took a look at Venice. There was lots of water but it wasn't very deep.

I found the Pearys at the Hotel Continental. I think I felt a little bit like an Eskimo when he sees his friends after a long winter. I burst in on them delighted to be with them again. They had long been like my family. The first thing they asked me was:

"Where's the mail, Bob?" A fatal question.

I felt like a boy who'd played hookey.

Hanged if I hadn't gone off and forgotten the mail! I was supposed to be in London all the time and, while there was no reason why I shouldn't, I had gone off on a spree to Paris and forgotten the very thing I was supposed to do. I hadn't any more alibi than a flying fish.

I think Rome's welcome to Peary was one of the greatest celebrations that was ever given in the old city. Mayor Nathan presided over the civic banquet. Three years before he had been toastmaster at the banquet given to Peary after his 1906 trip. So he welcomed the explorer as his "old comrade."

After eight or ten "orations" Peary was given the freedom of Rome, the Eternal City. The Latins are a sentimental people and they know how to make a man feel that he is a hero. No people in the world could have done the job better.

The high point of the visit was the luncheon the King gave us. To my dying day I will remember that meal, if I dare call it by so common a name. In the greatness of the guests, the splendour of the room, the efficiency of the service and hospitality of the King, I had a chance to see the most exquisite form human entertainment could take. We ate in a special dining hall in the Quirinal. It was a room of high windows and fine paintings. Heavy hangings and tapestries blanketed the doors and edged the windows. Just outside and below us was the Roman Forum. Dimly in the distance I could hear the hum of the great city.

There were twenty-eight guests. I have heard people called the flower of their profession, the flower of diplomacy, and so on. But if any collection I ever heard of was the flower of their outfit, these were the orchids. Of course there was the King at the head of the table. On both sides of him were arranged the grandest diplomats, the brainiest scientists, and the highest royalty of the land. Fine ladies alternated with the gentlemen. At each place was cut glass and glistening silver. Golden platters held our food.

Over the centre was suspended one of the most gorgeous chandeliers I have ever seen. It sparkled in the sunshine. Behind each place stood a liveried servant. Indeed, though the diplomats and scientists were impressive the liveried servants were even more so. They were big fine healthy men and each had a shiny uniform on. They were efficient too. I have seen the Life Guards changed by the Tower of London. I have seen the quick and silent efficiency of the shift of watches on an ocean liner. But never have I seen any better-drilled men or speedier service than I saw right there in the King's dining room. I was so hypnotized by the way those fellows got food on without a sound and whisked it off without a sign that I could hardly eat.

Next to me sat a fine lady, the wife of the English Ambassador, I think. She was impressive as a ship with stun-sails out; but she was human. She was just as jolly and intelligent and entertaining to me as if I'd belonged to royalty instead of to the sea. She asked me many questions, but every time I gave her some information she had some equally interesting facts to shoot back at me.

"Do Eskimos marry for love?" she asked.

"No. The man marries to get a seamstress, the woman to get meat."

She nodded. "So do we. Only the sewing is social and the meat more often finery. Did you ever get used to the hard life, Captain?"

"Yes. We Newfoundlanders can get used to anything."

She glanced around the table, darted a look at one man in particular, and sighed. "So can the rest of us, I suppose," she said in a low voice.

For a moment I thought I had put my foot in it and tried so hard to think what I had said that might have been wrong that I choked on a mouthful of fish.

"Sign of a guilty conscience," she said as I sputtered. "I didn't know seafaring men had consciences. Have they?"

"Sure," I said, my face the colour of a red-leaded capstan. "Else we'd found the North Pole years ago."

She got my point all right and laughed. It set me up a lot to make a lady of her station bubble her mirth right out in meeting. It put me at my ease and made me enjoy the party. Incidentally, she had the finest hair I ever saw on a person. Maybe she had something to do, too, with my not getting enough to eat. I even can remember the perfume she used—not too much and not too little. It was another part of the hypnotizing I was going through. Altogether, between the King and the efficient service and that fine lady I have a memory that I treasure almost above all other memories.

During this day I had a chance to know the King and Duke d'Abruzzi. I was especially interested in the King because people seemed to know so little about him. He proved to be a quiet retiring sort of man, not big physically, I think he came about to my shoulder. But mentally he was big, and spiritually bigger still. He impressed me as a student. His questions were quiet but they were comprehensive; and they were questions I could understand. He asked me about the fish trade of Newfoundland and about bad ice conditions near the Pole. He showed by other questions that he understood exactly what I was driving at in my answers. As soon as we had exhausted one subject he quickly and without effort went to another. His information seemed extraordinary. He must have read books all his life. I like that sort of man. It shows that in a world full of hurrying restless people there are some quiet minds sitting back and reflecting on what are the best things to do for the progress of mankind. That was how the King of Italy struck me. Somehow I never thought of a king being other than like the overdressed dummies in a nursery book.

The Duke d'Abruzzi was the exact opposite. He was a tall, slender, direct sort of man. He had the bearing and accent of an English gentleman, with the same ruddy features. I have no doubt he was a student, too, for his questions and quick grasp of what I said showed his great knowledge. But he did not impress me as an academic man. He was in the prime of his life; a vigourous naval officer far more interested at that time in leading other men to do big things than in settling back in a library to work out some theory. He was a sailor, too; had a sailor's air about him in the way he stood, his feet wide and his body tilted a little forward. He looked very much the athlete his reputation made him out to be. Naturally he was interested in Peary and me for he had led his Italian expedition which based on Spitzbergen and his men had broken the world's record towards the Pole only a few years before. His book was a fine piece of work. I told him this.

"Thank you, Captain Bartlett," he said. "Do you write much?" Meaning of course to inquire about my literary work.

"I write my mother pretty often," I said.

Instantly he laid his hand on my shoulder and exclaimed: "That's fine!"

I certainly liked him.

I asked him if he were going north again.

He shook his head. "No, I guess I'm getting too old," he said.

"But you are only forty-three, sir," I burst out, forgetting for the moment he was a duke.

He shook his head and smiled in such a friendly way that I went right on. "I think it is wonderful that you have done the fine work up there you did, sir. Now down in Newfoundland we are born and brought up on the ice and on board ship. Even then it's a hard drag to go through with Arctic work. Only the best of us can stand it. But here you are—" I felt I was getting in deep water. I think I blushed a little in my embarrassment.

But he nodded a little pensively. "I understand, Captain," he said, "and I want to thank you for your fine compliment."

The Duke's war record shows that I was right. He still had a lot of stuff in him even if he was forty-three.

Shortly after that wonderful day I left for home. Peary had a lot of ground to cover and I didn't feel up to the strain of any more royalty. Also my funds were getting low.

Besides I had a deep scheme preying on my mind. I had to get home and go to work on it.

CHAPTER XVI

MY BIG CHANCE COMES—AND GOES

You don't dare anchor a ship with big way on. That's what I was like now, after the North Pole trip. I was too full of exploring to stop.

In 1906, Peary was very optimistic. We had the ship on the edge of the Polar Sea where we wanted her and we had plenty of Eskimos, dogs, and food.

One day on the *Roosevelt* in the winter of 1905, Peary said to me: "Captain Bob, if we make a go of it this spring we'll tackle the South Pole."

I could hardly believe my ears; so deep was I in our present effort to get to the Pole that I hadn't even thought about what I would do when I got back to Brigus again. It was like Peary to be planning ahead.

"Yes," he went on, "the Stars and Stripes will some day fly at both poles."

We talked about it quite a little. The idea took our minds off the struggles and anxieties we were going through.

At that time we knew that the South Pole was on the crest of a great plateau about 10,000 feet in the air, as Shackleton proved when he reached a point only a few years before less than 140 miles from it. This made the task different from our Polar Sea work, which was all on a floating cake of ice about 2,000 miles in diameter with a depth of water at the Pole nearly the same as the 10,000-foot elevation at the other end of the globe.

"We might even take Eskimos," said Peary.

But that was a hard spring in 1906. As I have already told we nearly lost the ship and Peary's starvation party just got back by the skin of their teeth. So all our efforts and thoughts went into the future towards the same old goal.

In 1909, the subject came up again. Peary at last had won. The plan dear to his heart, of placing the American flag at both ends of the axis of the earth seemed now a possibility.

I should like to put in another point too, one that illuminates Peary's fine character. He knew that in the group of young men with him he had developed both capable leaders and executives; I mean men who could go out into the wilderness of the polar regions and make good. They, in turn, knew the Peary system and they understood the technique of Eskimo life. Marvin was good with dogs and Borup could handle the natives like a father. Naturally I had soaked in a good deal of Arctic lore. Peary felt that with such a nucleus America could have the other pole within a year or two.

On our way south in 1909, he said to me:

"Captain Bob, we've got this ship to start with. And we have the best natives in the north. Also there are plenty of dogs. If we do it right, we can make use of them all."

He then showed me his idea for a new ship. Her general lines would be those of the *Roosevelt*; but she would be bigger. She would have heavy oak cross timbers and a solid bow, with vertical steel stringers between her top deck and her keel, so that she could withstand the pressure of the pack ice known to exist off the Antarctic continent.

His idea was that the old *Roosevelt* would pick up Eskimos and dogs in the early fall and carry them south. She would pause in temperate latitudes during the colder months so that the northerners would not be out of their element. Then she would go on gradually and make a quick trip across the Equator in order to get her crew of brown hunters into the Antarctic at the end of the south polar summer, or about March.

The new ship, though built on the general lines of the *Roosevelt*, would have larger deck space fitted up for laboratories and oceanographic work. Peary's connection with big federal scientific bodies centring in Washington had made him see the enormous amount of research yet to be done in the far south. Moreover, as the Antarctic continent was discovered by an American naval officer, Captain Charles Wilkes, it was fitting that Americans should continue the work.

"It isn't just the pole that we want," said Peary. "We will go right on over the ice cap and down the other side. The Antarctic continent is twice the size of the United States. There's no telling what we may find there. Someday, of course, men will fly over it and see more than is possible with sledges. But by relay parties and by branching out we ought to bring back a pretty good picture of it to the world."

This is especially interesting because now, nearly twenty

years later, the job is still undone and my friend Dick Byrd is planning to do it all by air.

It was my big chance. I never thought that Peary wanted to go himself. He was willing to contribute his time and his energy without limit to organization. Certainly his genius for Arctic travel would always be at our disposal. But he had in his heart a desire to see the rest of us succeed as he had succeeded and probably without the tribulations he had gone through. I would go in command. For the first time in my life I felt I was going to do something big and run the show myself. Such is the "pride that goeth before a fall."

I held my dream until the fall of 1909. But the minute the controversy broke Peary realized that the storm of abuse heaped on him and his men would prevent our going ahead at once with Antarctic plans. It was a bitter disappointment, but there was no way out.

It bears on the scheme that Peary had planned to start off on his lecture tour the minute he got back from the Pole. This tour would raise funds and would give him a chance to spread the gospel of American Antarctic success on a par with what had been done in the Arctic.

"I know General Hubbard and the rest of them will want to come in," he said enthusiastically, "after we have finally cleaned things up in the north."

It was one of the unwritten tragedies in Peary's life that he didn't lecture after all. On the advice of ill-informed men he shifted his lecturing from the fine old Pond management connections to another bureau which soon went to pieces. His first taste of dismal failure came when he started off to Providence for an opening lecture and got there only to find that the hall was dark. The bureau had forgotten to make arrangements! The lecture tour never came off. The fortune that should have been awaiting the discovery of the Pole never materialized. As a result the financial and moral aid that would have backed up my Antarctic expedition went into stemming the tide of prejudice against Peary.

The rest is largely history; and it forms an anticlimax to my yarn. Amundsen reached the South Pole in 1911. Scott succeeded and died.

There is not much else to tell. When we got news that Amundsen had succeeded the wind was all taken out of my sails. When we heard of the Scott tragedy we knew the public would be opposed to any more Antarctic work for the time being.

Most of the work I had in mind is still undone. Shackleton in the *Endurance* was headed for the accomplishment of some of it. But he died. Byrd may next year do a good deal from aloft. But the heavy winds that scour the surface of that great Antarctic ice cap will make it very hard for him and I shall sleep better when he is back.

I still think there is justice for sending a ship equipped for oceanographic work to the waters skirting the Antarctic continent. Shore parties could at the same time explore some of the vast unknown interior, which is nearly twice the size of the United States.

I would still like to see some Eskimos taken down there. It might be interesting to colonize a spot in the Antarctic with them. The big handicap is that there is almost no land life on that whole continent; only the penguins. But on the edges of the ice cap and the land fringe there are in spots plenty of seal and sometimes whales. It is conceivable that both geographical and anthropological experiments could be carried out with the help of natives that would be impossible in the north polar regions. Certainly overland travel would be made immensely easier if they were always available with their skill at dog driving and their extraordinary endurance.

The next scheme I had for leading my own expedition was to drift across the unexplored area of the north polar basin. As I had to make a living, I couldn't dally around. But with the exploring bee still in my bonnet I couldn't go back to sea routine and be happy.

After my return from Europe I went over to see Herbert Bridgman in his office in the *Brooklyn Standard Union*. I remember it was August because of the heat; I melted down three collars between dawn and dusk. I don't ordinarily shift collars so often, but that day I wanted to be at my best. I had a big job at hand. I came right out about it to Mr. Bridgman.

"I want to drift across the Polar Sea," I told him.

"You mean the way *Fram* did?" he asked, taking my measure with his little grey eyes.

"Yes, sir. I believe if we enter the ice further eastward we shall be able to define the Polar Basin. The *Jeannette* was too far west. She was smashed by the ice and many of her men were lost, if you remember."

"I remember all right," he said reflectively. He looked up suddenly. "Well, what are you going to do about it?"

"I have already done a lot, sir," I told him. "I have got about $90,000 pledged towards my expedition."

"How much do you want?"

"Three hundred thousand, sir!"

He whistled a regular bos'n's pipe of surprise. "That's a good deal. What do you plan next?"

I told him that I was hanging in the bight. I had got so far and couldn't seem to get any further. Just then one of his staff broke in and said: "By the way, Mr. Bridgman, did you know James Gordon Bennett was back on this side?"

Like a flash I saw clear water ahead. I said to myself: "There's my man!"

Mr. Bridgman hove around in his swivel chair and with a sly look on his face said: "I'll give you $5.00, Captain Bartlett, if you get to see Mr. Bennett."

I won't admit it was the bribe, or even the dare; but I knew right then and there I was going to get to that notorious millionaire or break my neck in the attempt. With the impulsiveness that has been my curse as well as my virtue, I went right back to New York and got a stateroom on the Fall River boat bound for Newport. To be on the safe side, I dropped in at the *New York Times* where my friend, Mr. Graves, confirmed the report that Commodore Bennett was back. He said he was sending a man up to interview him. I was so excited that I didn't even wait to pack my bag but went off without it. The following morning, I landed in Newport.

The first man I met in town was James Connolly, the writer and war correspondent. "*Hello*, Bob!" he shouted at me across the hotel lobby. "What in the devil are you doing up in these shallows, anyway?"

"Just a little voyage of discovery," I told him truthfully enough.

He came over and took my arm and dragged me into the dining room. During breakfast he pumped me; but I didn't spill my big plan. When he told me how he was going out with the Atlantic fleet for manoeuvres off Cape Cod, I cautiously inquired about the habits of some of the millionaires. I thought maybe he would give me some valuable tips. He did. He said they went out to take the air every day. This helped, as I soon found out.

The next thing I did was to telephone my friend Charlie Leavy over in Jamestown. I told him I was up for a day or two and asked if it was all right to drop in.

"Sure, come right along. What's up?"

But I wouldn't let on. My game was too valuable to risk a leaky telephone wire.

As soon as I got settled in Jamestown—there wasn't much to settle, not having any baggage—I came back to Newport to scout around. I realized that my best bet was to get down into Commodore Bennett's sumptuous place on Bellevue Avenue and see him in his own home.

Luckily, I happened to look down at the duds I had on. At once I saw I was in no shape to call on a millionaire. I had to get some gear that would fit the scenery around his marble palace. So down I went to the smartest store in Newport. Luckily just before leaving New York I had cashed a cheque for $100. Now I went in and bought a whole rig, consisting of fine straw hat with a wide brim, a Palm Beach suit, and shoes the colour of the Albany grease you use in sounding lead. I got a shirt with purple stripes in it; and a sky-blue tie to match the blue hatband I had on the straw hat. I didn't forget to get some light blue socks. I want to say that once I got into the thing I went through it in fine style: I even bought some silk underwear!

My next move was to go to the hotel and get dressed up in my new duds. Then I went down into the lobby where they had a full length mirror and admired myself.

Next I drifted out and began to look around for a sea-going hack. I haven't much of an eye for horses, but I think I picked a good one. I spoke to the driver who turned out to be an Irishman named MacGinty. As he thought I was one too, from my Newfoundland brogue I suppose, he was very friendly. Anyway, my costume must have made an impression on him.

"I'm just out for a look at the town," I told him.

"Nobody knows it better than me."

"Shove off," I said and hopped in.

Presently we were going down Bellevue Avenue, the street where all the swells live.

"Tell me about them," I commanded my driver. He soon loosened up. The old nag drifted slowly while he pointed here and there with his whip. He told me how many millions each man was worth and how many wives he had had; how many servants, and what his yacht cost; and a whole lot more. I guess there wasn't anybody that ever knew as much about Newport as that driver.

Pretty soon we got down to where Jim Connolly had told me Mr. Bennett lived. I felt myself getting hot and cold with excitement. If I could only get Commodore Bennett interested my whole project for polar drift would go through. He could give me $100,000 and never miss it.

"And who lives there?" I sung out as we came abeam of the place.

"Oh that's where Commodore Bennett lives."

I asked for details. He told me how the old gentleman was eccentric but still active, despite his seventy-four years. He described him as a slender but erect old man who looked a good deal like a retired general.

"You know, sir, the commodore used to be a live chap about here and he was a good sport. When he would go on a bender and break up a wagon, or damage a man, or hurt a horse, he always made good. I tell you he was a generous fellow!"

Then I got out, explaining that I was now going to walk the rest of the way. I gave MacGinty $3.00 and he drove away happy.

I now began to scout around the place, feeling more like a burglar than an explorer. It was a huge estate with trees and lawns and hedges. In the middle reposed a handsome residence. After I got the lay of the land I went in and rang the bell. A fine-looking butler in uniform opened the door. He eyed me up and down.

"What will you have," he asked coldly.

"I want to see Commodore Bennett."

"He isn't here."

"But I am an old friend of his. I mean that I know him and I think he knows me."

"What's your name?"

I didn't like that butler. I didn't like the way he talked to me.

"My name's Bartlett," I told him.

He disappeared. While he was gone I began to think matters over. I figured that the best thing to do was to try to win over this hard-boiled guardian. When he came back I handed him $5.00 before he could start to talk. He took it without hesitation. (There went my $5.00 bet with Mr. Bridgman.) He loosened up a little bit then.

"Commodore Bennett cannot see you now," he said. "The thing to do is to come around tomorrow morning. He usually takes a walk out on the Avenue. Perhaps I can arrange for you to see him at that time."

I thanked the archangel and went back to the hotel. I walked slowly so as not to spoil the fine condition of my new clothes. As soon as I got back I took them off and stowed them carefully away in my locker.

Sharp at four bells next morning I was on hand. My friend, the butler, to whom I had given the $5.00, appeared when I rang. He nodded and disappeared, leaving the door open. Presently I heard an irascible voice, that of an elderly man:

"Never heard of him! Send him away!"

This didn't sound promising. I gathered it was the commodore.

The butler came back and told me that he was sorry the commodore wasn't feeling well and that I would have to postpone my visit until some later date. But I was not to be discouraged. I had staked everything on getting to see my man. So instead of going away I anchored right there. I couldn't think of any moves to make that might be successful. Also I was afraid that if I made any bad mistake in my strategy it might end everything.

Much depressed I sat down on a bench hidden amongst the hedge just outside the entrance to the estate. Who should come along but my friend Paul Rainey. He slammed the brakes on his car and I looked up just as he came to a stop.

"Hello, Bob!" he shouted. "What in heaven's name are you doing here?"

Not wanting to yell about my game, I went out and told him that I was trying to see Commodore Bennett. He pooh-poohed the whole plan.

"Chuck it, old man! Don't you realize that this Polar game is all off? Cook put the kibosh on it. Why I wouldn't dare to be associated with you Arctic explorers after all that mess!"

I didn't like to hear my friend talk this way. I tried to tell him something about my proposed trip to the Polar Sea. But all I got from him was:

"All right, if you want to be bullheaded about it, Bob. Keep on and you are going to end as a night watchman on a dock." Still shaking his head he drove off.

This incident only made me all the more determined. I sauntered back to the seat, racking my brains. If I only could think up some master move, I thought. Then Fate moved for me.

The door opened. Out came a slender figure, which I recognized as that of Commodore Bennett. He had two little woolly dogs—Pomeranians I think they were. One was under his arm and one he was leading by a string.

I went up to him and doffed my new straw hat.

"Good morning, Commodore," said I.

He gave me a hard look.

"Who are you?"

"I am Robert Bartlett, and I came to see you, sir."

"What about?" he snapped.

"If you will let me sit down and talk to you a few minutes I'll tell you."

I think he knew enough about men to realize that I wasn't a journalist or a financial expert. After a few minutes' hesitation he shrugged his shoulders and said:

"All right. Come in."

He turned around and led the way. My heart was pounding against my ribs. At last I had won; at least so far as getting into the presence of the big man.

In his wake I went out to a piazza. There was a table there. I was ready for the test. In my pocket I carried a chart of the Polar Sea, showing the district from Alaska along Siberia and the polar basin below the Pole. I pulled it out and spread it on the table and said:

"You know this as well as I do, sir."

He looked at me inquiringly. I went on:

"You put the money into the *Jeannette* expedition, sir. That was a great expedition, even though many lives were lost."

The commodore looked more interested. I don't think many people know to this day how much money he contributed to the widows and orphans of the ill-fated *Jeannette*.

I went on at a great rate. For so many days my ideas had been boiling up in me that they came spouting out now that I had my chance.

"Good, good!" exclaimed the commodore, becoming more interested as I went on. I began to "heel to the breeze."

"It is one of the biggest things left to do in the Arctic," said I, "it is the last great geographical project in the world today!"

I won't repeat it all here. But I certainly put on a good performance. I was eloquent and I knew what I was talking about. And I felt I was really interesting the man before me. Suddenly he looked up and said:

"Do you know Peary?"

I was taken aback.

"Of course I know him, sir, I was captain of the *Roosevelt*. I started with Peary back in 1898."

"What kind of man is he?"

"One of the greatest men who ever lived, sir."

He leaned across the table at me. "Do you say that because you are in command of his ship, or because you really think it?"

"Because I know it, sir."

Then I did an impulsive thing. I put my face forward so that I was not far from Commodore Bennett's and said: "Sir, do you realize that some people speak of you as 'that old scoundrel'?" It was a wonder he didn't have his butler throw me out then and there. But not a muscle of his face twitched. I must say he took it well.

"Why do you mention that?"

The cat was out of the bag. But I didn't back water.

"Because, Commodore, I think you have attacked Peary without really knowing him. Had I not come here this morning and felt your hospitality and intelligence, and seen how kind a man you are, I should have believed what the people said about you."

He saw my point. Colour came to his face. He showed real emotion. He looked away.

"I think you are right, Captain," he said presently.

Somehow I felt he meant it.

The silence that followed was the climax of my visit. My strain and apprehension left me. I felt relaxed. The coolness and defiance, even arrogance, of the old gentleman before me evaporated. We were just two men facing one another over a problem of mutual interest. It wasn't rich and poor, old and young, master and hand; it was man to man.

He motioned me to a seat. He began to speak. His voice had lost its strength a little and sounded tired.

"I wish I could help you, Captain Bartlett. I wish I were a younger man and could jump into this thing and see you through. But I am no longer young." He paused.

"I am sorry, sir," I said just a little embarrassed at his frankness.

"At my age one doesn't know what will happen next." Again he paused. He shook his head. "No, Captain Bartlett, I cannot do it."

He rose, I got up. To my surprise I did not feel disappointed. There was so much justice in the old gentleman's point of view I couldn't feel that he had nipped my hopes in the bud by his simple statement.

As he shook my hand he said: "Won't you give me a story for the *Herald*?"

When I got back to New York, a *Herald* correspon-

dent, the late Mr. Jennings, called on me promptly. I began
to tell him the details of my plan. Presently he stopped me.

"Why I already have that whole story, Captain Bartlett.
I got it from Commodore Bennett."

So apparently I had driven my point home better than
I thought.

The war killed the whole project. I even forgot to collect my $5.00 from Mr. Bridgman. Thus ended my dreams
of leading my own expedition into polar regions.

CHAPTER XVII

SHIPWRECK AND DEATH

The spring of 1913 I spent with the sealing fleet. In June I got back to Brigus with a heavy heart. Things hadn't gone well. There were too many ships out and the seals had seemed nervous. I wanted to get back to exploring. I was spoiled for the grind of sealing and fishing.

As I walked up to the old house my father came down to meet me. He had a yellow envelope in his hand which he held out to me.

"Here, Bob," he said, "here's some business for you."

I don't like telegrams. They seem to bring bad news more often than good. When people have good news to tell you they sit down and write a long letter so as to get it all in. When they have bad news it seems to burn them like a hot coal. The quicker they get rid of it the better. So they telegraph.

I turned the envelope over two or three times in my hand before opening. I tried to figure out what had gone wrong. As a matter of fact nothing could go wrong. I didn't have any wife or any children and not much of a bank account. The law and I were good friends; and I didn't owe but one man money. Maybe he was hard up and wanted the few hundred dollars coming to him.

Like a diver on a springboard, I took a deep breath and plunged in—into the yellow envelope. It read:

```
    . . . Will you join me in the Karluk as
master?
                        (Signed) STEFANSSON.
```

My heart turned over a couple of times as I spelled the message through twice. I had heard that Stefansson was going north up the Alaskan side in command of a Canadian Arctic Expedition. He was headed for that big unexplored area above America which is still unknown. He had got Canada to back him and had plenty of money and many fine scientists. That he wanted me to be master of his leading ship was a great compliment. But it was more than that: it was just exactly the medicine I needed—a chance to go into the north again.

"Must be good news, boy," said Father.

I had forgotten him in my joy.

"Finest in the world!" I exclaimed. "I am going back north again!"

The old gentleman's face fell. I think he had hoped that I would stay home for a while. I heard a step. Mother came out on the porch. I hesitated. The old folks needed me. Though Father was hale and hearty he wasn't young anymore. He was nearing seventy. I know he had hoped that I could be a producing member of the family from now on.

But the north was in my blood. And I was the grandson of "Follow On" Bartlett. I couldn't help it; I had to "follow on."

"Guess I'll have to go, Father," I said.

The old gentleman put out his hand and gave mine a hard grip. Then he turned and walked up the path without saying a word. He felt deeply but he understood.

That was the beginning of my connection with the last voyage of the *Karluk*, the most tragic and ill-fated cruise in my whole career. We left Victoria, BC, in June and were in the ice by September. Fifteen months later the revenue cutter *Bear*, the Greely relief ship, brought only nine of our party back to Esquimault. These nine white men were the bedraggled survivors of twenty who had been aboard the *Karluk* when she was crushed in the Polar Sea in the preceding January. The disaster makes a sad story. It was particularly sad because we had such a fine outfit. Beside Stefansson we had some of the leading scientists of the whole world. There was Dr. Anderson, the famous zoologist. The Canadian Geological Survey had sent four men, all experts. James Murray of Glasgow was oceanographer; he had been with Sir Ernest Shackleton in the Antarctic. We had a fine fish man in Fritz Johanson who had spent some time in East Greenland. There was Bjarne Mamen from Norway whose work in Spitzbergen was well known. Dr. Forbes Mackay was the surgeon of the expedition. Altogether there were twelve on the scientific staff.

I must point out that some of the above men had never seen sea ice before. I do this because, without the slightest idea of criticism, I want to show how this very lack of experience ultimately led to the tragic death of a number of our party. It taught me a great lesson, too, as you shall presently see.

On June 17, we left Esquimault for Nome. It was a fine getaway with plenty of gay celebrations ashore and aboard. There is something in the spectacle of a ship sailing away that arouses the enthusiasm of the crowd. And when that ship is going out toward an adventurous goal everybody is thrilled.

I'd like to say in passing that I have sailed for the North Pole and for the war and for a lot of other unusual destinations, but curiously enough there is no excitement to be compared with the sailing of a sealer out of St. John's, Newfoundland. The explorer or the soldier is going to achieve something. But the sealer is going out to decide whether his wife and babies will have molasses cakes with their boiled codfish for the next eleven months. There is no phase of exploration or war that can be as important a thing in life as molasses cakes are to the outport kiddies of Newfoundland.

About seventy-five miles southwest of Point Barrow, we met floe ice. I was up in the crow's nest at the time. The first thing I spotted was a polar bear about three miles away on a big level pan. To an average man this would have been a good omen. But to a superstitious Newfoundlander the bear was but a beacon towards future disaster. Because the omen proved well founded, as I shall soon show. I am more than ever a believer in signs. Don't think I am a heathen. But there are certain signs that somehow always work out. So I cannot help thinking that they mean something.

What probably finished our future was that we went out and shot the bear.

Our bad luck took two months to reach us. In a sense

it started when Stefansson left the ship on September 18. We were tied up to the shore ice not far from Point Barrow. The Eskimos aboard as well as I understood what Stefansson was after. We all knew that we should have some fresh meat for the fall and winter months. I offered to go out with the leader and hunt with him. I had shot plenty of caribou in Grant Land and Ellesmere Land, as well as in Newfoundland. But Stefansson pointed out that he was the only one on board that knew how to hunt the animals in these parts. So on the morning of September 20, I helped him get fitted out. He left that afternoon.

When he left he gave me the following letter (I am not quoting it all because some of it does not bear particularly on the story):

Dear Captain Bartlett:
    On the trip for which I am leaving the Karluk today, I expect to make land on the largest second from the west of Jones Islands (Thetis Island). If the ice is strong enough I expect to cross thence to near Beechey Point to hunt caribou; if feasible I may go on to the mouth of the Itkulik River, known to the Eskimo as Itkilhkpe, to see if fish can be purchased there from the natives. Should the Karluk during our absence be driven from her present position it will be well for so soon as she has come to stop again, and as soon as it appears safe to send a party ashore, to erect one or more beacons, giving information of the ship's location. If she goes east, the beacons should be erected on accessible islands; if west they should be at Cape Halkett, Pitt Point, or Point Simpson, to facilitate the finding of the ship in fog or

blizzard by our party coming from shore, or by hunters who are overtaken by thick weather while away from the ship. It will be well to have established four lines of beacons, running in the four cardinal directions from the ship to as great a distance as practicable. There should be some arrangement by which these beacons indicate in what direction the ship is from each of them. And some of them should have the distance of the ship marked upon them. These beacons need not be large, but should not be over 100 yards apart to be of use in thick weather. Flags or other fluttering things should not be used, for bears might be scared away by them . . .

It is likely that we shall be back to the ship in ten days, if no accident happens.

I was much impressed by this letter. It certainly was in detail and it showed how thoroughly Stefansson thought things over before he acted. If I had any misgivings it was because I had been acquainted with the Arctic for a good many years. You can make all the plans you want in the far north and write them out on hundreds and hundreds of pages, using all the words in the dictionary. But the finer plan you have the worse it will go smash when wind and ice and drifting snow take charge. That's exactly what happened to Stefansson's plan.

Three days later the wind got busy and cooked up a forty-mile gale in a few hours. I noticed the natives were uneasy. We were frozen in the ice at the time, not tight, but fairly firm. The first night of the storm one of the natives came to me and declared that the pack was moving. He was very much frightened. At the time we had a dredge hole cut in the ice with a line and lead hanging down to the bottom. I checked up at once and found the Eskimo was right. We were under way with the pack. That polar bear we shot had begun to work.

It came on to snow. By the morning watch a fine full-blooded Arctic blizzard was upon us. On the main deck you couldn't breathe without holding your mitten over your mouth. When the gale softened a bit at noon, for a few hours our tenderfeet were encouraged. But the weather was, so to speak, just spitting on its hands and getting ready for a stronger pull. That night the wind rose to over seventy miles an hour. The ice began to grind and roar and snap. The *Karluk* had several chances to end herself then and there. Either she could go up on a nearby shoal under the ice pressure; or be cut in half by the heavy floes; or she could succumb to the blocks as big as bungalows which were upended by the pressure all about her. It was a tough jam all right. I never do like to see a ship suffer.

Of course we had to be ready to move at an instant's notice. I had all hands get the concentrated provisions up on deck and load our boats with supplies. If we were swept off-shore we might have to leave the ship and row in after the storm was over. I had sometimes seen several miles of open water between the pack and the Alaskan coast under such circumstances.

Fortunately we had some dogs on board. If we had to drive home they would save our lives. There were only enough for one good team; but a single sledge would carry food for at least a score of men several weeks if rations were reduced.

The storm continued for a week. It was the end of the

month before our situation cleared up. I say cleared up in the sense of our knowing what it was all about. So far as our future went the situation couldn't have been darker. It was this: the *Karluk* had drifted out into the ice-filled Polar Sea and there wasn't the chance of a snowball in Hades of our getting her back again to land. A nice mess, I thought to myself; Stefansson, the leader, ashore and his whole blooming expedition floating around here in the ice out of sight of land. It certainly would have been embarrassing for Stefansson if the Premier of Canada had met him on the beach about that time and said, "Sir, where's your expedition?"

The only thing Stefansson could have answered would have been to have waved his arm out over the polar pack and said nonchalantly: "They're out there waiting for me, sir," which we were.

We were waiting for him all right. We were stuck so hard and fast in that ice forty feet thick that all the motor trucks in Canada couldn't have pulled us out.

To make matters worse the little glimpse of clear sky we had at the end of September was followed by another blizzard. The wind howled through our rigging night and day; but its noise was usually drowned out by the roar of the ice. I don't think I have seen such ice pressure. It rafted on all sides of us, cracked and came again, and went through all kinds of contortions. Jack Hadley said one day it reminded him of a person with a louse in his shirt which couldn't be reached. It certainly wriggled.

The poor old *Karluk* began to suffer worse than ever. She creaked and groaned and, once or twice, actually sobbed as the water oozed through her seams. There is nothing more human than a ship in ice pressure. Sometimes I used to walk around on the floes out of sight of her because I couldn't stand to see the way she went on.

All the time I was worried more and more about my party of men who knew so little about the Arctic. I had a house built on the ice and most of our provisions put there on a thick floe in case the ship was crushed. I organized a fire party in case she caught on fire. I taught our people as well as I could how to take care of their clothes and I kept our Eskimo seamstress busy making boots and shirts.

On October 28, I gave up hope of getting out of our mess that fall. The sun was about to leave us; and the bad weather continued. I saw we were in for the winter.

I put the whole party on a two-meal basis; breakfast at nine in the morning and dinner at four-thirty. Being a Newfoundlander, I allowed them tea at one p.m. and at midnight. Also I made everybody except the watchman put light out at midnight. We didn't suffer because we had a great deal of fine food aboard. This was because it was a rich expedition and with generous backers and not a poor one such as nearly all of Peary's had been. For breakfast we had porridge and condensed milk with a choice of eggs, ham, bacon, and sausages to top off with. There was plenty of coffee. For dinner the cook would select from his large store of canned or dried vegetables and prepare a feast. We had carrots, parsnips, spinach, pickles, asparagus, beans, corn, and tomatoes. For dessert we used to have ice cream, pies, puddings, cakes, and canned fruits. There were times when I was almost glad to be there, with such fare to face twice a day.

We didn't waste anything. But we had too many different kinds of things to eat. That was another bad sign which, added to the bear we killed, made me sure we were in for it. We even had plenty of soap and razors and enough underwear to stock a store. We were a lot of dudes as compared with the ordinary seafaring man.

I tried to keep everybody busy. I must say that people accepted my routine in good spirit. By the time we settled down to a winter schedule on October 28, most of those with me realized what an uncomfortable mess we were in. So they took to my plan of action kindly.

From then on until after the new year life was without important incident.

It began to look to me at last as if we were headed for a fine big circus that would end in books and lectures and a lot of other money-making products. This would be the case if the *Karluk* only drifted out alive in the spring.

There was a circus all right, but the ice pack cracked the whip—and incidentally the old ship. Remember, the sun had left us and it had got really cold. You'd have to play around in that white desert for a while to know how fearfully cold it did get. Old Klondike miners used to say it got so cold that a loud crackle rent the air when they spat. Our weather now was just about that cold. It was around sixty below zero nearly every day.

On New Year's Day we were all below huddled around the little stove. Suddenly there rose a whining noise such as you hear singing along telegraph wires on a windy night in the country. This meant pressure again. With the pressure came an easterly gale. It lasted for ten days. At five o'clock in the morning of January 10, I was roused out of a sound sleep by a loud report like a rifle shot. A tremor ran through the ship. I threw on my parka and hopped on deck. I knew the end was near.

All that day the poor old *Karluk* struggled in the death grip of the pack. At half past seven that evening I went down to the engine room to have a look at our bottom. While I was on the ladder I heard a splitting and crashing below me. The engineer and I ran to a hatch and held a lantern down into the hold. We could see water rushing into the old girl. It was a terrible sight.

I hurried back on deck and ordered all hands abandon ship. There was no confusion. Our food and ammunition were already on the ice. I sent an Eskimo woman to our house for provision boxes to start a fire in the little stove we had placed there for emergency.

Then, all at once, I had a feeling that I wanted to be alone with the old ship during her last hours; so I sent all my men to the house. They were glad enough to go, between the storm and the depressing effect of their sinking vessel.

I went down into the cabin. I went down alone and sat and thought about what the *Karluk* had been through. We had a phonograph and about 150 records. With the cracking timbers and the rushing waters around me I played tune after tune. As I played the records, I threw them into the stove. I ate when I was hungry and had plenty of coffee and tea.

When I came to Chopin's Funeral March I laid it aside. I knew I would soon need it. About an hour or so later the ship began to settle in earnest. Pretty soon our lower decks were awash. Putting the Funeral March on the victrola I started the machine. When the water came trickling along the upper deck and began splashing into the hatch I ran up and stood on the rail. Slowly the *Karluk* dipped into a header. When her rail was level with the ice I stepped off. I turned and looked at her as she went down by the head into thirty-eight fathoms of water. I could hear the victrola in the galley sending out the strains of the Funeral March. Pushing my hood back I bared my head and said, "Goodbye, old girl."

CHAPTER XVIII

I GO FOR HELP

The first thing I did after the *Karluk* sank was to turn in to our igloo for a sleep. I had been up for thirty-six hours. The strain of suspense, the anxiety for our future and my personal distress at losing our fine ship had worn me out.

After twelve hours I woke. I was still in command; that's the law. But I was in command of a shipwrecked party. Had we been on a desert island things might have been brighter. But to be out there on the ever-shifting ice pack, far from land, and faced with the coldest months of the winter night, I could not look ahead without some uneasiness.

The first thing I did was to have the party rig up a tent for sheltering the last supplies we had hurried off the ship just before she went down. We had a pretty good collection of clothing; seventy suits of underwear, 200 pairs of stocking, 100 pairs of boots, etc. Our main supply of food consisted of over 9,000 pounds of pemmican to which were added 200 tins of milk and 250 pounds of sugar. Of general equipment we had the following: 250 sacks of coal, thirty-three cases of gasoline, nine sledges and 2,000 feet of lumber. Only the concentrated food and the newest and lightest clothing were of vital importance. Our safety lay in retreating south just as soon as possible.

I was familiar with the drift of the polar pack. I knew that if we stayed where we were we should likely slide westward and circle the Pole until, some years hence, we would possibly emerge down through the Greenland Sea. That's what Nansen's *Fram* did twenty years before. But by that time we should all be frozen stiff.

The temperature was not severe. The thermometer showed an average of about forty below zero. The wind was what hurt. Those who were not already hardened to it suffered.

On January 17, we made plans for an advance party to get off south. Wrangell Island above Siberia was the nearest land. There we would find driftwood and game. I had in mind transferring the entire party to the south shore of Wrangell Island. Then I could go on with two or three of the best men and work south to the mainland, and thence across to Alaska where I hoped I could secure a rescue ship that would take us off in the summer. The trouble was that not all of my party were strong enough to go through with a hard sledging journey. And there was some difference of opinion as to what was the best thing to do. The situation grew daily more uncomfortable.

It might be asked why I didn't have all hands just pack up and go south? The answer to this is that sledging conditions on the Polar Sea are pretty terrible in the sector north of Alaska. Even if we could have reached Wrangell Island alive it might be some weeks before we could secure game there. The thing to do was to relay some of our present food in. But during this relaying we had to be careful not to lose contact between small parties. I knew from experience with Peary how easy it would be to have the trail broken by movement of the ice. Then the first thing we knew we should be completely adrift from our food and equipment. In such condition we should probably be wiped out by a single bad storm.

It was not until the twenty-first that the first and second mates and two sailors with three sledges and eighteen dogs got under way toward Wrangell. I felt encouraged when I saw the teams disappear through the rough ice. At last we had made a move shoreward. Already there was good deal of whispering among the crowd. Inactivity was getting on everybody's nerves.

On January 25, the sun came back after nearly three months' absence. It didn't do any more than stick its nose up above the horizon. But it somehow put new hope in our hearts.

By January 28, I was getting anxious over my shore party. They were not yet back and there was no word from them. Moreover I was disturbed by one of our scientists, Mr. Murray, coming to me and asking for supplies for four men for fifty days with sledge. He said he and some of his friends had decided they would like to make an attempt to reach Alaska. These were Englishmen who had been with Shackleton in the Antarctic. They didn't altogether approve of my Arctic methods which I had learned under Peary. I don't pretend to criticize them. But on my own behalf I will say that Peary's methods largely originated with the Eskimos who have lived in regions of ice and snow for many centuries.

I told Murray that I thought he and his friends were taking a big chance. But I wanted to be absolutely fair. So I agreed to let them have their proportionate share of the dogs and food. At once the doctor, who was going too, began checking over the supplies and preparing for departure. Before Murray's party left I was handed the following letter:

CANADIAN ARCTIC EXPEDITION.
Sunday, Feb. 1st, 1914.

Captain Robert Bartlett,
    Sir: We, the undersigned, in consideration of the present critical situation, desire to make an attempt to reach the land. We ask you to assist us by issuing to us from the general stores all necessary sledging and camping provisions and equipment for the proposed journey as per separate requisition handed to you. On the understanding that you do so and continue as heretofore to supply us with our proportional share of provisions while we remain in camp, and in the event of our finding it necessary to return to the camp, we declare that we undertake the journey on our own initiative and absolve you from any responsibility whatever in the matter.

    A. FORBES MACKAY   H. BEUCHAT
    JAMES MURRAY   S. S. MORRIS

The party was equipped with sledge, dogs, tent, stove, fuel, rifle, and 100 rounds of ammunition. These supplies with other necessary equipment were quite sufficient to last the party fifty days. They got away on the morning of February 5, amid the cheers and good wishes of those left behind. I shook hands with each of them.

That was the last that was ever seen of those four fine brave men. Not a trace of them was ever discovered afterwards. I suspect they died of exhaustion. They were used to the Antarctic plateau which is level; but not to the terrific chaos of the Polar Sea. I picture their sledge breaking as Peary's sledges often broke, their dogs getting weaker, and frostbite hindering their work. For none was skilled in the handling of dogs or protection of their clothing and equipment in Polar Sea conditions. All this comprises a technique that takes years to learn.

Actual tragedy was closer to us, however, than to those departing.

The same afternoon my two men Mamen and Williams arrived back at Shipwreck Camp. Mamen had dislocated his kneecap. Williams had fallen through the young ice about four miles away. Fortunately the Eskimos with them didn't lose their heads. The temperature was thirty-five degrees below zero. Had there been wind or darkness the party might never have gotten back. I rushed Williams into the box house where he was filled up with tea and rolled up in dry blankets. Our second engineer, in the absence of our surgeon who was on his way over the ice to Alaska, massaged the sailor's knee and finally got it back to place. That's not the only time I have seen mechanical ability equal to a surgeon's skill.

The next day, the chief engineer and Malloch came in. They were in a sorry condition. Munro had broken through and was soaked. Their load of pemmican was lost and their camping outfit practically ruined.

By this time my skeptics were beginning to believe some of the things I had said about watching your step on the Polar Sea.

More proof came in next day when Chafe and his Eskimo arrived. Chafe said:

"Captain, I don't believe we'll ever see that sledge party again."

"What!" I almost yelled at him.

"That's right. I saw them twenty miles from Herald Island. Mackay, Murray, and Morris were pulling the sledge by hand. Beuchat was a mile behind with hands and feet frozen and half delirious from his suffering. Morris had blood poisoning from a knife cut in his hand. I think Beuchat must have died that same night."

I couldn't discuss the situation with Chafe. There was nothing we could do. It would have been a wild goose chase to try to reach the party. Certainly we never could have found them and gotten back. Moreover, a heavy gale was making. I knew the four men were probably dead by now. But I said nothing about it.

On the morning of February 19, we started our shore movement in earnest. There were two parties, each with a sledge and four dogs. The sledges carried as much food and clothing as we dared burden our animals with. On one of the sledges rode a black cat, a pet we took aboard at Esquimault.

The weeks that followed were a nightmare. As we approached Wrangell Island, the ice got rougher and rougher. High pressure ridges and impassable debris surrounded us. Time and again we smashed our sledges and bruised our bodies. The temperature was always between forty-five and fifty-five degrees below zero. Malloch and Maurer froze their feet. This was bad. A man has to have his feet to travel. Templeman got lost. Finally he turned up. I began to feel like the old woman in the shoe. The trouble was I knew what to do and most of the others didn't. I felt a great responsibility.

On March 12, we reached Wrangell Island. It is a desolate place, an eighty-mile-long mountainous and barren piece of land. But it was solid land at that and wasn't going to drift around or break up under our feet the way the ice pack did. One of the first things we did was to build a fine blazing fire with some driftwood.

It wasn't possible for the whole party to retreat from here. Some were in bad shape and all were inexperienced in polar travel. The safest thing to do was for them to make themselves comfortable with the food we had brought and with the driftwood while I went for help.

On March 18, I took seven dogs, one sledge, and the Eskimo Katiktovick, and started off for Siberia down over the southern horizon. We had food for forty-eight days for ourselves and for thirty days for the dogs. It was 109 miles from the southern edge of Wrangell to Siberia, but first we had to get around the shore of the island and extricate ourselves from the horrible ice in which it was embedded. We started off in a howling gale of drifting snow. We could have waited; but it was my belief that if you start in a snowstorm you are likely to have fair weather the rest of the trip.

That belief got knocked in the eye by the fact that we had a storm most of the way to the mainland.

On March 30, we sighted land; at least the Eskimo did; I was suffering acute pain from snow blindness and couldn't see very far.

On April 4, we reached land. We had probably travelled about 200 miles. It was snowing and the land was utterly and completely desolate and empty of every living thing. But it was the mainland. There was land for 5,000 miles right strait south of us. We wanted to use it. I tell you it was a pretty good feeling.

We started east towards Alaska and the next day fell in with four Eskimos. Katiktovick was sure they were going to kill him. He told me it was a tradition of his own people that the Siberian Eskimos were a bloodthirsty outfit. This wasn't encouraging but I didn't let on that I believed him. When the strangers came up I held out my hand and said:

"How do you do?"

Right away they rushed up and shook our hands enthusiastically. We did a lot of talking on both sides but none could understand the other.

They took us in an igloo made of heavy driftwood covered by walrus skins. It smelled worse than any Greenland igloo I have ever been in, which is saying a good deal. But Katiktovick seemed happy and inhaled great breaths of the odour. Our hosts served us up some rotten walrus meat and I made some tea.

I got out my chart and did a lot of sign language argument after supper trying to get somebody to go with us. Katiktovick was tired and wanted to stay around and rest. I realized that I should have to hurry if I was going to get across to Nome in time to start a relief vessel toward our party. My men on Wrangell Island didn't have much food. They would have to be rescued this spring.

I told one of the Siberian natives I wanted him to take me east.

"How much you pay me?" asked the native.

I figured it was pretty important that I hurry. So I said, "Forty dollars."

Right away I saw I had made a mistake. If I had been a businessman I would have said twenty dollars. I could tell this by the look in the fellow's face. He was used to trading fox skins and knew how a bargain should be made, each party beating the other party up or down. And here I had gone and left myself only five dollars leeway.

"Show me money," said the native.

But I had my dander up by this time. "No, by golly!" I said.

He said: "Maybe no got him."

I said, "You bring me to East Cape, I give you forty dollars."

Well, we kept this up for about two hours. Then he sort of got hoarse from yelling at me. I was hoarse too. But we were still at forty dollars so he decided to take me. We travelled by dog sledge over the rough ice. It was hard work and the weather was cold. But we kept warm arguing about that forty dollars. Part of the time we could argue whether it was the right price or not. When the native wasn't looking I'd count it to make sure. This way we went along about a week.

There was hardly anything to eat and my feet were all

played out. My guide seemed to be getting worried. I couldn't tell whether he was worrying about the forty dollars or about the danger of our getting to East Cape.

My fears were realized when he came to me and said: "I go home."

"How about the forty dollars?" I asked him.

He said he had been thinking things over and decided that he had a lot of deerskins back in the country that he had better get. He confessed that he knew forty dollars was too high a price in that part of the world for the job he had undertaken. He added he knew that if I got to a place where I could talk to some white men about it I would find this out and refuse to pay.

The funny part about it was that when we came to a stopping place that night at another native hotel my guide came to me and said, "Me want money now."

That made me mad. I yelled right back at him: "Not a cent!"

Well, we argued back and forth for about twenty minutes, he in his language and I in mine just as loud as we could shout. Finally I decided I would be a good sport and I gave him five dollars.

Then to make him feel bad I showed him the four ten-dollar gold pieces I had as well. His eyes stuck out but he never said a word. That shows how a shipwrecked sailor man is up against it in a strange land.

I finally got over to Nome and fell in with the revenue cutter *Bear*. Through the kindness of her captain she took me out towards Wrangell Island early in September. Working through the loose ice we sighted a little schooner dead ahead. It turned out to be the *King and Winge*, a small trading ship. She hove to and we were soon alongside. She had the *Karluk* survivors aboard.

"All of you here?" was my first question.

Then I learned sad news: "No," said McKinlay, "Malloch and Mamen and Breddy died on the island."

Inquiries up and down the Alaskan coast failed to give the slightest clue to whereabouts of the doctor's party which left us on the ice. We know now they all must have died.

CHAPTER XIX

BUT THE NORTH STILL CALLED

"Why don't you stay home and take it easy for a while?"

Everyone asks me the same question when I come back from a voyage north. After the *Karluk* tragedy and its aftermath of recrimination which always seems to follow Arctic work, I really thought I might settle down for a few years of sealing. My father and mother were still taking care of the old home, but there was need of us younger Bartletts at their side. So I went home and did enough sealing and fishing to keep my hand in and make a little money.

Perhaps I should have stayed home if there had not cropped up a brand new phase of Arctic exploration. It got to be a fad. People began to go north just for the fun of it.

But then people are like sheep. The minute one does something everybody else wants to do the same thing. Take razors. I used to use an ordinary respectable razor. Now I use one of these fancy mechanisms they call a safety razor. I guess I have used them all and one's as bad as another. But the reason is, I think, that people got started using safety razors and everybody followed suit.

That's the way it was with Arctic exploration. Peary was after the North Pole and Scott and Shackleton were after the South Pole. And the first thing you knew everybody wanted to smell an Eskimo and drive a dog team.

Nearly a dozen times now I've guided amateur expeditions into the polar regions. A typical case was when I came back from sealing one spring, having been in the ice since March in command of the *Algerine* and cleaned up a good load. I met Uncle John Bartlett in St. John's. He welcomed me a little more cordially than usual I thought. I knew something was up.

Uncle John Bartlett was one of the many striking characters in our part of the world. In Brigus he was always known as a great aristocrat. His wife was called "The Duchess." The couple lived in a fine frame house of Newfoundland home-cut lumber and their life was full of ceremony. Uncle John was one of the few citizens of Brigus who had servants. He was always immaculately groomed and finely dressed. Ashore in his gloves and stick, his well-tailored suit and high hat, he was a fine-cut figure. Father told me that once in Uncle John's cabin aboard ship he saw over 100 ties hanging ready for the master! I have been told that he wore gloves to bed to keep his hands soft and clean. That sounds effeminate, yet he was afraid of no one. I have seen him stand up tall and straight with his eyes flashing and tell a man twice his weight where to get off. And if the fellow knew no better than to fight, Uncle John would half-murder him in three minutes.

When I saw him in St. John's that spring I speak of, he

was about sixty. When stopping to greet me he said: "I've got a job for you, Bob."

"Yes sir," I answered, without any special enthusiasm. I was just back from sealing and wanted to go home.

"I'm going north this summer," he said, "and I've got a boatload of dudes for you."

"Boatload of what?" I said, not understanding him.

His eyes twinkled. "Some young sports from New York want to go exploring. Will you be my mate?"

I think if it had been anybody but Uncle John I wouldn't have agreed to go. I had been with tenderfeet before and knew how dangerous the game was. If things go wrong it's your fault—always.

"I'll go, sir," I said. "When do we leave?"

We left in June. The ship was the *Algerine*, the same one I had been sealing in. We picked our party up at Sydney. There were Harry Whitney, Arthur Moore, Stuart Hotchkiss, Bert McCormick, George Goss, Charlie Leavy, George Cox, Lindon Bates, and some others; all rich men, or sons of rich men. Yet Uncle John was wrong about their all being dudes. Some were hairy sailor men despite their brass. They were going north for a lark. Our destination was Hudson Bay. We were to be gone for the summer only, hoping for some of the bear, seal and walrus hunting usually found in those waters.

I must say that we went well equipped. For instance one day I thought I'd see if there was plenty of ammunition. Down the after lazarette I counted 100,000 rounds before I even started. We had enough guns to equip the Mexican army. We had them all prices and sizes. There was one rifle aboard that cost $1,600. There were some fine fishing rods, too; and every kind of fishing gear, flies, reels, and other doodads that you can think of.

I said to Uncle John: "Do you think there'll be anything left alive when we come back?"

"Possibly," he said. "I hope it's us, Bob." He was very serious, though.

He shook his head. It was like him that he would not joke about his passengers. He was determined to see them through the finest hunting voyage they had ever had. "They are paying for it, aren't they?" A bargain was a bargain to Uncle John; a sacred thing.

I don't know as you would exactly call it hunting but our passengers certainly were busy. They didn't waste any time taking pictures or keeping diaries.

They were up on deck with their guns at all times of the day and night. Anything that came along on legs or wings they took a potshot at. Before they would shoot they'd bet to see which way the bird would go, or whether they would drop him or not. I used to think it would take a public accountant to keep track of those bets. They'd pay them off too; though after a while currency ran out and it had to be on paper.

We went through the Strait of Belle Isle and down toward Cape Chidley. It was a bad year for ice. We dodged around a good deal but soon got into the big heavy fields coming down from the north. Uncle John and I didn't care much and the passengers were delighted—for a while. Then they began to get nervous because we weren't going north fast enough. Finally, just when their patience ran out, the ice opened up and we got around into Hudson Strait.

In Ungava Bay near Akpetok Island, our "explorers" shot seven bears. Two of the bears nearly got away because the hunters had to draw lots to see who got the first shot. Hard betting saved the lives of two more. I must say in justice to the hunters that they skinned the bears after the massacre. They did it pretty well too, although it took some time and a lot of arguments about the technique of it. I think Charlie Leavy was the best butcher; I believe he once took a course in surgery.

Down in Stupart Bay we ran ashore. Luckily it was only about half tide and we got off at high water. But the *Algerine* rolled over on her side in low water and nearly caved in her port bilge. The tide there is almost thirty-five feet. Fortunately our passengers were off hunting up in the hills when the accident happened so they didn't have to suffer the anxiety a man does the first time he sees his vessel high and dry.

Some of the hunters had a big thrill down near Cape Wostenholme. We had to shift coal out of our hold and into the bunkers. Uncle John suggested that our party leave the ship while we finished the dirty job. He took some on one boat and the chief engineer took others in another. I think there was a real rivalry between the two old Newfoundlanders as to which would give his crowd the best time.

It came on to blow while they were away. Uncle John got back all right, but the chief had some trouble. His party were close in under the cliffs, bent on shooting birds, and did not notice that the wind was freshening. When they tried to get back to the ship they met a strong tide race and headwind. The first thing they knew some of the thole-pins and oars broke and the boat was helpless. Providence steered then to a notch between a small islet less than fifty yards in diameter and the cliffs. The islet was formed by a mass of rock that had become detached from the mainland and fallen into the sea. A narrow channel separated the two. If the boat hadn't drifted into this channel it would have been swept out into Hudson Strait and swamped. All would have perished. Luckily the party was able to land since further progress was impossible with the wind blowing nearly a full gale. All hands began to explore around their small island and discovered a caribou and a polar bear. As usual there were plenty of guns and ammunition in the crowd. So the two castaway animals went to fill the stomachs of the shipwrecked party.

That night the gale nearly blew the sticks out of the *Algerine*. We had to drop a second anchor, veer chain and steam full speed ahead to save her from being driven on the rocks. We were seriously alarmed about the safety of our missing passengers and chief engineer. The next morning, we saw no signs of them. They couldn't move because the wreckage of their boat was jammed into the stony debris under the cliffs. We steamed alongshore and finally saw their smoke. As the sea was still running high we had to float a dory in to them and haul them out. I was surprised to find the New Yorkers very pleased at the whole incident despite their narrow escape from death. "Good adventure stuff," one of them explained to me later.

On July 30, we got into some loose ice and young Bates fell overboard. Nobody saw him go; and since we were moving along at about nine knots he was soon well astern. Luckily he climbed out on a small pan of ice and somebody happened to spot him. We turned around and went back. Uncle John was furious. It is the worst sort of form for anybody to fall overboard from a ship. As we hove up alongside the floe on which Bates was perched Uncle John glared down at him.

Bates looked up and blandly called: "Hello, Captain."

Uncle John, still so angry he could hardly speak, shouted back: "Are you all right?"

Bates replied with broad English accent: "Well, Captain, I've had a nice bawth."

The old man almost hit the sky.

We soon got into Rowsell's Harbour. Here we anchored while all hands went ashore to shoot caribou and Arctic hare. It was at this point that the Du Ponts later opened up a pyrites mine with Uncle John as manager. He brought a big crowd up from Newfoundland to operate it and stayed there a whole year. Later the mine was abandoned as the ore was too low grade to make it profitable. Our crowd scoured the hillsides for game and littered them with empty cartridge cases. I think eight hare was the bag.

On July 3, we had a bad row aboard. While most of the party had gone ashore hunting, the captain steamed off to sea several miles to have a look at the ice. Harry Whitney stayed on the ship. When two polar bears were sighted Harry shot them. On our return to pick up the rest of the party they claimed that Harry Whitney had privately fixed this up with the captain so that he could get some bears all by himself. The whole crowd argued for the better part of two days. There was much hard feeling and finally Uncle John had to step in to keep our passengers from coming to blows.

Luckily another rumpus took their minds off the bear trouble. Someone stole a case of ship's jam out of the lazarette. Nobody would confess he did it. The old man was furious. Had he known the guilty party he would certainly have put him in irons. Of course it didn't make any difference how rich our tourists were, Uncle John was captain of the ship.

This jam argument proved good Sunday conversation. I mention this point because Uncle John insisted that there be no work or play on Sunday. Even our passengers were not allowed to shoot. They were rebellious, but I noticed they didn't break the captain's rule. We never discovered who stole the jam. This sort of thing sounds silly in a serious account, but even jam may become a vital matter on an Arctic expedition. That Monday we saw a lot of old seals basking on the ice. It was warm and bright and most of them were asleep. Eleven of our passengers climbed up on the forecastle and opened fire with eleven rifles. They laid down a terrific barrage. Every seal escaped unscathed.

So it went until the end of September when we eased back into Sydney, our amateurs pretty well fed up with the North, and Uncle John and I relieved that we had brought our charges back safe and sound.

From 1913 to 1917, the Crocker Land Expedition under the direction of the American Museum of Natural History was basing on Etah, North Greenland, for its exploration of the Polar Sea to the northwest of Ellesmere Land. Fitzhugh Green led a party by sledge down the Greenland coast late in 1916, bringing news that the last relief ship had failed to escape from the ice. As a result I was sent north in the summer of 1917, to bring down the beleaguered party and their scientific collections.

Then came the great war.

CHAPTER XX

SKIPPER U.S.N.

I had a good time during the war. My start wasn't auspicious; but I came out all right in the end. At first I was a good deal like the fellow who plays extra parts in the theatre; he comes on in the first act as one thing and then runs out and shifts over to another for the second act. In the third act you recognize him in still another part.

I started out as a soldier (picture me a soldier!). Then I got into the navy. And I guess I didn't miss the Marine Corps very far. But after things got boiled down I found myself wearing the uniform of a Lieutenant Commander of the United States Navy and in command of a transport carrying troops.

In the fall of 1917, I landed back in the *Neptune* with the Crocker Land Party on board. As usual Peary was ready to look out for me. That's the kind of man he was: always ready to help his friends. As he knew more about red tape than any three average men he didn't have much trouble fixing me up with a job on the Hoboken docks.

I worked under the army transportation service. My boss was General Shanks. Right here I want to confess that the thing that scared me about war was never the enemy; it was the generals and admirals. Now that I have read a lot of modern books I realize this is what they call an "inferiority complex." I thought it over for a long time. A general or an admiral was a man just like me; often he wasn't any older than I was. I won't say he wasn't better looking, but certainly he wasn't any more of a man than I was and there were some admirals that couldn't have had any more seafaring experience than I had. But there was something about them, starting with their uniform and ending with the way they carried their shoulders, that sort of put me in wrong with myself before I ever started talking to them.

Now I have got it all figured out what was wrong. In a Newfoundland outfit like Brigus the head official for law and order is the constable. As a boy I grew up to fear the constable just about as much as I feared God. If we went skating on thin ice or ran off with a neighbour's dory or broke any other laws it was the constable that we had to look our for. I guess I have yet to feel any fear as great as I felt when as a boy I looked over my shoulder and saw the constable coming my way. He hadn't seen me do wrong. But I had a feeling he could look right inside me and know what I had been up to.

Well, what is an admiral or general but another kind of constable?

Another thing that was part of the picture was the terrible lot of complications in any Government business. Ordinarily you call this red tape. We have some red tape in our sealing. But comparing it to the tangle of army or navy business is like comparing the cat's cradle you make with string on your fingers to a radio wiring diagram. I don't know where I would have ended but I finally found a clerk in my end of things who could spin red tape the way Will Rogers spins his lasso. This fellow kept me out of jail.

My first job was to go around with some experts and investigate the condition of the ships. In those days this country was just waking up to the enormous army it would have to send to straighten out things in Europe. Our party was on the lookout for available ships that could be used by the army and navy. We had to work too fast to go very much into details. But, generally speaking, the conditions of the ships I saw were so much better than some of the old wrecks we took down sealing that I didn't have much fear in reporting them all right.

At sea my job had been to lay the course and let her go. Now I found myself in a stew something like this:

"You will inspect the *Seagull* this morning, Mr. Bartlett."

"Aye, aye, sir," from me.

I'd go aboard the *Seagull* or some such ship. I'd look around her decks and stumble over hatch covers and coils of rope and old fenders carrying two handfuls of paper and a pocketful of pencils. My first job was to get in the lee of some deckhouse and try to figure out the questions on the pieces of paper. Then I'd try to fill in intelligently the answers to some of these questions. Then I'd try to make some extra copies. By the time I had filled in five or six forms I'd have to get a new stock of pencils. After some hours I'd go back to the office.

"Report on the *Seagull*, sir," I'd say to the commanding officer."

"What is the *Seagull*?"

"She's the vessel I was supposed to report on this morning."

He'd punch a buzzer and a clerk would come in.

"Have you any record of the *Seagull?*"

The clerk would go out and get two other clerks and they would go through three or four files and come back and say: "The *Seagull* is in San Francisco, sir."

Then I'd have to get up and tell him that the *Seagull* was down at the end of the dock and I had just been making an inspection of her.

Then the commanding officer would ring another buzzer and another officer would come in.

"Correct your records on ships present," would command the commanding officer.

"Aye, aye, sir," would say the new officer and swallow a couple of times to give him a chance to collect an alibi. Then he'd clear his throat and ask if he couldn't bring in Captain So-and-so.

I won't go into more details but by the time I had got warmed up to the thing and convinced them that the *Seagull* was right outside the office instead of over in San Francisco there would be five or six officers and an office full of clerks and enough correspondence to stoke a sealer's furnace for twenty-four hours.

After some weeks of this sort of thing I wasn't quite so scared of generals and colonels as I had been before, especially because I found that underneath their uniform they had hearts like other men. I think I never got over the first time I discovered that a general had a sense of humour.

One morning I was on a tug going upriver. I had been

down the bay trying her out for duty overseas. I guess I felt a little flip for things having run so well and made the mistake of cutting in too close to a float ahead of me. I told my helmsman to take her out a bit. He put the wheel over in a direction that on an ocean-going vessel would have taken her in even closer. I didn't realize that the helm connections were reversed on the little ship.

Being a man of action I didn't wait to argue with the fellow but grabbed the wheel myself and hove her over hard—still in the *wrong direction*. The first thing I knew we took up against the float, my stem cutting deep into the other fellow's hull. We got clear but things were a mess. And the tug filled up rapidly. She didn't sink but we got her into the dock with the help of another tug.

I tell you I was scared. This meant I had to go up on the carpet before a colonel and maybe a general. It turned out to be a colonel; but that was almost as bad.

The colonel's orderly told me to come in the office. I went in and stood before Colonel McCabe who was in charge of one section of marine operations. He was not a tall man but he had a severe look. He looked at me hard for a minute or two before he said anything.

I stood right in front of his desk with my heels together. In the last forty years, my heels haven't been jammed up to one another many times. But they certainly were that morning. Pretty soon he said:

"How did this happen, Captain Bartlett?"

I didn't make any bones about it. I told him the story.

"Colonel, I was wrong. I shouldn't have grabbed the wheel."

He sort of grunted and looked just as severe as ever. "All right," he said. "We'll take the matter up later." I went out. I wasn't sure whether it meant jail or hanging at the yardarm. But I figured that this country needed good seafaring men so that I had a chance.

The trouble was, would they think I was a seafaring man after ramming a float right out in broad daylight? Apparently they did though; because I never heard anything more about it—not a word. Can you beat that?

I slaved along for several months after this and must say I was getting pretty sick of docks and old dirty ships out of commission. One day I was sent for and told I had to make a shift. It seemed that there was a tug up in the St. Lawrence River. If you remember, that winter was a terrible one. This tug had got jammed in the ice. She was needed in France because she was a wrecker. The Navy Department was casting about for somebody to bring her out. They hit on me.

The only trouble was I was a soldier at the time. You see I was still working with the army. But they soon fixed that by taking me over to another set of officers and shifting me from the army into the navy. (Sort of Act 2 stuff as I said in the beginning.)

It was a quick shift. At four o'clock I was a soldier. At eight o'clock I was a sailor, a naval officer on my way north again. As I sat in the train headed in my old direction I thought how nice it would be if I had time to get a uniform with gold stripes and everything and duck over home and see the folks. But there was no time for that. We were at war.

This was January. Navigation had closed this winter in the St. Lawrence in the late fall. This was almost unheard of. But then Hampton Roads froze over, that year which was like having a snowstorm in Havana.

The job on the tug was uneventful. It was a hard struggle to get her out but we finally made clear. What helped me was my years of sealing in these waters. I knew the prevailing wind at the time had jammed the ice down on the lee shore, so I made up to the northward and worked east until we reached clear water. In a week we were down in Boston.

Now that I was squared away as a naval officer I took up a whole new circle of associations. That "constable feeling" still held somewhat. I had learned about generals and colonels, but these fellows in blue uniforms with gold stripes discouraged me a little bit. I soon found that they too were human.

One thing that impressed me about the Navy crowd and the Army as well was their honesty. I don't mean they just weren't pickpockets or something like that. I mean that they were honest about the small things which a man sometimes finds himself slipping into without really meaning it. I have seen a Navy man on a bridge make a mistake and not have any reason especially for telling what he had done. But it was a matter of tradition, it seemed, not to try to hide behind any sort of alibi. I tell you that makes a big difference when you are trying to work with people.

I never stuck a bayonet into anybody. And I didn't shoot any torpedoes or fourteen-inch guns at the enemy fleet. In a way I am sorry to say I was not one of the thousands of brave Newfoundlanders who went over and died in the trenches. But I did my best. And I must say I saw a good deal of fighting without going into any trench.

I just want to give you a little picture of the warfare that came my way. Sometimes I wished I was under rifle fire instead of under tongue fire. And it would have been far simpler to have stood up and fought a man right out and out than to have struggled around in a nightmarish maze of complications, half of which there wasn't a living man knew all about.

When my friends who were soldiers start telling about the battle of San Mihiel I feel like telling them about the battle of the *Buford*. This battle isn't in any of the official archives; but it was a grand fight just the same and I wouldn't be surprised if we used more ammunition in it than they did in some of the actions on the western front.

The *Buford* was a transport. She was tied up over in Hoboken when she got orders to load up with ammunition labelled for Manila. I knew she was going because it was my job to know what vessels were in use. But you could have knocked me over with a feather when an orderly came out one day and handed me orders as commanding officer of the *Buford*. That was the opening gun of the battle.

I went aboard her. She lay at the army base with a cargo of everything from rifle cartridges to TNT. I was used to black powder in my ice work in the Newfoundland pack. But I had never got chummy with dynamite before and it was a new feeling to have a whole shipload of it between decks. The first couple of times I lit my pipe I sort of looked around when I struck the match to see if anything had gone off yet.

The first couple of days nothing more happened except a steady stream of letters and reports and telegrams and other usual details of red tape. Then the full action broke out. It seemed that some congressman got up in Washington and said he thought Japan wouldn't like our sending ammunition out across the Pacific. I guess the rest of the orators were a little tired of talking about Europe because they all took a hand and within twenty-four hours there was a fine row in progress. As a result, before I could get under way, they decided not to send the ship and had put me back in Hoboken. This was discouraging because I had hoped I was headed for the open sea.

Then somebody wrote a lot of letters and telegrams and before I knew it they had another man on the *Buford* and took her down to Norfolk where she was anchored in the open roadstead out in Lynnhaven Bay near Cape Charles. I mention this because it has a bearing on what comes next.

Then that orderly came along again and handed me another set of orders. I had to go to Philadelphia and take command of four transports that had just been built and were to go into commission. On Christmas Eve I had one of them out in the Delaware River trying her out. It was the *Chaumont*. We got back all right. I was all set to go below and shift for a quick run to New York where I had plans for spending a fine Christmas. Leave of absence had been granted me and the way was clear for a little rest after some strenuous months. But the enemy winged me with another set of orders.

"Report aboard the *Buford*, Lynnhaven Bay, Virginia, and take command," or words to that effect was the way the letter read.

This was a nice mess. I didn't have any gear and my base was still in New York. And here I was with a strong round turn of red tape about my neck hauling me southward.

The next few hours were pretty confused, but I managed to collect some clothes and with the help of Colonel Jackson, one of the finest men I ever met, I got away for Lynnhaven.

Then began the hand-to-hand fighting. Up to now there was so much smoke, so to speak that I wasn't quite sure where I stood. But when I got aboard the *Buford* I discovered that I had to take a definite part in the action. The ship was lying there crammed with explosives and orders to get away. The captain I was relieving said she couldn't go because her ventilation decks was not sufficient to make it safe to have explosives down there. This was a good basis for an argument. The trouble was we were lying right out there in the open in mid-winter with our holding gear snarled up and a northeaster coming on. In the old days, that fellow and I could have had it out properly. But with radio on board we were at the mercy of our masters up in Washington. I finally got word through that I was satisfied with the ventilation (which I was, not having carried dynamite around much in my life) and asked permission to leave. The answer came back for us to go and we went.

The straw that nearly broke the camel's back was a big barge they made us tow down. About the nastiest job I know is to tow a barge in the open sea at any time, but to have a light barge in winter weather tagging along after you is not so good. I could write a book about that trip. But we finally got her in Panama by the grace of Providence and I reported to the authorities.

I have never seen a man with leprosy pass through a crowd. But if I did it would be a good deal like the *Buford* going through the Panama Canal. They treated us just as if we had some loathsome disease.

They couldn't get us through quick enough. That reminded me again of the dynamite between decks, which our barge troubles had been making me forget.

On the western side we squared away for Honolulu and got in several weeks later. There I found orders for me to shift my cargo to another vessel and return. The commanding general took advantage of my brief stay there to show me around. By that time I had lost my fear of generals and really began to like them. This one was unusually nice.

I started out by calling this the battle of the *Buford*. As I read what I have written I realize it doesn't sound very bloody. But when I think back over the mass of radios and letters and reports, over the rows and squabbles and changes of plans, over the rumours and disputes, over the fact that I was working for both the Army and the Navy at the same time, and not forgetting that I was walking on some thousands of tons of high explosives through it all, I can say with all honesty that I feel that my coming through unscathed is almost as miraculous as the experience of a man who went over the top in heavy fire and lived to tell the tale.

The rest of my naval service was about the same, only more so. I commanded the *Madawaska* after I got back to San Francisco. I took her around to New York and got rammed in a fog on the way. I had the *Cantigny* and the

Somme and the *Eldena* in succession. I carried all kinds of things to all kinds of places. Towards the end I got so I could sit down and look through a basketful of official letters without getting mad. I even got so I could fill out reports with the best of them. The war may have left its mark on me; but sometimes I think it was an ink mark.

CHAPTER XXI

ALASKAN ADVENTURES

During the fall of 1923, I had several talks with Colonel E. Lester Jones re my Polar drift proposition. One day in Washington I saw the *Shenandoah* flying over the city. It then occurred to me, why not have her fly over the Polar Sea and decide if land is or is not there? The more I thought about it the more I was convinced that it could be done and it should be done by the navy.

So I got Colonel Jones to go with me to the Secretary, Mr. Denby. The secretary immediately saw the possibilities and said he would see the President, which he did.

Things began to move rapidly. Before I knew it I was up in a closed room with a lot of captains and admirals. We gathered around a table covered with charts and records of ships that had been in the Arctic. It was very impressive, but I cannot say I like it. I had been too much in the north to be willing to plan for an expedition by studying out of books. The trouble is the Arctic isn't anything like the books after you get there.

Anyway, we worked hard for many days. We averaged up all the barometer readings and the forces and directions of the winds around Point Barrow, Alaska, for the last fifty years. Engineers figured out how high a mast would have to be and how strong to hold the *Shenandoah* once she got to Nome.

The purpose of the expedition wasn't quite clear to me. It seemed that the people who thought the Navy should have dirigibles wanted to prove their usefulness. Also a good deal of stress was laid on the fact that one million square miles north of Alaska were still unexplored. If land were discovered in that big space it might prove a sort of halfway station between Europe and Asia after the trans-polar route came in.

I felt overawed at the extravagance of the whole plan. I don't mean extravagance from a money point of view. It would have cost plenty—probably $500,000. But I mean in making such a long trip from Lakehurst to San Francisco, Nome, North Pole, Spitzbergen, and down to London, in an airship that hardly got out of its own backyard yet. But I was all for being shown; and I believe to this day the Navy could have done it if they had ever got started.

The trouble was they never got started. We sent in a report pretty nearly as thick as the Bible and comparing favourably in interest with the book. But nothing ever came of it. Congress decided it didn't want to hold the bag; and Mr. Coolidge very properly refused to order the trip without the sanction of Congress.

So everything was postponed. But good came out of the party for me. The National Geographic Society in Washington, D.C., decided to send me up as a one-man expedition that spring and summer. They wanted me to collect information along the Alaskan air expedition which would lead to a successful air expedition next year. The Society published a bulletin which read in part as follows:

Will Study Aircraft Bases.

Captain Bartlett will study especially the locations available in Alaska for bases of operations for aircraft which would fly a zigzag course over the million-square-mile area between Point Barrow and the North Pole—which area is wholly unexplored. He will report upon harbour facilities for supply ships, possible landing places for various types of craft between Nome and Point Barrow, the terrain across country and along the coast between these points, and upon air and water temperature, wind and sea surface conditions.

"The Navy Department has extended Captain Bartlett every cooperation in his work, which will be of great value as a basis for explorations such as those proposed when the *Shenandoah*'s North Pole trip was planned.

It was good to be working for Gilbert Grosvenor again. He and his great Geographical Society had, for years, helped Arctic exploration; and when Peary was suffering at the hands and tongues of congress, it was the Society's staunch support that made any sort of justice possible.

Right away I began to collect instruments and gear for gathering as much scientific information as I could. The Navy let me have anemometer, barograph, thermograph, and other instruments. Through the Bureau of Fisheries I secured nets and trawls for collecting animals from the bottom of the sea. From the Department of Agriculture I got a flower press and blotters. The Coast Geodetic Survey let me have instruments for getting water samples, deep sea

271

thermometers, tide pole lines and a gauge. Altogether, I felt pretty important when I joined the revenue cutter *Bear* at San Francisco on the afternoon of April 24. We sailed on May 3.

The old *Bear* was one of the relief squadron that saved Greely's party in 1884 at Cape Sabine. Until recently each year she went north to Point Barrow, Alaska, carrying supplies, food, and mail to the isolated white families and natives in that far corner of the world.

Captain Cochrane of the *Bear* was one of the finest men I ever knew. I suppose it sounds egotistical but one reason I admired him was because he reminded me a good deal of myself. He liked nautical things. He loved a smart ship with clean sailors and clean decks aboard her. He wanted work done and finished once it was started. Some said he was a martinet. But I noticed those who said it were lazy loafers every time.

He was a big man with ruddy cheeks and white hair. He had a penetrating eye that stood him in good stead. When he went north each year all the unsettled quarrels that had started during the long dark winter were laid before Captain Cochrane for his opinion. His opinion carried enormous weight. When both sides had said their say he used to fix first one and then the other party with his hard sharp eye. The party that quailed was usually the guilty or unjust party. In this simple way he could usually decide the case right off the bat. His word was law. He was admired and respected by such men as Bishop Rowe, my friend Jim Ross, and many other of the old-timers, in the north. Certainly Captain Cochrane deserves enormous credit for the years and years of service he has put in helping the wretched dwellers of our Alaska territory and carrying help to whalers imprisoned in the ice. He has a fine wife; but out of over thirty years he hasn't spent more than two or three with her. *That's the trouble with being a seafaring man and married at one and the same time.*

When we cast off our decks were piled high. Every available space below was filled with coal, mailbags and provisions for a six months' cruise. On the topside were boxes of fruit, eggs, lettuce, tomatoes, potatoes, gasoline and more coal. In the mailbags were all the spring styles for the ladies and gentlemen of icebound Nome and cities north.

As we steamed out to sea, I opened a package that had been handed me just before we got up anchor. It was marked "Coffee." I supposed somebody had sent me an advertising sample. Imagine my surprise when it turned out to contain a fine coffee pot with a pleasing note from a young lady. *Moral: always open a package.*

One of the things that had pleased me about this expedition was the fact that we didn't have any dogs or whale meat aboard. Those two things were always tough shipmates, on the *Roosevelt.* But I was wrong. We hadn't got out of the Golden Gate before I heard a terrible dogfight going on in the waist of the ship. It turned out to be between an Irish terrier called "Paddy" belonging to the crew, and a pure white sheepdog named "Laddie" belonging to the captain. From then on "Paddy" and "Laddie" fought on an average of five or six times a day.

Another thing that was exciting about this expedition was that we had a bathtub. I wasn't used to taking a bath very often north of the Arctic Circle. Now I thought I could have one when I wanted it. But as soon as the captain's dog emerged from his first fight covered with blood and coal dust the steward took him down and put him in the tub. It turned out that "Laddie" had first claim on it.

The trip north was pretty tame compared with some of the hard voyages I have made. As a sample let me quote from my diary:

> May 17th. Fine and clear. Washed the pigs; these were for my friend Mr. Ross of Nome. Set jig, forestaysail and mainsail. Found stowaway cat in hold. To my surprise received wireless from captain of the *Roosevelt* on her way north: "Your old ship making progress to north and steaming ten knots. Signed *Roosevelt.*" Right away I sent an answer back: "That's faster than I ever saw her go. Signed Bartlett." Five dogfights today.

A few days later my scientific work had a setback. There was a quartermaster named Orme who kept his bright-work polish in a whisky bottle. The captain happened to see this and gave him hell. He said to the sailor: "It's all right to drink whisky but not to see or show it." Before Orme could remonstrate, the skipper made him throw the bottle overboard.

I discovered that Orme cut out little ships from soft wood and fastened them in empty whisky bottles by means of sealing wax. He got five dollars for such trinkets. After the captain's impulsive action one of my bottles of formaldehyde, on which I depended for preserving my specimens, disappeared. Now I guess it is on someone's mantelpiece with a ship model inside fastened with sealing wax. Little annoyances like that gradually made me sympathize with real scientists.

As we passed the northern limits of the United States and entered Alaskan waters the sky became overcast and fog increased. Winds were raw and we often had snow flurries. It took me back to my old days in Baffin Bay.

We had a passenger on board from Unalaska Island, a Mr. Larsen.

"Why don't you go into the fox business?" he asked me one day.

"Is there money in it?" said I.

"There's lots of money in it. You could raise from 150 to 200 blue foxes a year and get an average of $70 to $125 a skin."

Maybe if I ever got married and settled down this will be a good way to pass my declining years. I made a note of it.

In Unimak Pass we fell in with the *Haida*, a small vessel that had been chartered by the U. S. Army to stand by for the round-the-world fliers. Her deck was covered with gasoline drums in the centre of which stood a spare airplane. She told us the fliers had had a harder time up north here than people realized. Bitter cold, high winds, snow and all that. The Aleutian Islands are a cheerless group, poorly mapped. Everything is covered with fog and snow lies on them like a blanket clear to the high-water mark.

I went ashore at Unalaska for a look around. It is a depressing sort of town: squalid, rambling and dark in all its hues.

The High Priest's residence needed paint badly. The big wooden house, the Jess Lee Home for Orphans, that stands on a hill, is another building that ought to have some money spent on it. I walked through the town to the little cemetery beyond. Here are buried many of the Russians who came over centuries ago. Curious inscriptions mark many of the gravestones.

On my way back I visited my friend Nick Bolashin who has lived in Unalaska for twenty-five years. He married a teacher from Carlisle Indian College, a very fine lady. He told me the latest news:

"Last winter it blew a living gale, Captain, off and on for two moons. The children couldn't go to school for several weeks. When we had influenza people died so fast we took them to the cemetery in cartloads. When we put them in a common trench I marked a lot of them so we would know where friends and relatives were buried."

Remembering the advice I had had, I asked him about raising foxes. He has a fox farm on one of the outer islands.

"They are doing fine," he said. "I get good money for the skins. Why don't you come up here and start a fox farm?"

I think if a few more of them had asked me about it I should have been raising foxes by this time instead of wasting my good energy writing a book.

On May 31, we ran out to the open sea and headed north to pass fifteen miles to the westward of Nunivak Island. We had had a lot of rain but little wind. I don't know which was worse, the rain or the fog. Here the land was desolate and dark.

Here is another typical entry out of my diary. It shows some more of my troubles pretending to be a scientist:

May 31st. Begins with rain. Wind light, northwest. Maximum and minimum thermometers have bubbles. Had to broach two more. Why in hell I should get such poor instruments from the Navy Department is hard to understand. Clock mechanism of the thermograph is rusty. Have to take it apart and oil it. Sunset calm and small sea. Fog.

We had some more passengers now. There were fifteen Eskimo men, woman and children. Also there was a "squaw man"; that is, a white man who has married a native. The marshal told me he had been in jail several times and would not support his children. So the marshal got Captain Cochrane to take the whole kit and caboodle north into the reindeer country where the loafer might find employment and not be a charge on the government. This squaw man and his love for the ladies was offset by an Eskimo maid aboard who, the marshal said, was too fond of the sailors. All this gave Mr. Rhineberg, our executive officer, much concern. Finally, he had curfew rung for the squaw man and the Eskimo girl and appointed an old Eskimo woman to be chaperone for the latter. This scandal complicated shiplife on the *Bear* very much and was just one more thing to interfere with my scientific work.

By June 4, we were in the ice. As this was to be expected, we were not discouraged. But as we went on and the ice got thicker and no offshore wind came to clear it out, the captain began to get worried.

By June 6, the ice was not only heavy, but in very large sheets. Also there was plenty of fog. I occupied my time heaving my trawl and getting specimens of seals.

As I soon noticed that no one ate the seal meat I went to the captain and said: "Isn't it strange that our Eskimos are not faring on seal when we have two carcasses already in the rigging?"

"Why should they?" he asked. "We have plenty of beans and bread and 'Canned Willie' on board."

This made me boil over. "Because it's the kind of meat their forebears ate! And it's the kind of meat I have been eating all my life down the Labrador. It's fine meat, too!"

"All right," said the captain, "we'll have some seal meat for dinner."

So he got one of the old Eskimo women to go into the galley and cook up a fine mess of seal.

I am sorry to say that when it came on the table I was the only one who ate it. I laid down enough for three people.

Later on the same day Captain Cochrane came to me and said:

"My dog's ill."

"That's too bad," said I.

"It's all your fault."

"Why is it my fault?"

"Because he got hold of some of that dammed seal meat and he can't digest it."

"Well, that's funny," said I, "it didn't bother me."

Captain Cochrane got all purplish in the face and didn't say anything for a minute. Then he came out all in a bunch with: "Well, you have a cast-iron stomach,

Bartlett, and besides that I think you are a squaw man!"
Just the kind of trivial row that breaks up an Arctic expedition!

I'd like to add that I would rather be able to eat seal
meat than the richest plumduff that was ever put together.
When the captain cooled off I told him so.

After the seal meat episode sort of died away I asked
Captain Cochrane one day why he never had any duff.

"Down where I come from," I told him, "we tell the
day by the duff. We have plumduff every Sunday, Tuesday,
and Thursday. In fact I don't think a windjammer ever
knows what day it is except by this event."

Captain Cochrane laughed and said, "All right,
Bartlett, we'll have duff tomorrow."

The next day came on the table a marvellous creation.
Unfortunately it was a surprise, as I had thought we were
going to have some heavy crullers or something. So I had
loaded up and now couldn't eat any duff. In order not to
hurt the steward's feelings, Captain Cochrane ate two dish-
es himself and one of mine.

I didn't tell him so, but I preferred my seal meat to his
duff. The only audible comment came from him when he
mumbled: "There's no pleasing our Eskimo palate."

One day the mess cook said he was going to have snails
for dinner. I walked the deck all afternoon thinking about
what he said. It was the first time in my life I ever felt like
being seasick. I went to my spud-locker where I kept my
scientific specimens and looked at the bugs floating around
in formaldehyde solution. It unnerved me to think I had to
sit down to the table that night with something like them. I

had heard of people eating snails but I never dreamed I would have to face one on a plate.

Imagine my surprise when the snails turned out to be only a kind of cruller.

All through June and into July we struggled with the ice. I got more and more depressed. I had counted on spending some time at Point Barrow. Not only did I want again to see my old friends whom I had made on the *Karluk* voyage, but it was important that I look over the beach there for details that would help the Navy establish a landing field.

Ice smashed two blades off our propeller. It cracked a seam on our port side and also wrenched the rudder. The poor old *Bear* was having a rough time.

Towards the end of June we at last had some sunshine and calm weather, both favourable for dirigible work. By this time the captain and I had got pretty well talked out. He had a lot of records for his Victrola that he was taking north. But they seemed punk to me as most of them were jazz. Between these records and my anxiety to get further north I was nervous as an old maid. The cool weather soothed me a lot.

On the day after the Fourth of July all hands had a great laugh at me. As I had now been collecting scientific specimens for about six weeks, I was getting to know the names of a lot of things that take about two swallows and a snort to say. This morning I was looking over the taffrail when I saw something resembling a fish about four or five feet under water. It moved slowly and mysteriously in my direction. As I was afraid I should lose the strange specimen, or that it would pass under the bottom of the ship, I kept my eye nailed on it and yelled hard for one of the sailors to let me have a boathook. Meanwhile I jumped out into our whale boat hanging in the davits. With a grapnel I finally snagged my new specimen of animal.

As a result of my cries nearly everybody on board had gathered around to see me haul it up. With great effort I got it to the surface. Then there was a loud cheer. *I had hooked the intestines of one of our pigs which the butcher had just thrown over from the other side of the ship.*

Things began rapidly to get more and more uncomfortable. We had more dogfights and more fog and more ice. We lost another propeller blade. Baffled, we gave up, and at three p.m. on July 16, we sailed into Nome Harbour. The expedition was off. Ice had prevented us from going north. We had rain and fresh winds right up to July 24, when the captain finally decided that he would have to go south. By long walks ashore I gathered sufficient data for a dirigible station in this neighbourhood. The Point Barrow data will have to be collected by someone else. (Amundsen later flew to Teller, Alaska, southwest of Barrow.)

Just before we left Bishop Rowe came in. He was going on north in the *Boxer*, a little hermaphrodite brig. The thing I liked about Bishop Rowe was that he was such a sincere man. He was sincere in his love for the north as well as in his love for humanity. I should like to make a sledge journey with him someday. I believe he would stack up with the best of them.

On August 30, I got back to San Francisco. My films and flowers I expressed to the National Geographic Society at Washington. Then, with a somewhat heavy heart, I went over to Norton Lilly's office to get a bill of lading for my fish specimens. The People's Express brought it over to the dock and took my gear to the station. I travelled east alone, depressed and full of doubt about the future. On September 10, I reached Washington, D.C., and reported to the National Geographic Society that I had come back. They stood up well under the shock.

CHAPTER XXII

NORTH AGAIN!

In July 1926, we nosed into North Star Bay, up in North
Greenland, on the far side of Cape York. That was on my
two-masted schooner, the *Morrissey*, north that summer for
the American Museum Greenland Expedition, with my
friend George Palmer Putnam as leader.

It was about two o'clock in the morning, a fine bright
sunlit morning, too, when we pushed through the bay, ice
choking the upper end of the bight just outside the big
headland that marks the location of the trading station,
Thule, like a monument.

The folks ashore put out in a launch, dragging it across
the ice until they found a lead of open water. Then in a few
moments Neilson, the Danish trader, and his gang of
Eskimos were aboard. Neilson was in charge there for Dr.
Knud Rasmussen, the great Danish explorer and authority
on Eskimos, who conducts this trading station—the most
northerly in the world—for the benefit of the Smith Sound
tribe of Eskimos.

As a favour to Rasmussen we had brought up a lot of
provisions for the station, and Neilson was mighty glad to see
us. In fact he had been there six years running. He hadn't

seen a white man for fourteen months. I remember the way he sank his teeth into an apple that we gave him; the first apple he had seen in nearly seven years.

Then through one of our crowd, Carl Dunrud, the cowboy who spoke Danish, they began asking us questions. One of the first was, "Is anyone going to try the North Pole this year?" That was in July, mind you. And so we were able to tell him about Byrd and Amundsen flying over the Pole in the plane and the dirigible only a few months before. In a way they had been flying pretty nearly over Thule itself, but these people, absolutely shut off from the world, of course knew nothing at all about it.

And a great year 1926 was for aviation. Especially aviation in the Arctic. Of course in a way it made me sort of heartsick, because so many years I had had my mind set on getting the Navy Department to send the *Shenandoah* over the Pole; I have told something of that before. But the Navy couldn't see it; so, after all, it was the Norwegians and the Italians who got the dirigible there first. Anyway, it was Dick Byrd who actually won out in his heavier-than-air machine, even though a lot of so-called experts had predicted it was utterly impossible to use one in the Arctic.

Just a year before, in 1925, Byrd had been up in this same North Greenland region doing a lot of experimental flying out of Etah. It was what he learned then, largely, that convinced him the polar hop was feasible. And from that time on he went right ahead making his plans, which result-ed in his magnificent flight from Spitzbergen to the Pole and back, and so beautifully showed up those who had kept saying right up until the last moment that he couldn't possibly do it. A brave man, Byrd, and a grand navigator and explorer.

Of course, our own was just a summer expedition. It didn't have any large pretensions. But I must say it got away pretty well, at that. We went for the American Museum of Natural History, primarily to get specimens for exhibition in the new Hall of Ocean Life, and, by great luck, we brought back everything we went after, which is more than many a more elaborate expedition can say.

We started out from New York in mid-June. The *Morrissey* had been refitted with a fine standard diesel engine, excellent gear, radio outfit, and all the rest of it. Nothing fancy or extravagant. Just a good sensible seamanly outfit, not for looks or comfort, but for service.

In all, the little vessel covered about 8,500 miles in that long summer. I suppose we drove her a bit. Anyway, it's not hard to cover a lot of ground when you have twenty-four hours of daylight. And on top of that, we struck a grand summer—about the best weather that there has been in North Greenland perhaps for fifty years.

Thanks to the amazing ice conditions, we hung up a record or two. For instance, we actually crossed Melville Bay three times; which I don't think has ever been done before in a single season.

Up in Upernivik, we picked up Dr. Knud Rasmussen who came over from Denmark to meet us. That is, we picked him up there after we had first gone on to North Greenland and pretty nearly lost the *Morrissey* when she got stuck on a rock. We had to bring her back from

Northumberland Island to Upernivik, where she was repaired largely thanks to the generous help of the Danes.

We got Dr. Rasmussen and went back to his friends, the Eskimos of the Smith Sound tribe—the fine people who had worked with Peary so splendidly in years gone by, and so many of whom I knew intimately.

Indeed, the boys on board called it an "Old Home Week" for me! It actually did seem like getting home. It made me young again to visit the places and the people so bright in my memories of the days on the *Roosevelt*. We were in close to Redcliff where Marie Peary was born. Among the Eskimos who visited and worked with us were a lot of old Peary men, fine chaps like Kudlooktoo, Pooadloona, Metak, Sipsu, Inyoughitog. It made me sit up a bit to find them with grown-up sons and daughters. You see I hadn't been up there for years.

One feature of that *Morrissey* expedition was especially pleasant. I mean finding my old Eskimo friends in the Smith Sound tribe in such good shape.

It seems to me the Danes have done a fine job in taking care of North Greenland, and in the successful handling of the problem Knud Rasmussen had had a large hand.

The Smith Sound tribe, you know, is about the most isolated and primitive people in the world. There are, perhaps, 250 of them. They are practically shut off from South Greenland, and any access to the outer world, by Melville Bay. They live a life absolutely remote and entirely their own. Their centre of population is only about 750 miles from the North Pole. They live there, right in the shadow of the Pole, and pretty much as they existed centuries ago.

Fifty years ago these Eskimos lived literally in a stone age. Their one food was the meat which they killed. That, practically, is still true. But before the coming of the white man, their hunting implements were made entirely of bone and ivory and flint, with occasionally arrowheads and harpoon points beaten out of the meteorites. They had no wood whatsoever. Nothing but the stone, together with the bone and ivory of the animals they killed.

And they prospered. Certainly they were happy. Indeed, by and large, I think they are still far happier than the average run of so-called civilized people in the softer environments of the south.

I have said things have changed for them. Chiefly that is because in the last thirty years or so their hunting has been made easier. Rifles have replaced the bows and arrows. They have had wood for their kayaks, harpoon handles and the like.

In a way it was a blessing, I suppose. But not an unmixed blessing. For as killing became easier, they have killed, probably, too much. Of course, Eskimos are simple-minded people, pretty well without forethought. The word "conservation" means nothing to them. So they have gone ahead, and with sheer waste have cleaned out their game pretty well. At least, it seems to me to be getting cleaned out. It's pretty pathetic.

There is about one polar bear where there used to be ten or twenty, even in my time. Of course, the muskox are about all gone. Seal, I imagine, hold out well. But I think that the walrus and narwhal are much scarcer than they used to be. The results of that are inevitable.

Just last summer we saw some startling examples of the falling off in bird life. And for comparative statistics in this sort of thing it is easy enough to check up with the records of the old whalers and explorers. It is only guesswork, of course, but I would hazard that Duck Islands, there to the south of Melville Bay, haven't one-fiftieth of the eider ducks which they supported fifty years ago. That is largely because the Eskimos come over from the mainland in June and gather up all the eggs.

What comes next for these northern Eskimos is hard to say. It is not like our own country where the carrying off of game is followed by the development of agriculture. There can be nothing in that territory but game. No food supply but meat.

Already I found Dr. Rasmussen was working on the importation of reindeer hides from Alaska to be used for clothing and bedding, in place of the bear and muskox skins no longer available. Ultimately, perhaps reindeer will be imported and developed in North Greenland, much as they have been in Alaska. That is a possible solution of the food and clothing problem.

It's not only the ducks and the game animals of the Eskimos that have been disappearing from the northern waters. More important, from the standpoint of everyday economics, has been the extermination of whales. And nowhere perhaps in the north do you get a better realization of the difference between today and yesterday than up there at the Duck Islands, in north Baffin Bay, where the real Arctic begins.

In a manner of speaking, that was the centre of old-time whaling, and often the stopping place, too, of polar expeditions. Once back in 1888 Admiral Peary visited the Islands. I remember the admiral told me that his skipper of those days, Captain Jackman, and he each buried a fifty cent piece in a cairn with their records. Just last summer I climbed the hill, and found the cairn all right, but the records and fifty cent pieces were gone.

In the golden days of the Duck Islands, a fleet of whalers made the islets their regular headquarters. Great names in Arctic history, south as well as north, are those of the whaling visitors of the last century. There was the *Terra Nova*, wrecked off Franz Joseph Land, and the *Falcon* in which Uncle Harry Bartlett was later lost. I have told you the *Windward* was given to Peary by Lord Northcliffe. Well, in the old days, she whaled in these waters too. The *Aurora*, Mawson's famous Antarctic vessel, Fiala's *Eskimo*, and the old *Bear* too, lately a coast guard vessel on Bering Sea patrol.

They reckoned that in the old days upward of 2,000 men sometimes were on and around the Islands. Today there are only a few piles of stones, and a dismal bleak grayness.

We found one broken headboard. On it was written, "William Stewart, A.B., 24, S.S. *Triune* of Dundee, June 11, 1886."

The old Scotch ship *Triune* was one of the last of them. And likely this lad was about the last of the Scotch whalers to be buried there.

That lonely, stony grave on that lonely rocky island marked the end of the colourful story of those brave days which went before. And after all, if your job and your joy is to go down to the sea in ships, wouldn't a man rather relish putting into the final harbour at some such clean faraway place like that?

We struck a submerged reef off Northumberland Island and had a rough time. We had to put all our cargo on the beach and nearly lost the ship. Finally at high tide we got her off.

This kept us from going on to Etah. We went back across the ice-filled waters of Melville Bay into Upernivik. There we found a Danish vessel that had a diving suit aboard. The Danes loaned us the diver and I used the suit myself. We soon found that, though damaged, the old *Morrissey* was good for the trip home. We took her back across Melville Bay, a record for any ship—three crossings in a season. After a few weeks with the Eskimos we went on across to Jones Sound, got some bears and then came home down the Labrador.

CHAPTER XXIII

THE SEA IS MADE OF MOTHERS' TEARS

"*The Sea is made of mothers' tears*," is an old Newfoundland proverb.

As a matter of fact in my nearly forty years the most terrible thing I've encountered in all my hard voyages has not been fire or shipwreck, gale or blizzard or starvation. It has been the horrible sense of helpless grief that comes when men sail away and never come back.

If you know your husband or father or brother is dead, you can bear the loss. But if you picture him year in year out dying by inches on some desert island or wandering with lost memory on some distant shore, a bitter anguish haunts you night and day.

From this cause I have seen aged men die; gay young wives grow old and grim; mothers weep their hearts out until the grave relieves their despair; and both sisters and brothers turn cold shoulders to a happy world in the awful thrall of a never-ending hope.

A pretty terrible thing happened in the fall of 1890. I was just a boy. Several of us were digging a cave down at the end of the street on which I lived. We stopped our labours one afternoon to go down and see a big schooner, the

Treasurer, sail out of Brigus. She was going to Sydney for coal. The father of one of the boys commanded her. The father of another boy was first mate. A brother of another boy was one of her hands. It was a nice family party that gathered on the dock to wave goodbye.

"Gee, I wish I were going," said one of the boys. "Me too," said another.

I loved the sea and I wanted to spend my life on it.

But I remember a queer feeling that came over me while I was listening to those boys talk. I had a premonition that I should die were I to have gone on the voyage. I felt it so strongly that I turned away.

"Come on," said I, "let's go back to the cave."

Two weeks later the cave was finished. We sat around in it talking in low tones about the *Treasurer*. The schooner had not been heard from since the day she left.

"I bet my father comes back all right," boasted the son of the skipper. "My brother would never let his ship go down!" declared the other boy. But his lips closed tight after the words came out.

Two weeks later the mothers of those boys gathered in our front parlour. I remember going and peeping in. Both women were sobbing. My mother was trying to comfort them. There was still no news of the *Treasurer*. There hasn't been to this day.

Her ballast shifted and she rolled over, was the way my father explained it. That's what the U.S. Navy thinks happened to the USS *Cyclops*.

Then there was a strange case of the *Lion*. She was an auxiliary steam sealer. One pleasant January evening she left St. John's with passengers, mails, and a full cargo of sealing supplies for Trinity about sixty miles north.

For three days and nights fine, clear weather prevailed at St. John's. There was a good moon every night. Ships came and went as ships always did. There was no indication of any strange tidal wave, local hurricane, or ice pack in the vicinity. In short it was one of those brief placid trips when the seafaring man can enjoy life. But in those three days the *Lion* disappeared and was never heard from again.

Did she strike an isolated berg? Was there mutiny? And if mutiny did the rebels seize her and take her into distant waters only to be lost themselves? There are no answers to these questions as yet, and there probably never will be.

When the *Lion* did not turn up at Trinity there was anxiety among the families of her human freight. Her sister ship the *Tiger* left a few hours afterward. She arrived at Trinity all right.

Two weeks later a strange thing happened. A man rushed into the shipping office and signalled his friend to come out.

"Do you know what happened to the *Lion?*" he whispered hoarsely.

His friend shook his head. Running the facts over his fingers he said: "It couldn't have been ice. The old man knew too much about it. It couldn't have been mutiny. The gang wasn't that kind."

"No," went on the excited informer, "it was none of them. The *Lion* rammed the *Tiger*. She is now en route to another harbour to be patched up. She will be back in a week. Great news, ain't it?"

"Great!" almost sobbed the other. Men and women wept for joy and hugged one another. But, alas, the *Lion* never came back. And when the *Tiger* showed up it was found that the rumours were wholly unfounded.

It's that sort of thing that makes you suffer. Any Newfoundlander could tell a score of stories of wrecks and mysteries of the sealing ground, but they will not talk of them. The stories come too close to home. Too many men—too many friends—too many fathers and brothers involved.

In April 1914, the *Southern Cross*, a fine steam sealer, went down the Labrador with a crew of seventeen men. They were the sons of the best families of Newfoundland. They were strong, fine young boys. I knew many of them intimately. They were eager and happy and we heard them singing as they pulled in their mooring lines before cutting out to the harbour.

The *Southern Cross* had no wireless aboard her. So when the rest of us got radio reports of an approaching storm she was unaware of the peril. Maybe she would not have paid any attention to it anyway. Her captain, George Clark, was a fire-eater. He had loaded her early in the game and her cargo hatches were flush with oily skins. The rest of the fleet ran for the pack ice when the barometer began to drop. The sky blackened and flurries of snow cut across it as we huddled against the ice. Darkness came on with the thermometer near zero.

The *Southern Cross* ran for St. John's. She was logy with the big cargo she had on board. Seas must have swept over her. She did not have the buoyancy to recover when the weight of water crushed her down.

I suppose the main hatch must have burst while she was yet far from port. I have seen it happen when the slimy cargo of seals and fat gets to rolling around the entrails of a giant.

They no doubt manned the pumps but the water rose in the hold, finally reaching the fires. I guess the captain headed her for the beach. But it was too late. She went lower and lower. One hundred and seventy-six fine young Newfoundlanders swarmed into the rigging; all frantic with fear, but calm. But there was no hope. Slowly the hull sunk beneath them and the black sea cruelly licked them off the shrouds. Many a widow and orphan was made that tragic day. In at least three homes spirits of the lost mariners were seen that night.

Not all the ships that don't come back are annihilated by the sea. Disappearance of master and crew can't always be laid to storm or fire.

I was carrying bananas on a tramp ship up from the West Indies when I fell in with a mate who had been on the *Marie Celeste* twenty years before when she had made her last voyage. Her case is the strangest of which I have ever heard. She sailed from New York for Genoa with a cargo of alcohol in 1872. The master was a fine man with a splendid reputation both as a mariner and a gentleman. He had his family with him.

The *Marie Celeste* made a good passage almost to the Mediterranean. Early in December two vessels recorded in their logs that they had sighted her 300 miles off Gibraltar. She had her canvas spread.

A British brigantine fell in with her. The English captain with a keen eye noted that the *Marie Celeste*'s yards were trimmed properly, but that her course was queer. He sent a boarding party over to see if she needed help. His men found the ship completely deserted. Every soul aboard her had disappeared!

There was no sign of violence, nor of any sort of trouble. Her ship's papers and her chronometer were the only articles of importance that had been taken away. The captain's gold watch was found hanging by his bunk. A child's dress was still in the sewing machine, and there were four half-eaten breakfasts on the mess-room table. But not a clue was visible or even indicated that might lead to the solution of the riddle of where had gone those two score souls. To this day, and I have inquired from seafaring men all over the world, I have never heard a whispered word that threw sensible light on this extraordinary mystery.

We Newfoundlanders know of a number of cases where smaller vessels on fishing voyages were found in a condition similar to that of the *Marie Celeste*. But this sort of thing is more easily accounted for.

For instance, not so long ago, there was a schooner loaded with salt from Cadiz bound to Labrador for dry fish. She was discovered by one of our own vessels on the high seas with all sails set and a fire burning in the galley. Her crew could not have left her over four hours before.

But there were indications of excitement. A pot of soup was overturned. Clothes were found lying on the deck. Somebody had knocked a chart off the chartboard. And the captain had broken his parallel rulers. It wasn't a fight. In a fight somebody wins and lives. And seafaring men spill blood in a fight. No, it was something different.

What we figured happened was that a whale or a school of fish were sighted. All hands rushed up and manned the dories leaving only the skipper and helmsmen aboard.

It is just possible that the skipper and helmsmen did what a seafaring man should never do. They went over the side in a flattie or dory to get something out of the water. First thing they knew a gust of wind had caught the ship and swept it away from them. They couldn't overtake it. Fog came. The fog continued. Darkness descended.

Out on the ocean scattered and wretched, heaved in the groundswell a dozen dories with shivering men aboard. When daylight came and the fog lifted, *the ship had disappeared.* A gale rose. The dories one by one swamped. The men drowned. And because a fishing vessel is a foolproof ship the derelict sailed through the tempest unmanned.

But that, after all, is only a guess.

Occasionally, a case of this sort is cleared up definitely after a lapse of years by the confession of a dying man or by the discovery of some accidental clue.

About the end of 1924, the Norwegian sealer *Isstjernen* was found drifting off the coast of Newfoundland without a soul on board. The table in the mess room was set ready for a meal, the lamps all properly lighted, and everything was in perfect order. It was a case as puzzling, if not quite as tantalizing as that of the *Marie Celeste.*

For two years no satisfactory theory was offered. But in January of this year a German sailor died at Oslo after telling a story which there is no reason to doubt. It appears that he was one of a gang of smugglers doing a miscellaneous business in liquor, jewels and fur. This gang fell in with the *Isstjernen* and tried to make a deal with her for their spirits. The Norwegians refused. A dispute rose, and the smugglers threw the entire crew of the *Isstjernen* into the sea. They then carefully destroyed all traces of the fight and prepared the vessel as she was later found.

Speaking of the *Isstjernen* reminds me of another shipwreck I went through. One spring a friend of mine at St. John's offered me his ship, the *Leopard*, for the coming seal hunt down the Labrador. Early in March I went aboard the *Leopard* with 150 men I had secured for the cruise. On a raw morning two days later the old ship was ready for sea.

I wanted to get away as early in the day as possible, because the gin mills would soon be open. It was then a custom among seal fishermen to have a last drink or two, sometimes five or six, just before weighing anchor. This meant a lot of trouble on the dock and always considerable lost time getting the madmen aboard.

Another reason for my hurry was that the harbour was still frozen over and there was a good deal of drift ice at the entrance. My father's ship, the *Viking*, larger than the *Leopard*, was due to leave the same day. If we could follow her, she would make a way for us through the ice. That meant we could probably get down to Cape Race before dark.

After a couple of rough-and-tumble fights, I managed to get my gang aboard. We got under way and followed the *Viking* out and headed down the coast. As she was a bigger ship, she had no deckload of coal as I had, so when the sea began to rise with a strong easterly wind, she had no difficulty working offshore. I had to set my sails to help the

Leopard. But I soon found that the green water coming over the bulwarks was carrying my deck cargo overboard.

Things went from bad to worse. Pretty soon I had to nose in among the shore ice in order to handle the water which was rising rapidly in the hold from the water that leaked down from the hatches. Before I knew it we got in among the slob ice, thousands of small pieces all pressed in together by the wind. This ice had formed a sludge fathoms deep, so that we couldn't even use our hand lead.

Along about midnight, it began to snow a perfect smother. As the sky was overcast and there was no moon, it was pitch-dark. You couldn't see your hand before your face.

I thought the ice would hold her until morning, and we could work our way out slowly. But along about two a.m. there was a crash.

"That's a heavy pan," said the mate.

"Pan, my eye!" I yelled. "*That's the bottom!*"

A couple of more big thumps came, and we were hard and fast on the rocks.

The poor ship didn't have a chance in the world. The heavy gale piled ice up against her with a pressure that couldn't be measured. Her weather side bulged in as if it had been made of rubber. One by one the timbers gave away with sickening crashes. She began to fill rapidly.

About fifty fathoms on our starboard bow was a shelf of rock in which lay the forward part of the steamer *Delmar*, wrecked some years previously. There was only one chance to save my 150 shivering men.

I set them to work right away ripping off deck sheathing, oars, spars and other spare timbers. These they laid on the slush ice, forming a sort of roadway over to the other wreck. It sounds simple enough, but the ice was just wet slush, a sort of snowy quicksand with water all through it. It was 1:30 a.m. when we struck. At three a.m. when it was still black as your hat, she was gone.

Gorry, how cold we were! The boards sank down with the men. Every one was soaked when we reached the *Delmar.* We huddled up together inside the old hulk, nearly dying of cold. For the blizzard was still howling around us. When daylight came we climbed the steep cliff with aid of rope let down by the fishermen living nearby.

It is bad enough to be shipwrecked yourself. But to be wrecked and saved and then to have to look back and see another ship going down with all on board is the most terrible feeling in the world.

One bad winter several of our fleet were down around Battle Harbour when it came on to blow straight out of Baffin Bay. Three thousand miles the howling wind sizzled across the bleak Atlantic and built up a sea big enough to wear away a mountain. Uncle Isaac had done well with the *Retriever* that year. By his glass he knew the gale was coming. So he ran for Battle Harbour. But he got there too late. The *Retriever,* solid oak that she was, was crushed on the harbour boulders and sunk. All hands were saved.

Within twenty-four hours the *Monticello,* of considerably greater tonnage, laid her bones alongside the *Retriever.* Her crew was also saved, but only after terrible sufferings.

Despite my many harrowing experiences in shipwrecks and in the far north, some of my closest shaves of recent years have been aboard ships that weren't in trouble at all.

Sooner or later a sailor man has to know how to handle himself after he falls overboard. The great danger is not being seen. Many a good sailor man has disappeared off his ship when nobody happened to be looking. I can imagine his feelings when he sees her sailing away and leaving him to the sharks.

A funny thing happened to me one day. Just before Christmas when I was mate in a barquentine we sailed out of Sydney, Cape Breton, in a stiff northwester and the thermometer almost down to zero. In heaving up the anchor the fluke became caught in the ship's forefoot. We couldn't get it free. So I had a block put at the end of the bowsprit, a line rove through it and made fast to the anchor. The weather was so nasty and cold that none of us were very spry. I climbed down on a backrope and stood on the anchor ring. First thing I knew I lost my balance and tumbled off into the sea. As I was all snarled up in oilskins and pilot suit I was in no condition to swim.

By luck the starboard forebrace happened to be hanging over the side and the ship was listed a little that way. I grabbed the rope and went up like a monkey, glad of the exercise after the shock of the ice water. In about six seconds I was sitting on the topgallant forecastle. Just then a cry broke out in the well deck amidship: "*Man overboard! The mate's gone over the side!*"

When the excitement started up I waited a bit. Then just when all hands were figuring I'd drowned I let out a yell: "*Yes, but I'm back again! Now, turn to, you cockeyed loafers!*"

As sailors are a pretty superstitious crowd a disaster like

a man disappearing over the side means to them Divine punishment.

When I'm on it, let me say that superstition is one of the worst things among sailor folk. It nearly did for a great friend of my family's, a Captain Halfyard of Western Bay near where we lived.

The fall work was just over and Captain Halfyard sailed from St. John's for home where he was going to spend Christmas. Uncle John left the same December afternoon a few hours later.

The next day, a visitor to Western Bay would have seen a sad-looking group gathered around Captain Halfyard's house. Crepe was on the door. His ship had just come in and reported he had fallen overboard in the midst of a gale during the dark winter night before off Cape Conception. The poor widow and children were crushed with grief. They had looked forward to a happy Christmas. Now Death had put his black hand on their celebration.

Right about this time Uncle John came in, rounded to all standing and dropped his hook. He had a dory already over the side and hurried ashore. He ran all the way from the landing to the widow's house.

When he reached the edge of the mourning crowd he filled his lungs and hollered as loud as he could: "*Captain Halfyard is alive!*"

There was wild excitement. And while the village wept for joy Uncle John explained things. It seemed his lookout had heard a "spirit" in the mid watch of the night before. Luckily Uncle John happened to be on deck at that moment. He had the helm put down and nosed his vessel up in the direction of the "spirit." Five minutes later he pulled Captain Halfyard out of the sea, a pretty cold and tired ghost, but a very solid one.

Imagine the vitality of a man overboard during December in the North Atlantic swimming around for four hours in gale and blizzard without even a life preserver to hold him up.

I am often asked if I believe in ghosts. Sometimes I do and sometimes I don't. When there's a bad shipwreck I do; especially if the ship disappears.

Take the case of the brigantine *Berkeley*, Captain John Penney, out of Francis Harbour, Labrador, to Brigus, Newfoundland. She met a howling gale down near Green Bay. Most all the vessels hove to to save their deckload of herring, but Captain Penney kept right on. He was a driver and wanted to get to port.

That night in three different families of the crew the absent members who were aboard the brigantine appeared at home.

In one case the mother of one of the boys was sitting darning a sock by her lamp. She was rocking in her chair thinking how happy she would be next week when her lad came back. Suddenly the door clicked. In walked her only son with soaking clothes and his boots squeaking with water. He stood there swaying before her as if terribly exhausted. But before she could speak to him he disappeared.

Pat Clancy was in the same crew. His wife lived at Cape Ann. She was just getting supper when in walked Pat, the water running off him. He didn't say a word. He just staggered over to the cradle where lay his two baby boys and looked down at them. Sadly he shook his head. Then he faded away.

The brigantine *Berkeley* never came back; not a trace of her was ever found. Ninety-seven souls were aboard her, counting Pat Clancy.

Then there was the *Gertrude*, another brigantine. Captain Thomas Carew took her out of St. John's bound for Cape Broyle to pick up sealing crews. She was due back in a few weeks. But she didn't come. All that spring, all summer and all fall the families of her officers and crew waited for her to return. Alas, she never was seen again.

In the following winter, a brother of one of her crew was out hunting. Coming out of the woods he was startled to find on the edge of the path his missing brother sitting on a rock. He was dumbfounded. He knew it could only be the ghost of his brother because the *Gertrude* had long ago disappeared without a trace.

Finally, he controlled his voice enough to ask: "How far did you get, brother? Did you make Renews Rock?" This rock was just outside Renews harbour.

The spirit of his brother replied in hollow tones: "Too true, too true," and vanished. That told us where lay the *Gertrude*'s skeleton.

A similar case was that of the *Magnolia* en route from Sydney to St. John's laden with coal. Captain W. T. Percey commanded her. He was a fine man too: a God-fearing mariner of the best description.

There was no reason to feel that disaster had overtaken the ship. But Mrs. Percey announced one morning that she would never see her husband again.

"I was out walking last evening after school (which she taught) and I saw him in the path," she told my mother. "But he could not speak to me. So I know he is dead."

Here is another incident my mother told me about a little while ago:

In 1894, under Uncle Harry Bartlett, the steamer *Falcon* left Philadelphia for St. John's with a load of coal. She had there disembarked Peary's polar party and was bound home after a long hard trip. A few days later a neighbour of my mother's ran in and said: "I was just passing the home of Harry Smith (a sailor on the *Falcon*) and I saw him at his window!"

"But the ship won't be in until next week!" exclaimed Mother.

The lady wrung her hands. "I know it," she said. "What I have just seen is Harry's spirit! He's dead and so are probably all the others!"

Her premonition turned out to be correct. The *Falcon* never reached port and no trace of her was ever found.

When rats leave a ship before she sails it is one of the worst possible omens. Sometimes when this happens the sailors pack their bags and ditty boxes and promptly desert. Risking jail seems far less dangerous than a cruise in a hoodooed ship.

The rats all left the *Treasurer* back in 1901, when Captain James Gushue took her out of Brigus for Sydney where he was to load coal. Three days later one of the crew walked in on his wife, threw his bag on the floor, and sat down in his favourite armchair, with water dripping from his face. The poor woman tried to throw her arms around him but grasped only thin air. The next moment the appari-tion turned and walked out.

It's things like that that make me believe in ghosts even though I don't want to.

But, as I said in the beginning, the terrible thing is not the temporary grief that comes with the first bad news, but the anguish of picturing your father or husband or brother dying by inches on some deserted island.

CHAPTER XXIV

HOMEWARD BOUND

If I had it all to do over again I should be a sailor just the same. There is nothing so satisfying as the sea.

On shore a man is always worried because he hasn't twice as much as he has already got. It's not like that on board ship. You can only have just so much. No amount of money on any but a passenger ship will get you quarters better than your rank deserves. Once you have warm dry clothes there is no use having any more. You can only eat only just so much food. As a result of this you are contented with your life simply because you are living. The sheer joy of being alive and working hard is your reward.

In this way I largely account for the remarkable health I have had all these years. You wouldn't think to look at me that I was once a runt and sickly. I am not fat but I weigh over 200 pounds, and wear a No. 17 collar; and I think I could hold my own with pretty nearly any other man my age. I have already told how I almost died when I was a child. But that isn't the whole thing. Just to come out of childhood alive. You have got to keep at your own machine if you want to have it run properly.

While we were down sealing and fishing we gave our

bodies a good deal of punishment. There were the long hours and the steady toil. We were wet and cold and miserable a great deal of the time and I cannot hand the food very much. But those were the years when I was in my 'teens. They corresponded to the years when other young men are in college and more or less under the direction of a physical instructor. A lad ought to get along all right then.

But what counts for the main part of his life is how he takes care of himself from, say, twenty-five onward. What does he eat? How does he get his exercise? What does he do when he plays? What effect did his work have on his health? I had to handle this problem for myself when I began to cruise around the globe on steamers.

Being officer on a tramp steamer as compared with going sealing or cod-fishing is just about the same as going into office work as compared with college. I found pretty soon that it was better if I watched what I ate. Not that I didn't have a good digestion. I guess my inner plumbing could handle wire nails if I didn't eat them too often. But I learned it wasn't so good to overload my stomach.

I still followed the fisherman's plan and had a light mug-up in the afternoon; some tea and biscuit, perhaps. I eat my big meal in the middle of the day. I avoid hot bread. And when I am not doing heavy physical work I don't eat too much meat. I vary my beef and mutton with fish. When I am at the end of my runs I go ashore and sample all the vegetables of the port. In other words, I balance things pretty well and am moderate. I don't have any foolish diet plans that keep me to this or that or the other.

There was a time in my life when I thought it didn't

make any difference whether you used your muscles or not. In spite of my fine health and the great strength which happily is still mine, I give quite a little thought to muscular exercise. I don't swing dumb-bells or do anything graceful like that. But when I have a choice between walking or riding, I walk. If there is a job that I have time to do that requires lifting or pushing or pulling, I try to do it myself instead of giving someone a half dollar to do it for me. I like to carry my own bag, for instance. The heavier the better.

That takes care of food and exercise. Now here's the most important thing of all. That's the state of mind I am in. If I get in a bad humour I might just as well never come to the dinner table. What's the sense of fretting and fuming on the outside and expecting your stomach to do its job inside? I don't know much about anatomy but I figure there is a pretty close telephone connection between a fellow's brain and his stomach. If I have had a row with somebody and feel myself ruffled up I prefer to take a walk rather than sit down and eat. Better save the eats until you can smile at the waiter who brings them.

I am not trying to parade my morals and good health all over the place. That's my own business and I don't see anybody else should be interested in them. But I find that I like to hear a well man say how he keeps well and I like a good man to give some idea of why he chooses to steer a straight course; and I rarely see a happy man that I don't take a squint behind the scenes if I can and find out how he enjoys life. So it may not be amiss if I add a word here, while I am on such things, about my religion.

In a sense I haven't got a religion. In another sense I am one of the most religious men in the world.

Like most seafaring people from down my way I was brought up in the church. My mother and father, who are still alive and hearty despite their great age, are very religious people. I have often thought that their long and happy life has been largely the result of their fine association with the church.

But when I went to sea and began to drive around from one port to another, staying ashore only a few days at a time, I gradually veered away from the routine religion in which I had been brought up. This worried me at first. I used to wonder if the devil had me. But I soon found he didn't. And as the years went on I found that it wasn't necessary always to go inside the church and sing hymns to be close to God.

My idea now is that a seafaring man is closer to the Almighty when he goes out to sea, with the sky overhead and nothing in sight, than he is when he is jostling his way though a crowd of struggling human beings in a city.

Again I say, if I had it all to do over again, I should be a sailor just the same. There is nothing so satisfying as the sea.

Squidding along the Labrador. Holloway photo.

Brigus, Newfoundland. Home of the Bartletts. Holloway photo.

Sealing steamers jammed in the Narrows.

Drying fish in Newfoundland. Holloway photo.

Splitting cod fish. Holloway photo.

Tracking the *Panther* through the ice.

SS *Grand Lake* in the ice. Holloway photo.

Barquentine *Corisande*. Lockart Auld image.

Mrs. William Bartlett, Captain Bob's mother. Holloway photo.

Captain William Bartlett, Captain Bob's father.

Captain Rupert W. Bartlett. Killed at Vimy Ridge. Lafayette photo.

Captain John Bartlett.

Captain Abram Bartlett.

A stern view of the *Roosevelt*.

Ada Blackjack. Seamstress on the *Karluk*.

The *Karluk* imprisioned in the ice floe.

The *Karluk* beset in the ice.

The Hubbard Medal (front and back).

A model of the *Terra Nova*.

The *Neptune*.

Captain Bob turns diver.

Dr. Knud Rasmussen and Captain Bartlett on the *Morrissey*.

The *Morrissey* at Turnavik. The Bartletts' old fishing station on the
Labrador Coast

Captain Bob Bartlett gazing through his sextant.

INDEX

INDEX

INDEX

INDEX